Cities, Sagebrush, and Solitude

THE URBAN WEST SERIES

Cities, Sagebrush, and Solitude

*Urbanization and Cultural Conflict
in the Great Basin*

EDITED BY

Dennis R. Judd and
Stephanie L. Witt

UNIVERSITY OF NEVADA PRESS
RENO & LAS VEGAS

THE URBAN WEST SERIES

Series Editors: Eugene P. Moehring and Amy L. Scott

University of Nevada Press, Reno, Nevada 89557 USA
Copyright © 2015 by University of Nevada Press
All rights reserved
Manufactured in the United States of America

Library of Congress Cataloging-in-Publication Data

Cities, sagebrush, and solitude : urbanization and cultural
conflict in the Great Basin / [edited by] Dennis R. Judd,
Stephanie L. Witt.
pages cm. — (The urban West series)
Includes bibliographical references and index.
ISBN 978-0-87417-969-9 (paperback) —
ISBN 978-0-87417-970-5 (e-book)
1. Urbanization—Great Basin. 2. Urban policy—Great Basin.
3. Sustainable urban development—Great Basin. 4. Great
Basin—Environmental conditions. 5. Great Basin—Economic
conditions. 6. Great Basin—Politics and government.
I. Judd, Dennis R. II. Witt, Stephanie L.
HT384.U52G743   2014
307.760979—dc23   2014035961

The paper used in this book meets the requirements of
American National Standard for Information Sciences—
Permanence of Paper for Printed Library Materials,
ANSI/NISO Z39.48-1992 (R2002). Binding materials were
selected for strength and durability.

FIRST PRINTING
23   22   21   20   19   18   17   16   15
5   4   3   2   1

Contents

Preface

Cities, Sagebrush, and Solitude addresses a much-neglected topic: the environmental consequences and political conflicts arising from the recent and rapid urbanization of the largest of the four deserts of North America, the Great Basin. In recent decades the rapidly spreading urban agglomerations within this arid landscape make it, in statistical terms, the fastest-growing urban region in the United States. The four metropolitan areas situated at the cardinal points of the Basin's rim—Boise, Reno, Salt Lake City, and Las Vegas—must cope with the problems associated with rapid growth, but attempts to do so provoke conflict between urban residents and the people who live in the thinly populated desert outback. In the Great Basin, policies to address the environmental and resource limitations imposed by the desert environment may be incompatible with a deeply entrenched political culture that resists all cooperative or governmental effort. The alchemical mixture of three ingredients—cities (which are morphing into sprawling metropolitan regions), sagebrush (the ubiquitous signifier of aridity and resource scarcity), and solitude (which has nurtured a libertarian political outlook)—makes the Great Basin a compelling place to study. Each chapter of this book traces the way that the tensions among cities, sagebrush, and solitude inform contemporary policy debates and public policies of the region through an analysis of the environmental stresses connected to economic change, resource extraction, land management, and urban development.

The conversations that created the community of scholars who contributed to this book took place at two conferences held on the campus of Boise State University in 2011 and 2012. Nearly all of the participants had written about the West, but only three of them had previously focused their research specifically upon the Great Basin. These conferences provided an opportunity to engage in the kind of animated give-and-take necessary for giving a consistent thematic structure to a project as unique as this one. The tenor of those lively exchanges informs our approach to the subject matter. The editors encouraged authors to step a bit outside their academic roles and write for a diverse audience of scholars, policy makers, and educated readers. We believe the topic of the book will interest scholars across several disciplines (especially social scientists and urban and policy specialists), plus scholars and informed readers interested in the history, politics, culture, and environmental issues of the American West. This book should be especially appealing to residents and policy makers living in the Great Basin, one of the most beautiful, sometimes desolate, and misunderstood ecological regions of the United States.

We appreciate the generous hospitality provided by Boise State University for the two conferences that brought scholars together from six western universities. In particular, we want to express our thanks to Melissa Lavitt, who was then dean of the College of Social Sciences and Public Affairs at Boise State University, for offering enthusiastic encouragement at every step of the way. This book would not have been possible without the critical support of Dean Lavitt and the college.

Cities, Sagebrush, and Solitude

The Last Urban Frontier

DENNIS R. JUDD AND STEPHANIE L. WITT

IN THE SECOND HALF OF THE TWENTIETH CENTURY, a historic redistribution of the American population brought into being the New American West. The "opulent, energetic, mobile, and individualist" cities of Southern California seemed to perfectly project America's national future,[1] but there were troubling signs, too. Images of urban sprawl and clogged freeways and highly publicized incidents of racial violence and ethnic tension signaled a gradual "withering of California's Pacific Idyll."[2] An increasing number of the state's residents began to spill into the Intermountain West, and at the same time people moving from other parts of the country began stopping short of the Pacific. Today, four rapidly growing urban constellations located at the margins of the Great Basin Desert constitute the most recent, and perhaps the last, of the series of urban frontiers that have shaped America's cultural and political outlook.[3]

Despite its vast expanses of thinly populated desert, the Great Basin is the fastest-growing urban region in the United States. In only a fourteen-year period from 1990 to 2004, the population of the Great Basin Desert increased from 2.9 to 4.9 million people.[4] In the early 1990s a Nevada boom took off, fueled by the maturing of Las Vegas as the nation's entertainment capital and by Reno, with its growing legions of California expatriates. At the same time, a sprawling corridor of urban development scribed a path through Salt Lake City and along the foot of the Wasatch Range of Utah; in the southwest corner of the state a smaller one, Little Dixie, stretched through the red rock country. On the desert's northern rim, Boise, Idaho, began a remarkable transformation from an obscure agricultural center to a city celebrated for its high-tech economy and hip urban culture. Small towns in and near these areas of the Basin experienced "stupefying rates of growth" in the 1990s, and they did not moderate their population binge much even during the 2008 recession.[5]

The Great Basin is the largest of the four deserts of North America (the

1

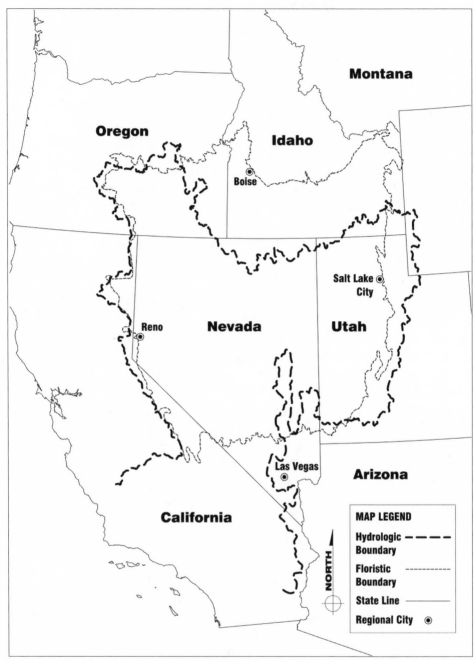

Map 1: The Hydrological Great Basin (bold boundary) overlaps but is not the same as the Great Basin Desert, which is defined by its floral communities (light boundary).

others are the Mojave, Sonoran, and Chihuahuan), and it would not seem to be a friendly place to build cities. In 1843 explorer John C. Frémont coined the term *the great basin* to refer to a desiccated inland region where the water drains inland rather to the sea. By his reckoning this vast area stretched from a range of mountains in southern Idaho and a portion of southeastern Oregon almost to Baja California (see map 1). Later, it became apparent that the basin identified by Frémont covered two separate desert regions divided by distinctive assemblages of floral communities. The vast sagebrush ocean that defines the Great Basin Desert runs west from the Wasatch Mountains of Utah to the Sierra Nevada of California; on the southern edge it gives way to the stunning redrock country and the creosote, blackbrush, and rabbitbrush barrens of the Mojave Desert of southern Utah-Nevada; in the desert's northern reaches the sea of sagebrush goes beyond Frémont's hydrological boundary and embraces the Snake River Plateau and Owyhee Highlands of southern Idaho and southeastern Oregon.[6] Extremes of aridity, heat, cold, and alkali are the main ingredients that produce a desolate and forbidding landscape.

Extreme aridity imposed an oasis pattern of settlement that differed significantly from the American historical experience. Instead of the small towns and fertile fields that marked westward expansion and progress in milder climates, the towns and tiny hamlets of the Great Basin were widely scattered, each located wherever a water source and a patch of arable land made a permanent human presence possible. For this reason, *rural* does not work well to describe the lightly settled reaches of this desert region; terms such as *frontier* and *outback* come more easily to mind.

The Great Basin is littered with ghost towns, physical reminders that people have found it difficult to permanently settle there. "Environmental limitation was the ultimate lesson of the harsh, empty, desert country, and the ethos of those people who endured was extractive rather than nurturing."[7] In the mining era, as soon as the ore played out towns that had popped up almost overnight vanished just as quickly. For the Mormons, a unifying theology produced the disciplined cooperation needed to make the desert bloom in a few irrigated slopes and valleys along the Wasatch Range. In three other places on the Basin's rim, the history of stymied progress ended in the twentieth century, when massive federal reclamation projects brought water to the foot of the Sierra Nevada at Reno, dams and canals to the Snake River Plain and, in the late 1950s, when Las Vegas completed a pipeline to Lake Mead, a meandering 110-mile-long reservoir backed up behind Hoover

Dam, one of the largest dams ever constructed by the Bureau of Reclamation. These were the four areas of the desert where cities of a significant size might prosper.

Even in these locations urbanization presents significant challenges, in part because managing the impact of urban growth requires a level of coordination and planning that contradicts a long-established political culture that resists and resents all governmental authority. This culture of solitude is an important ingredient in a volatile mixture made up of cities, sage, and solitude. The combination of these elements produces a fascinating and unpredictable experiment to see if it is possible to break the bonds historically imposed by a withholding environment.

Cities and nature do not operate in parallel universes, although in the Great Basin there may be a temptation to think they do. The website of Nevada's Public Lands Information Center reflects a perspective that fits comfortably in a desert landscape: "Mention the name Nevada and for many people it conjures up images of Las Vegas, Reno, neon-lit nights and casinos. Others will think of a vast, empty land where mountain ranges stand like mirages on the horizon and the sky seems to be bigger than anywhere else." Despite these visual impressions, however, there is a growing realization that these contrasting worlds are not as separate as they may appear.

The Great Basin Desert

Like a boulder in midstream, the Great Basin Desert[8] sits squarely in the middle of the West, so that anything that does not wash over is swept to either side. In the history of westward expansion, people avoided it. It was the last place in the United States subdued by the surveyors' chains, and even today it is unknown to large numbers of Americans. Pouring over nighttime satellite images, writer Peter Stark found four spots on the map of the United States that were almost devoid of light; one of those is the portion of the Basin that thrusts north into eastern Oregon. There, fewer than seven thousand people live in a county of ten thousand square miles.[9] This corner of the Basin was visited by writer Dayton Duncan when he roamed around the country in search of counties with fewer than two people per square mile.[10] In the Great Basin his search truly hit paydirt; if he had wanted to, he could have wandered through thousands of square miles without even that many people to account for.

For thousands of years the environmental conditions of the Basin limited the human population to a few thousand people kept on the move in search of water and whatever meager sustenance the desert might offer.[11] Nineteenth-century explorers and emigrants who encountered the Paiute, Goshiute, and Washoe referred to them as "Diggers" because they survived on a diet of roots, insects, and an assortment of birds and small creatures. Unlike the Pueblo cultures of the Southwest, the inhabitants of the Great Basin did not build permanent structures or engage in agriculture, and the volume of artifacts left to mark their passage is comparatively small. The harshness of their environment found silent but eloquent expression in a blanket discovered in a cave in northwestern Nevada. It was sewn from six hundred mouse skins.[12] Aridity was the singular characteristic of an environment so extreme as to require such extraordinary resourcefulness.

Despite a popular fascination with the American West that goes back to the era of the mountain men, gold seekers, and wagon trains, the Great Basin never fitted comfortably into the American story of westward expansion. From the early explorers to the present, the reports of those who encountered it have been mostly unfavorable.[13] Jedediah Smith, the first white man to cross it in 1827, would have died if he and his companions had not chanced upon a spring, and nearly twenty years later its reputation as a fatal desert entered the national consciousness when the Donner Party, having survived a harrowing desert crossing, became trapped on the eastern slopes of the snowbound Sierra. Their story became the most tragic, lurid, and oft-repeated episode of the nineteenth-century westward movement. Forty-five of the eighty-nine members of the party died, and survivors resorted to cannibalism to stay alive. Three years later a gold seeker on his way to California exclaimed, "This is the poorest and most worthless country that man ever saw," worse than God-forsaken because "He never had anything to do with it."[14]

The Basin's dismal reputation has survived the test of time. During the Cold War era, the fire-blasted landscapes produced by nuclear testing became the archetypal images of the Basin.[15] Between 1951 and 1962, when one hundred atmospheric explosions shook the desert, many people would have agreed with a prominent historian's view that "at least it [now] serves some useful purpose."[16] During the Cold War years large tracts of land were "bristling with military bases and sequestered into huge bombing ranges, many pockmarked with craters from both regular ordinance and nuclear weapons. . . . [I]t helped call popular or public attention to the area as a place *set aside* from the rest of America. In other words, the image of the region as one of desolation was exacerbated by its marginalization as a sacrifice zone."[17]

More recently, the battle over Yucca Mountain as a nuclear waste depository produced stylized images in the American press, with (for example) a *Washington Post* reporter calling it a "hellishly dry desert ridge" and a reporter for the *New York Times* employing descriptors such as "remote," "barren," and "desolate."[18]

Most outsiders form their impressions of the Great Basin when they drive through at high speed on the narrow ribbon of I-80. Few of them stop for long. In the summer months, while visitors by the million fill to overflowing the Grand Canyon, Bryce Canyon, the Canyonlands, Yellowstone National Park, and Glacier National Park, the Great Basin sees few vacationers. Because it has virtually no iconic tourist destinations, it remains largely invisible, an enigma for those encountering it for the first time, "the broad brush-covered plain seem[ing] as vast as the ocean, the distant mountains appearing like islands. It can be unnerving. A European traveler driving through in 2000 was moved to say, "God, that country's dull, and so much of it."[19] The Nevada section of US Route 50, which runs from Ocean City, Maryland, to Sacramento, California, is known as "The Loneliest Road in America," and curiosity seekers who travel it can testify why.

Few people visit the Great Basin because it does not offer the picturesque images that people generally associate with the American West. The Great Basin National Park, the only national park located within the Basin, attracted 69,235 in 2008 (a decline from 80,477 visitors in 1998); in the same year more than 4.4 million visited the Grand Canyon.[20] On describing the park on its website the National Park Service seems obliged to say, "Called dead, barren, and desolate, visitors are surprised to find it's alive, fruitful, and full of wonders."[21] Evidently, this kind of public relations has not been especially effective. Interstate I-80 runs close by the scenic Ruby Mountains, but despite being easily accessible, this oasis attracts only 40,000 visitors each year. It is a curious paradox that a region greeted with such indifference should be in the process of becoming the nation's newest urban frontier.

Cities

Depending upon one's perspective, claiming that the Great Basin is the most rapidly urbanizing region in the United States may seem to some people like little more than a clever statistical trick. Federally owned public lands constitute 70.6 percent of the region, leaving just under 30 percent of its landmass for settlement, agriculture, and commercial and industrial uses.[22] This constraint imposes a settlement pattern in which densely populated urban areas are surrounded by a nearly empty desert landscape. The urbanization of the Basin is occurring almost entirely within the cities and towns that sit on its rim. Over the past quarter century or more, three of its four cities have managed to make the top-ten list of fastest-growing cities in the nation, with Las Vegas consistently in the lead. The pace of urban growth seems startling because it has come so late, and so fast. In midcentury Boise had a population of a little more than 34,000 residents, which made it bigger than Reno by a couple of thousand people. Despite the shot in the arm provided by the construction of Hoover Dam in the 1930s, Las Vegas was still a dusty and isolated town of scarcely more than 8,000 in 1940 and barely topped 24,000 a decade later. At varying times in the next few years all three of the four cities entered a period of extraordinary growth. By 2010 the city of Las Vegas had grown to 584,000, Reno had reached 225,000, and Boise had become a city of more than 205,000 residents. Salt Lake City offers a contrasting case of population loss, mainly because it failed to adjust its boundaries during the fastest period of regional growth. In 1950 it already had a population of 182,000, but like older cities elsewhere in the nation it slid into decline in the 1970s and 1980s; since then it has made a sustained recovery, exceeding 186,000 by the time the 2010 census was conducted.

A more dramatic story of the urbanizing Great Basin is revealed in regional population figures. By the 2010 census the Salt Lake Metropolitan Statistical Area had topped 1.1 million, but the interlinked corridor of development reaching north through the Ogden MSA and south through the Provo MSA made up an urban conurbation of twice that size. By then Salt Lake City accounted for only 17 percent of the population of its own MSA and a meager 8 percent of the urban dwellers distributed among the three MSAs that sprawled along the foot of the mountains. The 2010 census revealed that the Boise MSA had grown to more than 600,000 and that only 30 percent of them lived within the Boise city limits. The same census showed that of the nearly 2 million residents of the Las Vegas MSA, only one-third resided in the city of Las Vegas. With a population of 435,417 in 2010, Reno was the one city on the Basin's rim to capture as much as half (53 percent) of the population that lived within the metropolitan region.

Each of the four cities has a distinctive history. In the late 1840s the Mormons were attracted to the Great Basin because it was so isolated. Although desolate landscapes were near at hand, the particular spot they chose for settlement was favorable: legend has it that "Brigham Young, when he came through a neighboring canyon and saw rivers flowing out on an alluvial fans from the wall of the Wasatch to the flats beyond, made a quick decision and said, 'This is the place.'"[23] Salt Lake City's original town site was located around City Creek to take advantage of this valuable source of fresh water. The symbolic significance attached to this water source is reflected in the fact that there are now three "fake versions of City Creek flowing through downtown Salt Lake: the one going through the park at the mouth of the park at the mouth of the canyon near Brigham Young's grave; the one going in front of the conference center by the elm trees; and now the one going through the mall."[24]

The looming wall of the Wasatch Front is central to Utah's urban economy and identity. The outdoor industry employed 36,000 people and contributed $4.5 billion to the Wasatch Front economy in 2007.[25] The Winter Olympics in 2002 prompted huge infrastructural investments, including the Utah Trax light rail and Frontrunner train system that will eventually move people along the Wasatch Front from Ogden to Provo. Today the Salt Lake City economy relies upon tourism and is dominated by education, medical, and professional services.[26]

Boise began in the early 1840s as an outpost for travelers on the Oregon Trail, but quickly became a service center for mining, farming, and ranching that took hold in the mountains and fields surrounding the city. Although it was never large, Boise's regional importance was reflected in a busy downtown containing block after block of ornate stone buildings. Unfortunately, a love affair with urban renewal clearance in the 1970s removed several square blocks of architecturally significant structures, which prompted a feature story in a 1974 issue of *Harper's* declaring that Boise had destroyed itself.[27] City leaders remained deadlocked over the development of the empty lots for more than a decade. Eventually, a new convention center and a popular pedestrian mall provided an anchor for a redevelopment process that is still unfolding.

Sometime in the 1990s Boise began attracting attention in national publications as a city offering an exceptional quality of life. Albertsons, Morrison-Knudsen Construction, Ore-Ida Foods, Micron Technology, and the Hewlett-Packard printing division were all located within the metropolitan area in the 1990s, and the presence of so many corporate headquarters turned the city into a magnet for young people working in managerial and high-tech services. Its natural surroundings provide a context for a distinctive western lifestyle revolving around a high level of urban amenities and outdoor pursuits.

Nevada's urban development has followed an utterly unique path. Beginning in the late nineteenth century, Las Vegas, Reno, and a scattering of small towns and crossroads in Nevada were able to prosper by projecting an image "as the last bastion of the individualist morality of the Old West."[28] For a long time Reno was the state's leading city, and it gained notoriety as an entrepôt for easy divorce, gambling, and prostitution. Generations of boosters have tried to shed those early associations. In the early twentieth century there were failed schemes to promote irrigated agriculture, and a century later civic leaders were trying a new tack, this time promoting an image of a city offering an exceptional blend of indoor and outdoor pursuits: "Day or night, indoors or out—winter, spring, summer or fall—Reno-Tahoe is filled with adventures. There's no other place like it on the planet."[29] Since the early 1990s California expats have been pouring across the border. Sprawling subdivisions have been invading horse pastures and sagebrush hills, but the city itself has continued to struggle.

Las Vegas is the city that "now symbolizes the new America, the latest in American dream capitals." Today it appears as a city of opulence and excess because it offers a twenty-first-century blend of fantasy, leisure, consumption, and culture. It was possible to bring all these elements together here because it is a newly minted city rising in a sere desert landscape, a blank slate waiting to be written upon. Driving into Winnemucca at night, writer John McPhee thought the desert was a natural place for this kind of city because "neon looks good in Nevada. The tawdriness is refined out of it in so much wide black space."[30]

There are no big cities or metropolitan areas in the desert interior; it cannot support them. Even so, for the first time since the boomtowns of the mining era, a few towns have begun to grow, filling in the interstitial spaces between expanses of public land. From 1980 to 2010 Elko County, Nevada, increased its population from 20,000 to more than 49,000 people. It sits in the middle of a triangle right in the heart of the desert: Boise is a 193-mile drive, just a little closer than Reno, which is 231 miles away, and Salt Lake City, at 226 miles. Elko's growth reprises a long Nevada history because it is a boomtown that relies upon a latter-day gold rush. A few places are growing in response to the same forces that are sweeping across the rest of the nation: "As telecommuting becomes a viable employment option, more people choose to live in more isolated areas within a few hours of urban centers."[31] Retirees have also been flocking to smaller towns in and near the Basin. For example, the communities of St. George and others in Washington County,

Utah, added 53 percent to their populations in the single decade from 2000 to 2010.

The growth of cities, large and small, places increasing demands on water and other scarce resources. In the past environmental limitation frustrated human aspirations to tame the desert. As Elizabeth Raymond has noted, for much of its history the Great Basin stubbornly defied a national "environmental ethos" that equated agricultural settlement with progress and abundance.[32] The explosion of urban population in recent decades might be interpreted as the fulfillment of a long-delayed ambition that the desert shall not be allowed to stand in the way of progress.

Sagebrush

The Great Basin supports endless expanses of sagebrush because it lacks enough water to grow anything else in such amazing profusion. Even to the present day the problem of water scarcity has not been overcome except at the desert's edges. The four cities of the rim have prospered by planting one foot in the Basin and the other in a nearby ecological system where water is more plentiful. Salt Lake City escapes the limitations imposed by the desert because it sits on the alluvial fan at the base of the Wasatch Mountains. Within hours of arriving in the Salt Lake Valley in July 1847 the Mormons began digging irrigation ditches to carry water from mountain-fed streams to their newly planted fields. The Mormons succeeded so well in developing a system of water rights and distribution that by 1910 more than a million acres of land were under irrigation.[33] Likewise, Boise and the agricultural arc of southern Idaho are watered by rivers and streams flowing from nearby mountains—although, it should be noted, the Owyhee River, with its headwaters in the Owyhee Plateau of northern Nevada, also supplies an important share. Reno extracts water from the Truckee River and groundwater from a series of small basins running along the foot of the Sierra Nevada. Likewise, Las Vegas would not have been able to morph into a neon metropolis without its lifeline to the Colorado River.

The network of dams, canals, and pipelines that sprawl almost everywhere else in the West bypassed most of the Great Basin Desert. The Snake River Plain is the one notable exception because it sits outside the area of internal drainage first noted by Frémont. Shortly after the turn of the twentieth century, the US Reclamation Service embarked on a program to bring water to the broad floodplain of the Snake River. Twelve major dams and thousands of miles of canals, pipelines, and ditches water the fertile crescent of southern

Idaho. Equally audacious irrigation schemes promoted by Reno's boosters and funded by the US Reclamation Service were frustrated because there was no great river to sustain them. Reno's promoters were eager to develop an agricultural alternative to an economy based on gaming and the itinerant riffraff and sin it brought in its wake. Amid an extravagant fanfare announcing a bounteous agricultural future, the first water from the federal government's first major reclamation project was turned onto fields near Reno in 1905, but the desert soils, which quickly leached salt and toxic minerals to the surface, ultimately proved to be poor candidates for irrigation. Unlike Idaho, which has rich alluvial soils in the floodplain of the Snake River, the desert around Reno "did *not* blossom like the proverbial rose."[34]

Despite a long history of frustrated hopes, the Basin may yet offer an unexpected bounty. The desiccated landscape hides a treasure trove of underground water, and ultimately it will surely prove to be a resource too precious to leave alone. A system of aquifers stretches from Death Valley upward through the eastern half of Nevada and western Utah and farther north into a corner of Idaho.[35] Already the "megapolitan" corridors sprawling along the desert's outer seams are beginning to look to groundwater to support their future growth.[36] Since 1990 "water withdrawals for urban and suburban use have increased from 8 to 20% of all withdrawals in the state of Nevada, and urban centers are increasingly acquiring water from distant, rural areas."[37] When it begins to yield up water to its thirsty cities, the driest desert of North America will become ever more desiccated, and a cascade of ecological changes are sure to follow.

Urbanization increases the pressure to make use of whatever water the desert may be hiding, but past experience shows the surface will feel its effects. The pumping of groundwater beneath Las Vegas has lowered the water table by three hundred feet and dried up the meadows and marshes that gave the city its name. Over a century the dams and water diversions built on the Truckee River downstream from Reno lowered Pyramid Lake, the largest freshwater lake in the Great Basin, by seventy feet; wiped out a major trout fishery; and set in motion a slow dying of the lake's ecology. Only recently has this process been slowed by efforts to increase stream flows into the lake. These environmental disasters open a window onto the dramatic changes that urbanization is likely to bring to the Basin in the years ahead, but there are other gathering threats as well.

The long-term drying of the West is being accelerated by global warming.[38] As snowpack and river flows decline in the watersheds on the Basin's rim, the cities of Nevada and Utah are desperately searching for new sources of water. St. George, Utah, has been pressing for approval for a pipeline to Lake Powell, but even if this massive project is ultimately constructed, the Colorado River's declining flows make that source increasingly precarious. Groundwater is the obvious last resort, which is why Las Vegas has been seeking rights to the Basin's hidden treasure for more than two decades.

From 1970 to 2010 Las Vegas and its region grew nearly twice as fast as any other US metropolitan area, and Clark County is expected to increase by an additional 53 percent by midcentury, to 3.6 million people.[39] For decades the population boom in southern Nevada has relied upon the unexamined assumption that enough water will be found to satisfy the region's demands. Local public officials, in any case, do not seem in the mood to challenge this prevailing attitude. Patricia Mulroy, the general manager of the Southern Nevada Water Authority, is the one person who might plausibly chart a different course, but she has expressed her conviction that "you can't take a community as thriving as this one and put a stop sign out there. The train will run right over you."[40]

This exercise in realpolitik collides with the fact that Las Vegas is "the only other place on earth [except Egypt] where so many people are so helplessly dependent upon one river's flow."[41] The shaky foundation for Las Vegas's development was laid with the completion of the Hoover Dam in 1935, which gave it access to Lake Mead and the Colorado River. The looming issue now facing the city is that the river has been oversubscribed by its potential users for almost a century, the demands on it have steadily grown, and the river's flow is unreliable and is projected to fall, perhaps sharply, in the coming decades.[42] Authors of a leading study conclude that there is a 50 percent chance Lake Mead will become a "dead pool" by 2021, which would happen if water levels fall below the dam's outlet tunnels.[43] To forestall the possibility that one of the city's two pipelines might soon be suspended in air, the Southern Nevada Water Authority moved forward with a plan to build a $1 billion intake to take water from the bottom of the lake.

The city's "ultimate lifeline" is the water lying beneath the Great Basin.[44] Las Vegas's attempts to secure water from other sources besides the Colorado River began in 1989, when the Las Vegas Valley Water Authority (as it was then called) submitted a filing to the Nevada Division of Water Resources for the right to reserve water from designated surface and groundwater sources throughout the state. The Nevada state engineer, who is empowered to approve water filings for the division, approved the application and thus effectively awarded half of the state's water resources to Las Vegas. By 2004 Mulroy had persuaded the Nevada congressional delegation to introduce a bill to provide rights-of-way across federal lands for the building of a pipeline to tap into an aquifer lying below Utah and Nevada. Utah's delegation offered support on the condition that the two states reach an agreement on the amount of water that could be withdrawn. Negotiations began in 2005 and seemed to conclude in 2009 when officials representing Nevada and Utah announced an accord that would allow Las Vegas permission to pump water from the shared aquifer.[45] The agreement ignited a raging controversy. Opponents cited evidence that falling groundwater levels would disrupt the functioning of watersheds, profoundly alter ecological systems, intensify wildfires, compromise air quality along the front range of the Wasatch Mountains, and threaten the Great Basin National Park.[46]

On April 4, 2013, the drawn-out debate culminated in an unexpected decision by Utah's governor not to sign the compact. The Southern Nevada Water Authority (snwa) protested, but it was clear the governor's decision made it certain that the pipeline project would be significantly delayed, possibly indefinitely.[47] In December 2013 opponents scored another victory when a Nevada state judge ruled that the state engineer had to show that water withdrawals from four valleys in the eastern part of the state would not deplete the groundwater.[48] The controversy took still another turn in February 2014, when the Center for Biological Diversity filed a suit in federal court to overturn an earlier decision by the Bureau of Land Management to award the snwa a right-of-way across federal lands for the pipeline project.

Over the long run it is unlikely that Las Vegas's search for Great Basin water will be denied. The city long ago asserted legal claims over the surface water in watersheds scattered throughout. In the meantime, water withdrawals in the Basin are already increasing. Rising gold prices have brought a boom in open-pit gold mining, and the leaching process required to process the huge quantities of earth moved in these operations requires enough water to supply medium-size cities. In northern Nevada, for example, one mining operation has drawn down the underground aquifer twelve hundred feet.[49]

Water diversion accelerates a drying trend that has been occurring for centuries. Already the Department of Interior considers the Great Basin as more "at risk" than any other ecological region in the United States,[50] and climate models predict a 10 to 20 percent drop from present precipitation levels by midcentury.[51] These changes can already be observed in "declining snowpack, earlier peak spring streamflows, lower summer streamflows, and elevated stream temperatures."[52] The ecological systems of the Basin face threats not only from climate change, but also from the urban development spreading along its rim. There may be ways to turn away from the collision course between nature and man, but it would require a level of governmental activism that has been notably absent throughout the Basin's history.

Solitude

The dean of western writers, Wallace Stegner, mocked as myth the idea that western settlement required special qualities of individualism and self-reliance; even so, he held a fondness for the Great Basin because, by his account, "that desert has in very truth been sanctuary to outlaw and zealot and artist and scientist and White Indian and Nephite." Stegner's colorful cast of characters provides some insight into a distinctive regional culture that many others have also noted. According to historian Elizabeth Raymond, "Residents of the Great Basin . . . developed in self-defense a regional identity that grew from their pride in the basic accomplishment of simply having endured in such an unlikely place."[53] Like Stegner, Raymond emphasizes a stark contradiction between cultural myth and environmental reality: in actual practice, survival in the Basin has always required collective endeavor. Mormons solved the problem by bringing with them a shared sense of communal destiny and an authoritarian leadership structure. In the twentieth century, the ability to marshal collective effort was achieved by the giant reclamation projects that brought irrigation water to southern Idaho, eastern Nevada, and Las Vegas. Federal policies also subsidized mining and grazing on public lands. The Great Basin has been so powerfully shaped by federal authority that it is scarcely possible to imagine how it could have developed without it.

Seventy percent of the land in the Basin is owned by agencies of the federal government. The ubiquitous federal presence has given rise to a political culture that distrusts governmental efforts of all kinds.[54] Anti-Washington rhetoric is a fundamental feature of politics throughout the West, but conflicts play out more intensely in the Basin than elsewhere. The Great Basin is the original home of the Sagebrush Rebellion, which became a national cause during Ronald Reagan's presidency. As early as the 1960s the State of Nevada had unsuccessfully challenged federal control of land within its borders. By the late 1970s the resistance to federal authority had coalesced into a coalition that brought together state and local officials, developers, and industrial interests across the western states. What energized opposition was that federal land management policies placed increasing emphasis on environmental protection at the expense of ranching, mining, and energy development. State officials were convinced that policy makers inside the Beltway did not understand the "conditions and concerns" they faced and even that federal officials "displayed outright animosity toward the west."[55]

Conflict between state and local officials and federal land managers took a new turn in the 1990s when hundreds of western counties passed "county supremacy ordinances" asserting that they possessed sovereignty over federally owned lands within their borders.[56] These ordinances often cited "the wise use of resources" doctrine advanced by Gifford Pinchot early in the twentieth century, which made free access and multiple uses on public lands a founding principle of the US Forest Service.[57] Although they failed to pass judicial review, the County Supremacy ordinances succeeded in focusing and energizing the opposition to federal land management policies.

In 1998 Congress passed the Southern Nevada Public Lands Management Act, which allowed the Bureau of Land Management to auction public lands in the Las Vegas region, and subsequent legislation was passed or proposed for four other counties in the Great Basin.[58] If anything, modest concessions such as these encouraged the rebellion. On March 23, 2012, Utah's governor signed a bill asking the federal government to cede twenty million acres of federal land to the state. Other states rushed to press similar demands, and Utah and Arizona began preparing lawsuits.[59] The legal challenges were not likely to change the facts on the ground, but the symbolic value for western public officials was too good to pass up.

Like malaria, conflict with the federal government is a recurring fever, and it will continue to flare up from time to time because public lands hold resources that powerful interests covet. The resentment has purely local origins as well. In many Nevada counties more than 90 percent of the land is owned by the federal government, and none of it is subject to taxation. These counties depend heavily upon federal payments in lieu of taxes to help sustain governmental services. Although federal payments provide critical services and jobs, they are viewed by local officials as an entitlement. Any parent with teenagers will instantly recognize the syndrome.

The isolation of many desert communities and the thinly scattered settlement pattern make government seem distant, but at the same time governmental services for people are needed. Four Nevada counties contain fewer than two thousand residents and eight have fewer than five thousand.

Although western rural counties have few resources, those that begin to grow must deal with newcomers who are shocked to learn that even the most basic public services are sometimes absent. In such a circumstance, any policy problems that may arise must be either ignored or, if possible, passed on to the state or federal government. The irony is that when federal officials try to help, they often find that local officials and residents relish the opportunity to bite the hand that feeds them.

The Desert Future

Those who love deserts often speak of the spiritually healing qualities of solitude and empty spaces. Scholar and writer Richard Francaviglia has traveled throughout the Great Basin and is one of its most passionate and eloquent spokesmen: "In this desert land, the forces that had originally been unleashed by God in creating the universe were still everywhere visible." Driving a lonely road at night, he is uplifted by the "stunning desert landscapes" of the Basin and confesses that "I thrive on the openness of the landscape and the momentary separation from civilization."[60] Francaviglia's reflections are shared by a host of writers who have connected the austerity and even bleakness of desert landscapes with a sense of timelessness and spirituality.[61]

Sentiments such as these are hard to square with the changes now coming to the Great Basin. Urban growth and the aridity that makes empty spaces possible are on a collision course. Because this desert seems utterly unique, it may be tempting to regard its problems as merely regional in interest and scope. It should be noted, however, that one-third of the earth's land surface is covered by arid and semiarid regions, and virtually all of them are experiencing population growth and ecological disruption.[62] On a global scale, climate change and water supply will be among the most pressing problems of the twenty-first century. The Basin has been warming for centuries, and global climate change is accelerating this long-term trend. Because warmer air holds less water by volume, water availability is projected to fall by as much as 20 percent by midcentury in the West, with the drying regime intensely concentrated in a broad arc stretching the length of Nevada and sweeping east to the Rockies.[63] Climate change is also affecting the Great Plains, Texas, Oklahoma, and the southeastern United States.[64] Understanding the impact of urbanization within the largest desert in North America may yield insights about how cities can be built in ways that preserve natural environments, not only in the Great Basin, but elsewhere as well.

NOTES

1. Carl Abbott, *The New Urban America: Growth and Politics in Sunbelt Cities* (Chapel Hill: University of North Carolina Press, 1987), 6.

2. Paul F. Starrs and John B. Wright, "Great Basin Growth and the Withering of California's Pacific Idyll," *American Geographical Society* 85, no. 4 (1995), http//www.jstor.org/stable/215918.

3. It has not always been acknowledged that much of America's national development has depended upon the growth of its cities. At the time the US Constitution was ratified, the five cities perched on the Atlantic Seaboard dominated national social, economic, and political life. In the first half of the nineteenth century, the continental interior was opened up by cities and towns fighting for power and primacy on the nation's frontier. After the Civil War, the industrial cities emerged as the powerhouses of the national economy, and their ascendant status was not eclipsed until the rise of the Sunbelt cities in the post–World War II period. The growth of large cities in the interior West may signal the closing of the final urban frontier because there are no large regions left in the United States that have not already been settled.

4. Alicia Torregrosa and Nora Devoe, "Urbanization and Changing Land Use in the Great Basin," USDA *Forest Service General Technical Report*, RMRS-GTR-204 (2008): 10.

5. Starrs and Wright, "Great Basin Growth," 422.

6. As Donald K. Grayson notes, defining the Basin strictly as an area of internal drainage achieves a measure of precision, but it is not useful for every purpose. Grayson recognizes three definitions of the Great Basin: the hydrographic, the physiographic, and the floristic. The area of internal drainage is the one most often displayed in maps (for example, on *Wikipedia*), but these differ substantially depending upon whether the Salton Basin of Southern California is included (Grayson does not think it should be). Much confusion occurs because the hydrological basin includes both the Mojave Desert and the Great Basin Desert, which are defined by their floristic communities. A Great Basin region is also defined by its main physiographic feature, an alternating sequence of basin and ranges. The dynamic geological processes underlying this unique topography are elegantly explained by writer John McPhee in his book *Basin and Range* (New York: Farrar, Straus, and Giroux, 1980). Finally, the floristic Great Basin is defined by its "relatively distinctive assemblages of plants," with sagebrush the most ubiquitous. The definition we employ in this book, the Great Basin Desert, includes the Snake River Plateau of Idaho and the Owyhee highlands of southeastern Oregon, but because the rivers in these regions drain to the sea, they do not lie within the hydrographic boundaries of the Basin. The definition employed by scholars and writers varies depending upon their interests; none, in the abstract, is singularly "correct." See

Donald K. Grayson, *The Great Basin: A Natural Prehistory* (Berkeley: University of California Press, 2011), 22.

7. Elizabeth Raymond, "When the Desert Won't Bloom: Environmental Limitation and the Great Basin," in *Many Wests: Place, Culture, and Regional Identity*, edited by David M. Wrobel and Michael C. Steiner (Lawrence: University Press of Kansas, 1997), 81.

8. Besides the Mojave there are the Sonoran and the Chihuahuan Deserts. (For a precise map of these deserts, see Grayson, *Great Basin*, 21.) In her book *The Mysterious Lands* (New York: Truman Talley Books/Plume, 1990), naturalist Ann Raymond Zwinger offers a colorful and personal portrait of these four biotic regions. An especially enlightening history of mapping in the Great Basin can be found in Richard V. Francaviglia, *Mapping the Great Basin: A Cartographic History* (Reno: University of Nevada Press, 2005). His map of the hydrographic boundaries of the Basin contains 165,000 square miles and encompasses Death Valley and much of the Mojave Desert (3–4). In his extraordinary photo-essay book on the Great Basin, *The Sagebrush Ocean: A Natural History of the Great Basin*, 10th anniversary ed. (Reno: University of Nevada Press, 1999), naturalist Stephen Trimble excludes the Snake River Plain (or Plateau). His discussion of the various attempts to delineate precise boundaries illustrates the many variations on the theme.

9. Peter Stark, *The Last Empty Places: A Past and Present Journey Through the Blank Spots on the American Map* (New York: Ballantine Books, 2010).

10. Dayton Duncan, *Miles from Nowhere: In Search of the American Frontier* (New York: Penguin Books, 1993).

11. Denzel Ferguson and Nancy Ferguson, *Oregon's Great Basin Country* (Burns, OR: Gail Graphics, 1978), 18–21.

12. Richard W. Etulain, *Beyond the Missouri: The Story of the American West* (Albuquerque: University of New Mexico Press, 28).

13. See, for example, this assessment by Soren C. Larsen and Timothy J. Brock: "For most Americans, the Great Basin is nothingness. In the popular imagination the basin is a dry, crater-pocked land of endless scrub populated by tarantulas and jackrabbits. It is seen as a place without use or value, a wasteland that has intimidated the most intrepid of travelers." Larsen and Brock, "Great Basin Imagery in Newspaper Coverage of Yucca Mountain," *Geographical Review* 95, no. 4 (2005): 517.

14. Cited in Francaviglia, *Mapping the Great Basin*, 5.

15. Richard V. Francaviglia, *Believing in Place: A Spiritual Geography of the Great Basin* (Reno: University of Nevada Press, 2003), 197.

16. Raymond, "When the Desert Won't Bloom," 86, quoting W. Eugene Hollon.

17. See Francaviglia, *Believing in Place*, 201–2. After the test ban treaty of 1962, 828 underground explosions were set off at the site. Ironically, it is now becoming a tourist destination.

18. Quoted in Larsen and Brock, "Great Basin Imagery," 530.

19. Francaviglia, *Believing in Place,* 3, 59.

20. http://www.nps.gov/grba/parkmgmt/statistics.htm.

21. http://www.nps.gov, Great Basin.

22. This percentage is calculated using the definition of the Great Basin Desert as defined by Grayson and utilizing county-level statistics on public lands as provided by the US Census Bureau.

23. McPhee, *Basin and Range,* 18. Here, McPhee is restating a time-honored myth. It is not known what Brigham Young said when he saw the Salt Lake Valley, but the phrase attributed to him did not make an appearance for more than twenty years after he entered the Basin and some years after his death.

24. Tim Sullivan, *No Communication with the Sea: Searching for an Urban Future in the Great Basin* (Tucson: University of Arizona Press, 2010), 30.

25. Sullivan, *No Communication with the Sea,* 25.

26. Office of Economic Development, Salt Lake City, "Statistics: Facts at a Glance," http://www.slcclassic.com/ed/pages/states/morestats.htm.

27. L. J. Davis, "Tearing Down Boise," *Harper's,* November 1974, 32–38.

28. Ibid., 83.

29. Alicia Barber, *Reno's Big Gamble: Image and Reputation in the Biggest Little City* (Lawrence: University Press of Kansas, 2008), 237. The quote is from a 2004 publication by the Reno-Sparks Convention and Visitors Authority.

30. Hal K. Rothman, *Neon Metropolis: How Las Vegas Started the Twenty-First Century* (New York: Routledge, 2002), xxvii; McPhee, *Basin and Range,* 54.

31. Torregrosa and Devoe, "Urbanization and Changing Land Use," 9.

32. Raymond, "When the Desert Won't Bloom," 73.

33. James Lawrence Powell, *Dead Pool: Lake Powell, Global Warming, and the Future of Water in the West* (Berkeley: University of California Press, 2008), 35.

34. Raymond, "When the Desert Won't Bloom," 81.

35. "Great Basin Carbonate-Alluvial Aquifer System (GBCAAS) Water Availability," US Department of the Interior, US Geological Survey, http://water.usgs.gov/projects/greatbasin/index.html.

36. *Megapolitan* has entered the literature as a way of referring to the "super-regions" that are emerging in many different areas of the United States. The term is interchangeable with *Consolidated Statistical Areas,* which the US Census Bureau uses to refer to interlinked metropolitan areas that exchange at least 15 percent of their workers as measured by commuting.

37. Jeanne C. Chambers and Michael J. Wisdom, "Priority Research and Management Issues for the Imperiled Great Basin of the Western United States," *Restoration Ecology* 17, no. 5 (2009): 507–714.

38. Gregory T. Pederson et al., "The Unusual Nature of Recent Snowpack Declines in the North American Cordillera," *Science* 333, no. 6040 (2011): 332–35, doi: 10.1126/science.1201570.

39. Center for Business and Economic Research, University of Nevada–Las Vegas, *Clark County Population Forecasts* (2011).

40. Quoted in William deBuys, *A Great Aridness: Climate Change and the Future of the American Southwest* (New York: Oxford University Press, 2011), 155.

41. Marc Reisner, *Cadillac Desert: The American West and Its Disappearing Water* (New York: Penguin Books, 1993).

42. Andrew Ross, *Bird on Fire: Lessons from the World's Least Sustainable City* (New York: Oxford University Press, 2011), 139ff; Powell, *Dead Pool*, 163–201.

43. A reservoir becomes a dead pool when the water level falls below the dam's outlet pipes. See Tim P. Barnett and David W. Pierce, "When Will Lake Mead Begin to Dry?," *Water Resources Research* 44 (2008). Subsequent studies by these authors and others moved the window a bit further out, but not by much. See deBuys, *Great Aridness*, 138–39.

44. DeBuys, *Great Aridness*, 153.

45. Ibid., 138, 150–51.

46. Henry Brean, "Pipelines Seen as Threat to Great Basin National Park," *Las Vegas Review-Journal*, November 9, 2011; news release, *Great Basin Water Network*, October 31, 2011; Great Basin Water Issues, "Water Grabs Threaten the Future of Rural Communities and Wildlife Throughout the Great Basin," *Great Basin Water Network*, http://www.greatbasinwater.net/issues/index.php.

47. Robert Gehrke, "Utah's Rejection of Water Deal Leaves Nevada with Few Good Options," *Salt Lake Tribune*, April 5, 2013, http://www.sltrib.com/csp/cms /sites/sltrib.

48. Brian Maffly, "Court Rejects Las Vegas' Groundwater Rights to Rural Valleys," *Salt Lake Tribune*, December 11, 2013, http:/www.sltrib.com/sltrib/politics /57251310-90/com-decision.

49. Christopher J. Huggard, "Squeezing Out the Profits: Mining and the Environment in the U.S. West, 1945–2000," in *The American West in 2000*, edited by Richard W. Etulain and Ferenc M. Szasz (Albuquerque: University of New Mexico Press, 2003), 118–19.

50. According to a "Watershed Condition Classification" published by the US Department of the Interior, all the major watersheds of the central parts of the Great Basin are "functioning at risk" or operating with "impaired function." See the watershed map displayed in *High Country News*, February 20, 2012, 6.

51. Douglas Fox, "Omens from a Vanished Sea," *High Country News*, October 31, 2011, 11–17.

52. Statement of Mike Pellant, the Great Basin Restoration Initiative Coordinator, Bureau of Land Management, before the Senate Subcommittee on Public Lands and Forests, October 11, 2007, http://energy.senate.gov/.../CBRICClimate Change/FieldHearingFinal10007.doc, 2. See also Chambers and Wisdom, "Priority Research and Management Issues."

53. Wallace Stegner, *Mormon Country* (1942; reprint, Lincoln: University of Nebraska Press, 1970), 349; Raymond, "When the Desert Won't Bloom," 83.

54. For a definitive historical treatment, see Charles F. Wilkinson, *Crossing the Next Meridian: Land, Water, and the Future of the West* (Washington, DC: Island Press, 1992).

55. "Questions and Answers" on the "Sagebrush Rebellion" fact sheet, folder 4, Guide to the Records of Sagebrush Rebellion, Collection no. 85-04 (University of Nevada, Reno, Special Collections), http://knowledgecenter.unr.edu/specoll /mss/85-04.html.

56. Stephanie L. Witt and Leslie R. Alm, "County Government and the Public Lands: A Review of the County Supremacy Movement in Four Western States," in *Public Lands Management in the West: Citizens, Interest Groups, and Values*, edited by Brent S. Steel (Westport, CT: Greenwood Press, 1997).

57. R. McGreggor Cawley, *Federal Land, Western Anger: The Sagebrush Rebellion and Environmental Politics* (Lawrence: University Press of Kansas, 1993), 166.

58. Torregrosa and Devoe, "Urbanization and Changing Land Use," 11.

59. Kirk Johnson, "Utah Asks U.S. to Return 20 Million Acres of Land," *New York Times*, March 23, 2012, http;//www.nytimes.com/2012/03/24/us/utah-bill-asks -government-to-give-back.

60. Francaviglia, *Believing in Place*, 17, 120.

61. See, for example, Belden C. Lane, *The Solace of Fierce Landscapes: Exploring Mountain and Desert Spirituality* (New York: Oxford University Press, 1998).

62. Ibid.

63. Fox, "Omens from a Vanished Sea," 10–17.

64. The US Global Change Research Program predicts "continued rising temperature, more frequent droughts, depleted water supplies and an influx of invasive plant species across the High Plains." Joe Wilkins, "Saving the Holocene," *High Country News*, January 23, 2012, 23.

Solitude

Framing the Empty

Technology and Progress in Photography and Art

TODD SHALLAT

ON MAY 10, 1869, when Union Pacific met Central Pacific at Promontory in Utah Territory, the driving of a golden spike became America's first live coast-to-coast multimedia extravaganza. Western Union broadcast the final thud of the ceremonial hammer via a wire attached to the spike. Cannons simultaneously boomed in Boston and San Francisco. Fire engines with screeching whistles circled Philadelphia's statehouse for the ringing of the Liberty Bell.

A. J. Russell of the Union Pacific preserved the euphoric moment in a wet-plate photograph called *East Meets West at the Laying of the Last Rail* (fig. 1). Composed as a tribute to the unifying spirit of e pluribus unum, with tycoons grasping hands below workmen on locomotives, the photo confirmed the technological magic of wasteland transformed into wealth. No matter that the photo was staged. No matter that the final spike was actually iron, that the railroad was far from finished, that the Union Pacific's man with the silver hammer had been kidnapped while his workers demanded their wages, or that the slaving Chinese—earning about a dollar a day—were excluded outside the frame. And no matter if the champagne bottles, toasted in celebration, mysteriously disappeared from later reproductions as if to mollify temperance crusaders. Russell's image was allegory. Neither fact nor entirely fiction, it strived for cultural truths. "Nature and Man shall be disjoin'd and diffused no more," wrote Walt Whitman, who saw the photo as a wood engraving in *Frank Leslie's Illustrated*. Engineering was cited by the poet as proof that the pious would inevitably triumph. The driving of the golden spike in Russell's heroic framing was God's mighty purpose revealed.[1]

The pale blankness of Utah-Nevada made the metaphor visually stark. Stretched from nowhere to nowhere, from the Wasatch Front to the Sierra Nevada across 210,000 square miles of rivers draining inward, through sun-drenched shadeless mountains and pools that mysteriously disappeared through sinks of alkaline sand, the Great Basin of Utah-Nevada was the

Figure 1. Chinese laborers stand outside the frame in A. J. Russell's *East Meets West at the Laying of the Last Rail* (May 10, 1869). (Library of Congress)

highest and driest of North America's deserts, the largest and least populated, the most disparaged and misunderstood. It was the Big Empty. The Void. The Great Unknown. Its character was "dreary and savage," said US topographical engineer John Charles Frémont from the Bear Lake corner of Utah in 1843. It was "worthless, valueless, d[amne]d mean God forsaken country," said a peddler on the overland trail. Mark Twain imagined "a vast, waveless ocean stricken dead and turned to ashes." For cowboy novelist Owen Wister, writing in 1897, the high desert of Utah-Nevada was an "abomination of desolation . . . a mean ash-dump landscape . . . lacquered with paltry, unimportant ugliness . . . not a drop of water to a mile of sand."[2]

The strangeness repelled the first generation of landscape painters. Even as giants such as Frederic Remington, Maynard Dixon, and Georgia O'Keeffe began to incorporate mesas and canyons, painters avoided the sagebrush. Printmakers and photographers compensated. Prints and photos of big machines and big engineering promoted tourism as they advertised land that financed the railroads. Hell-in-harness scenes of smelters and trestles, of shovels devouring hillsides, of dams and the laying of track were images of American prowess, a chronicle of popular thought. Some of the images cheered and others denounced industrial progress. Some pined for the landscapes lost to smokestack industrialization. Some viewed irrigation as a scientific sensation. Some imagined a mechanized Eden reclaimed by the faithful for God.

Images of machines advanced the discovery process through which Americans learned to perceive the enigma beyond the Rockies as something more than a hideous void. Mixing the real and the ideal, the imagery left a culturally coded appraisal of the highest and best use of land. Our sampling, herein, features landscapes from three historical eras. First, from the era of the golden spike, are pictures of barrens redeemed by steel and big engineering. Second, from paintings of agrarian Utah, are landscapes of farming's surrender to industrialization. Third, from postmodern Nevada, are forebodings of the toxic Sahara the Great Basin might one day become.

Deserts and Determinism

The frontier itself was a kind of machine that sputtered in arid places and had to be overhauled. So said Texas historian Walter Prescott Webb, writing in 1930. The machine with its axes and saws had moved west through swampy woodlands, clearing the timber, turning the sod. But the engine had stalled at the base of the Rockies, and there the process gave way to a motive capitalist force that Webb called the cattle kingdom. "It was a machine, too," said Webb, "but entirely different from the agricultural one undergoing repairs on the timber line." Corporate and industrial, it crossed into Utah on rails. Its vital parts were windmills, barbed wire, steam engines, the McCormick Reaper, and the Colt revolver. Its triumph was to sustain the garden myth of the West as a Land of Plenty on a frontier that was factory made.[3]

Webb sang for a chorus of western writers to fill the chasm between the promise of technology's progress and the peril of what progress had wrought. From the chasm's hopeful side came utopians such as Nebraska's William E. Smythe, who predicted, in 1905, that irrigation and big hydraulics would make the rising state of Nevada "politically untrammeled" and "economically freed." From the chasm's brooding side came a literature protesting the loss of agrarian landscapes. Novelist Frank Norris, writing in 1901, recoiled at the "soulless force" of trains crossing the prairie, their "tentacles of steel clutching into the soil."[4] Divergent thought they were, the writings of Norris

and Smythe anticipated a deterministic Webbian view of factory-made innovation. As if machines dictated culture, as if factories and their tools were
agents independent of hope, fear, politics, and scientific conjecture, technology had motive power.[5]

Technological determinism is the term scholars have used to describe this
view of machines as the force behind civilization. Determinists claim that
the six-shooter conquered the prairie, that the Pill (or hardtop automobile)
caused the sexual revolution, that cars created the suburbs, that Gutten-
berg's movable type brought the Protestant Reformation, that the A-bomb
divested Congress of its constitutional authority to make declarations of war.
In each case the implication is that the social consequences of invention are
far-reaching, uncontrollable, and irreversible. In each a tool or device is the
cause or precondition of some inevitable transformation. Things, not nature
or culture, are the decisive agents of change.[6]

It's a comforting belief. Born in the European Enlightenment, reborn
in the wishful thinking of Alexander Hamilton and image makers such as
Currier and Ives, the gospel of progress through innovation squared nicely
with the American myth of a clever, inventive people predestined to uproot
the sagebrush and plow. Critics respond by evoking the peril of devastation.
Thus philosopher Lewis Mumford compared twentieth-century man to a
drunken conductor of a runaway train. The train's conductor was "plunging
through the darkness at a hundred miles an hour, going past the danger signals without realizing that our speed, which springs from mechanical facility,
only increases our danger and will make more fatal the crash."[7]

Determinism pervaded the imagery of yeomen drawn west by the pull of
empty places. In the era of Manifest Destiny, when the "destiny" of Protestant civilization seemed "manifest" in the prowess of wondrous machines,
the railroad was an obvious symbol of national triumph. Painters Thomas
Cole, Asher Durand, George Inness, and others were no longer content with
puffs of steam in the distant horizon. Railroads took center stage. In 1860, in
a landscape commission by a railroad mogul, Philadelphian Thomas Otter
featured a west-bound Baldwin locomotive crossing a bridge as it overtook
an emigrant's covered wagon. Satirist Thomas Nast depicted an Indian flee-
ing before a charging locomotive in his frontispiece to a popular guidebook
called *Beyond the Mississippi* (1867). Another Nast illustration had an Indian
warrior prone and helpless, his feathered head on the steel rail. Black smoke
engulfed two cartoonish natives in a celebrated engraving called *Across
the Continent: Westward the Course of Empire Takes Its Way* (1868; fig. 2).

Engraved after a sketch by Frances "Fanny" Palmer and colorized "for the masses" by the New York publishing giant Currier & Ives, *Across the Continent* showed the route of the Union Pacific as a line of demarcation between savage and civilized worlds. Parallel lines of steel slanted west toward a treeless horizon. Unchallenged and pulling its mighty train of Anglo-Saxon values, the railroad moved from the past (as represented by cabins and toiling yeomen) into the nation's industrial future along the base of snowy mountains across a waterless plain.[8]

The most famously garish of the genre's colorized prints was John Gast's *American Progress* (1872). First painted as oil on canvas, it reappeared as the frontispiece for *Crofutt's Trans-continental Tourist Guide* (1874). The print, said its publisher, depicted the Goddess of Civilization. Blond and scantily clad in flowing classical robes, she floated through a grassy landscape. Her right hand held a schoolbook; her left strung telegraph wire. Indians and buffalo escaped through a dark corner at the edge of the canvas. Golden rays of heavenly light blessed the icons of national greatness: the river steamboat, the wagon train, the prospector with his pick, the trapper with his rifle, the yeoman with his plow. Three locomotives pushed west.[9]

Figure 2. Rails freight destiny in Frances Palmer's *Across the Continent: Westward the Course of Empire Takes Its Way* (1868). (Library of Congress)

Iron machines crossed canvas prairies with a heavy cargo of visual misinformation about the desert's flattest terrain. Seldom did the heroic school of metaphorical painters incorporate scrub vegetation. Romantics such as Albert Bierstadt and Thomas Moran preferred the alpine and the operatic. Indifferent to gray-green sagebrush, they reached instead for the jewels on the rim of the Basin: Lake Tahoe, Zion, the Green River, the Grand Canyon of the Colorado, the Shoshone Falls of the Snake. "Culture work[ed] as a lens providing focus," wrote historian Anne F. Hyde in an essay about western landscapes, and thus the history of artistic perception was also the story of willful misperception.[10] It remained for the photo savants of topographical science to reframe Utah-Nevada as a distinct geophysical place.

Among the first to mule-pack a camera in the service of science was a Sephardic Jew of Spanish-Portuguese decent. In 1853–54, Solomon Carvalho scaled the Rockies with a privately funded scientific survey under Colonel Frémont's command. Frostbit and surviving on horse meat above Utah's Cathedral Valley, the surveyors were forced to abandon their scientific equipment. Daguerreotype cameras were left in the snow. The misadventure spread skepticism about photographic documentation. US geographers John Wesley Powell and Ferdinand Vandeveer Hayden both came to prefer the imaginative grandeur of woodcut engravings. Photography, many believed, was too literal. Book publishers such as William Cullen Bryant of the *New York Evening Post* dismissed the camera because "mere topographical accuracy" would likely obscure "animation and beauty." Photography, Bryant maintained, "lack[ed] the spirit and personal quality which the accomplished painter or draughtsman infuses into his work."[11]

Not until photographer Timothy O'Sullivan met geographer Clarence King did the camera come into its own as a medium of scientific documentation. Irish-born O'Sullivan of Staten Island had campaigned with Union generals McClellan and Grant in the Army of the Potomac's photographic corps. O'Sullivan's silver prints of the Confederate dead, their corpses shoeless and posed, remain unsurpassed as testimony to the horror of war. Letters from the War Department brought O'Sullivan to the attention of King in the wake of Lee's surrender. In July 1867, via steamer and Isthmus railroad from New York to Panama, San Francisco, and Sacramento, O'Sullivan followed King and his party of ten surveyors into Nevada across Donner Pass.[12]

O'Sullivan did more than produce a stunning visual record. Shunning romantic convention, he extended the vision of science. Precise and meticulous but hardly objective, he supplemented the charts, graphs, fossil sketches, stratigraphic diagrams, contour topographical maps, and cross-sectional schematics that gave geology its visual power. In 1867, however, the camera was an afterthought for explorers whose primary task was the search for mineral wealth. Clarence King of Yale, age twenty-five, had orders to survey in advance of the railroad from Lake Tahoe to Colorado. King's United States Geological and Geographical Exploration of the Fortieth Parallel (1867–73) became the first to establish that Nevada's Humboldt River drainage was a watershed distinct from the Great Salt Lake. The Great Basin discovered by Frémont was, according to King, many dozens of smaller basins where primordial lakes had drained into the ocean, leaving alkali playas of sand. Science aside, it was the booming importance of mining that kept the survey funded by Congress. In Utah's Green River basin, the expedition found rich deposits of "practically inexhaustible" coal.[13] In Colorado, where swindlers had salted a mesa with chips from South African diamonds, King won international fame for exposing a mining hoax.[14]

The Fortieth Parallel Survey was also theoretical science. Basalt flows in impossible canyons with toothed and twisted formations were offered as proof of the crumbling and crushing that had sculpted and resurfaced the globe. King's *Systematic Geology* (1878), in part a challenge to Charles Darwin, advanced the theory that "moments of great catastrophe" had accelerated the life-altering process of natural selection. Volcanism drove evolution. Fractures, faults, fissures, and floods had forced the biota to cope or die.[15]

The violence of geologic events also focused the photographer's lens. Where King reported catastrophe, O'Sullivan accentuated the cataclysmic bizarre. In the Humboldt Sink of Nevada, where King used the word *picturesque* to describe volcanic fissures, O'Sullivan supplied what the scientists called "picturesque evidence."[16] At Witches Rocks, Utah, where, according to King, the crashing of tectonic plates had upthrusted spires of sandstone, O'Sullivan exaggerated the height of the weird formation in a skewed low-angle shot. Another photograph of the fingerlike Witches formation used a paper masking to isolate a single teetering spire. Returning to the Comstock Lode at the western edge of the Basin, O'Sullivan framed lunar landscapes as if the scientists were the first to encounter the Basin. An 1867 O'Sullivan print called *Sand Dunes, Carson Desert* showed mules pulling a wagon. Boot prints were tracked in the sand to emphasize isolation (fig. 3). Dark wedges of rock were engulfed by the whiteness of sky. Hailed for its minimalism, *Sand Dunes,* said historian William Goetzmann, "was one of the great matter-of-fact photos of all time."[17] Yet the photo was nevertheless a staged

Figure 3. Boot prints trail away from Timothy O'Sullivan's darkroom wagon in *Sand Dunes, Carson Desert* (1867). (Library of Congress)

misrepresentation. The dunes of the Carson Desert had long been an emigrant landmark in a farming region near a Pony Express station. O'Sullivan had composed the photograph to exclude a well-traveled emigrant road.[18]

Changing photography as he changed the perception of Utah-Nevada, O'Sullivan pioneered an aesthetic of distance and space. His panoramas, bleak and edgeless, showed men in improbable places that looked nothing like El Dorado. And when the focus of the survey turned to the silver bonanza in western Nevada, the documentation defied the romantic sublime. Squalid mills trailing factory smoke seemed "hideous," even "satanic."[19] One dark print from Virginia City showed six despondent miners as they waited to be lowered in cages through a shaft of the Savage Mine. A print of a mine disaster showed a miner's severed leg. Below the surface, danger was ever present. In February 1868, in a dark, gaseous tunnel below the Gould & Curry Mill in Virginia City, the photographer risked explosion by igniting magnesium flares. Historians have hailed the flare-lit mining study as the world's first exposures of men working deep underground.[20]

O'Sullivan exposed the counterintuitive fact that the Basin, like much of the West, was urban before it was rural, its settlement clustered in towns. From Carson City to Reno through ore and lumber centers, from Galena to Washoe City, Virginia City, Franktown, Devils Gate, and Ophir, the Comstock's scarred industrial landscape spread through the urban core. In Utah it was Brigham Young and the overland trails that made Salt Lake City the point of debarkation. Walled cities had effectively colonized the Ute and Shoshone homelands before the coming of the Union Pacific. Waterpower drove foundries and gristmills. A church-owned public utility called the Deseret Telegraph linked the five-hundred-mile Latter-day Saint (LDS) urban network from Logan to St. George.[21]

Railroad photographers did the most to document the transformation. Alfred A. Hart of Sacramento, formerly a portrait painter, sold stereo cards of the Central Pacific as it crossed northern Nevada. Determinism pervaded Hart's 1869 print of a Paiute posed alone on a cliff overlooking the Humboldt and the inevitable railroad skirting its banks (fig. 4). Another master photographer of the Ute and Paiute was the English-born Charles R. Savage of Salt Lake City. Savage rode circuit through the Mormon country, taking portraits and selling stereographic pictures of men with their heavy sledges breaking stone for the Mormon shrines. In 1867, at soon-to-be-famous Promontory Summit in Utah, Savage joined photographers Hart and A. J. Russell for the recording of the joining of rails. Mythology still shrouds the event.

Figure 4. Primitive man contemplates the doom of his civilization in Alfred A. Hart's *Indian Viewing RR from Top of Palisades* (albumen stereograph print, 1869). (Library of Congress)

One persistent fable is that the Chinese workmen were excluded from the famous photos because they were camera shy. Legend has it that the Chinese dropped the rail and scattered when a bystander yelled at Savage, "Now's the time, Charlie! Take a shot!"[22]

The lesson within the legend is that historians and photographers faced a common interpretive challenge when framing symbolic events. With images, with words, they sought balance between reproduction and construction, between the passive mining of data and the sequencing of that information into narratives with emotional power. The photographer's viewfinder became, as Yale's Alan Trachtenberg phrased it, "a political instrument" for validating the expansionist need to fence and subdivide land.[23] When icons of obsolescence were juxtaposed against the mechanical emblems of progress—when the covered wagon was overtaken, when Chinese fled before the hooded camera, when the Paiute alone on his cliff saw doom in the form of a freight train—territorial conquest, being inevitable, seemed pridefully justified.

Of the three photographers at Promontory, it was A. J. Russell more than Savage or Hart who milked the most metaphorical meaning from the power of the western landscape. Soldier, correspondent, salesman, and diorama artist, Russell, like O'Sullivan, had photographed machinery for the Union army during the Civil War. In 1868, from his base camp in Echo City, Wyoming, he had documented the last six hundred miles of the advance of the Union Pacific en route to the joining of rails. Fifty of Russell's most sensational prints graced a silvery album formally titled *The Great West Illustrated in a Series of Photographic Views Across the Continent*. Lavishly published with leather binding in 1869, the album sold in Manhattan bookstores for more than a month's worth of a rail worker's wage. The Far West with its trestles, tunnels, and trains appeared an astonishing and even "luxuriant" region of "colossal grandeur."[24] The desert, no longer wretched, appeared subdued and commoditized. Geographer Hayden cited *Great West* as proof that Utah was potentially fertile. Journalist Samuel Bowles, who traveled with Russell and witnessed the joining of rails, saw the photography as documentation of commercial and political virtues. The transcontinental, Bowles insisted, was more than a remarkable feat of American engineering; it was the single greatest engineering achievement of all time.[25]

There were no buffalo storming the prairie in A. J. Russell's grand presentation. No coolie-hatted Chinese. No Paiute dwarfed by trains. In the futuristic Utah that photography framed in its moment of industrial triumph, the primitive was anachronistic and too distant to be perceived as a threat.

Machines in the Garden of Zion

A desert and elsewhere a garden, a Silverado, a cattle frontier, a passage, a pariah, a bleak and shifting mirage, the strangeness at the foot of the Rockies fed towering expectations for the West's most perplexing terrain. Its discovery—a process, not an event—was visceral and subjective, an act of the mind as well of the eyes. Where tycoons saw industrial conquest, geographers saw cataclysm. Where engineers found canyons for dams and flatness for irrigation, artist George Catlin, a painter of Ute and Shoshone, confirmed the defeat of a vanishing race. Always a West of the imagination, a projection of heartbreak and dreams, the Great Basin was also a biblical Zion for the chosen but persecuted who found in that chaste isolation God's plan for restoring the Earth. Latter-day Saints in flight and seeking salvation escaped from the factory cities to preordained sanctuary. "Their spirit was inward, practical, and agricultural," wrote historian Ronald W. Walker. Even now, according to geographer Richard Francaviglia, "life in the Intermountain West is somehow buffered or sequestered from the terrors of the outside world."[26]

Aridity and farming in the kingdom of the Latter-day Saints gave rise to a variant telling of the industrial fable about the inevitability of megamachines. As developed in the western writings of American masters such as Emerson, Whitman, and Hawthorne, the story featured pioneers who fretted about modernization without losing faith in modern machines. Compelled, even predestined, to dominate wild places, they yearned for sylvan landscapes and pined for a lost way of life. Farmers mostly, they recoiled at uncut nature. They turned to nature for inspiration without wanting to return to it on a permanent basis. Historian Leo Marx, in an important book about cultural symbols, linked the narrative to a pastoral longing for order in chaotic places. "Pastoralism," as Marx defined it, held out the hope that the conquest of empty places would reconcile conflicting ideals. One ideal was progress through mass production—the machine. Another was tranquil living—the garden. The machine in the garden became a metaphor for balance between nature and industrialization. Blurring old into new, simplicity into sophistication, the machine would work in tandem with agrarian virtue to recover the green republic lost to the industrial age.[27]

God had given Mormons that desert garden because, said Brigham Young, it suited no other people on Earth. Treeless and semiarid, it was topography starkly foreign to yeomen from a woodland culture. Even the native population was sparse. Yet the sloping valley at the foot of the Wasatch Mountains showed agricultural promise. Black soil supported a cover of vegetation so thick that the first pioneers, in July 1847, waded a considerable distance before finding a camping ground. Bunchgrass towered over the oxen. Feeders to the Jordan River seemed well suited for gristmills. Sagebrush could be burned. The air seemed "good and pure, sweetened by healthy breezes." Geothermal springs bubbled up from the earth with medicinal powers enough to "heal all who bathe no matter what their complaint."[28]

Most miraculous of all in the marvel that was Utah was the wondrous Great Salt Lake. An American Galilee, the lake was "an ocean," said a rail tourist, "of majestic mystery clad in beauty divine." Parisian tourist Albert Tissandier found it "impossible to dream of anything more poetic."[29] Currier & Ives published an 1870 lithograph that imagined surreal snowy mountains rising from the luminous lake. Painters Albert Bierstadt and Englishman Alfred Lambourne depicted the lake with shorebirds as it appeared in the Utah legend about crickets vanquished by seagulls. By 1883, with the arrival of the Denver & Rio Grande Railroad, the "strange beauty" of the Great Salt Lake was being promoted in *Harper's* as "one of the points in the United States that all tourists think should not be missed."[30]

Storytellers of later times downplayed the wealth of the valley to heighten the drama of conquest. "There was little to invite and much to repel," wrote Orson Whitney in his 1892 *History of Utah*. "A seemingly interminable waste of sagebrush," the future site of the Mormon city was "baked and burning . . . the paradise of the lizard, the cricket, and the rattlesnake."[31] But Mormon artists told another story. Most of the best from the pioneer generation were converts from distant places such as Denmark, Norway, and England. Carl C. A. Christensen of Copenhagen, a painter of portraits and panoramas, had trekked one thousand miles from Iowa City to Utah while pulling an emigrant's handcart flying the Danish flag. Danquart Anthon Weggeland, missionary and educator, was a Norwegian trained in Denmark and perhaps the only pioneer painter in Utah busy enough to make most of his income from art. George Ottinger, American born, had wandered the globe as a whaler and forty-niner before his conversion to Mormonism. Reaching Utah with his mother by covered wagon, he tinted photographs for Charles Savage and established himself as an all-purpose painter of mountains and genre scenes.

"Romantic realists," they have been called: romantic because they painted the Salt Lake Valley as a biblical Canaan, realists because their paintings documented folkways and customs of Mormon pioneer life.[32]

The first generation painted Utah cartoonishly but with reverence for the communitarian work of subduing the wild. Few of the paintings were overtly religious, but many showed pious devotion to Mormon teachings about beautification, self-reliance, and the virtue of pooling labor. Weggeland emphasized work toward common objectives in *Old Fisher Folks* (1870s), *Rosebank Cottage* (1881), *Manti Temple* (1884), and pioneer epics such as *Mormon Emigrants Crossing the Plains* (1912). Christensen and Ottinger likewise glorified Utah in formulaic landscapes of praise for the holy work of reclaiming the Garden lost to the Fall. Christensen's *Wheat Harvest in Ephraim* (undated) pictured three of his well-fed children smiling with armfuls of grain. In the distant village of Ephraim was a tabernacle peaked above a horizon of gable-roofed and chimneyed houses that Mormons called Nauvoo style. Waterworks and modern equipment were excluded from the original painting. In 1904, however, when Christensen repainted the harvest, he added a hatless young man on his knees with a cup of water at the wooden gate of the homestead's canal.[33]

Paintings of the Utah harvest told parables of regeneration that were hardly unique to the Latter-day Saints. Strong in the Puritan heritage of Brigham Young's native New England, where the metaphor for earthly Zion had been "the city upon a hill," the iconography of regeneration had migrated west in the Mormon gospel of order vanquishing chaos, of wildness defeated and Eden restored.[34] "Make beautiful everything around you," Young had directed his people. "Build cites, adorn your habitations, make gardens, orchards and vineyards, and render the earth so pleasant that when you look upon your labors you may do so with pleasure and that angels may delight."[35]

Town planning echoed that piety of regenerative beautification. Villages right with the compass were said to be right with God. Rectangular townships "that lieth four-square" soon checkered the desert wherever the Saints methodically platted: in Salt Lake City, with its ten-acre blocks symmetrically subdivided; in Spring City, where LDS converts from Denmark built a cemetery in the rectangular shape of Utah; in Snowflake, Arizona, where the standardized streets were wide enough for a team of oxen to circle a wagon; in Franklin on the Idaho line, where the Gothic limestone houses followed the rectangular patterns that Latter-day prophets proscribed.[36]

Gridded towns with gridded fields framed the orderly sameness of hay

derricks and haystacks, of regimented orchards and sheep grazing with cattle, of cedar-post fences and cavernous barns. Scholars of Great Basin settlement patterns have called it the "Mormon landscape." For geographer Richard Francaviglia, who coined the term in his dissertation, the pattern was
symmetry, parallel lines, wide streets, central plazas, and geometrical repetition. For novelist Wallace Stegner, it was red-dusted fields of alfalfa, onions,
and beets with row after parallel row of Lombardy poplars planted as fence
lines. These fast-growing trees, Stegner explained, "were practically never
planted singly, but always in groups [that] took the form of straight lines and
ranks." Gardens were also important. "A Mormon who creates something
green," wrote Mark Leone of Princeton, "has shown his inner state."[37]

That the state of a man's religion was the state of his village and farm
became the driving premise of Utah's agrarian art. Weggeland's *Bishop Sam
Bennion Farm, Taylorsville,* painted in 1879, praised the virtue of Mormon
farming in a compact symbolic composite of the emerging settlement pattern (fig. 5). A painting in three parts, it honored the trinity of mountain,
field, and home: the mountain, reddish brown, that the Saints called Mount

Figure 5. Orderly places were blessed in Danquart Anthon Weggeland's paintings
of the Salt Lake Valley. *Pictured: Bishop Sam Bennion Farm, Taylorsville* (1879).
(Springville Museum of Art, Utah)

Olympus; the orderly field with domes of haystacks; the home of salt-white stucco with double chimneys and multiple doors. Fruit trees shaded the homestead. Children played. A farmer hoed. Cottonwood Creek fed a canal as it branched toward the Jordan River. A train bound for Provo trailed smoke at the base of the mountains as if crossing between the yearning for tranquil nature and the questing for material wealth.[38]

The motif of the train puffing smoke was a visual concession to the Walter Prescott Webbian realization that utopians looking backward still needed forward motion, that farmers needed the railroads, and that even Canaans with biblical place-names—Ephraim, Lehi, Manti, Nephi, Moroni—were inevitably forced to rely on factory-made tools and machines. Regimented orchards and windbreaks, because they depended on ditch irrigation, measured growing reliance on sophisticated dams and canals. Reclamation in Mormon doctrine became divinely providential. For Apostle John A. Widtsoe, a biologist and educator, the "science" of reclamation was more than an economic necessity. It was a Christian duty, a religious rite. "There can be no full conquest of the earth, and no real satisfaction to humanity," Widtsoe explained, "if large portions of the earth remain beyond his highest control." That God dwelled in dams and canals was also apparent to journalist William Smythe who, in 1905, defended the science of big hydraulics as "religious" and "divine."[39]

Publicists rushed in to prove the promise of a mechanized Eden where minimal physical labor produced a perpetual abundance of crops. Color advertisements for the Oregon Short Line posed modern-day Adams and Eves near machines and irrigation equipment. Lombardy poplars framed the perfect square of a Utah orchard on the cover of 1915 brochure for the Denver & Rio Grande. Idaho photographer Clarence Bisbee, meanwhile, aggressively courted the US Reclamation Service with postcards of water rushing through geometric canyons that seemed ideal for hydro dams. Factory and garden elsewhere converged in photography of symmetrical orchards dissected by highways and flanked telegraph wires (fig. 6).[40]

But machines in the garden of Zion still presented a modernist challenge to the tranquil aesthetic of Mormon art. In the 1890s, when five LDS painters were "called" to study in Paris at the Académie Julian, the art of Utah began to absorb a pastoral naturalism of muted colors and peasant themes. Art missionary John Hafen found in opulent Paris a model for the grander things that God had divined for Utah. Hafen's *Harvest Time Near Sugar House* (1897), *Girl Among the Hollyhocks* (1902), and *Corn Stocks* (1905) were

Figure 6. Clarence Bisbee of Twin Falls, Idaho, featured the power of steam in photo promotions for irrigation projects. *Pictured:* freighting equipment from Twin Falls to Salmon Falls Creek, 1908. (Twin Falls Public Library S-61)

tributes to Zion's glory, peaceful and devoid of machines. Fellow missionary Lorus Pratt, who sailed to Paris with Hafen, returned a devotee of the "toilers of the soil" tradition with its emphasis on sturdy peasant with primitive tools. Pratt, nevertheless, belatedly came to acknowledge Utah's changing folkways. In *Harvest Time in Cache Valley,* painted in 1913, Pratt posed yeomen under the log boom of a primitive derrick near a gas-chugging threshing machine. Impressionism, postimpressionism, expressionism, and modernism were all adapted to Mormon landscapes. Expressionist Mabel Frazer mixed Mormon symbols into her praise of self-reliance in a vibrant painting called *The Furrow* (1929). Utah's Philip Barkdull imported the fauvism of Henri Matisse in the saturated hues of the thick impasto he squeezed directly onto the canvas. Barkdull's *Designed Landscape: Symphony in Colour* (1930) isolated a Mormon homestead on the banks of what appears to be Bear River irrigation (fig. 7). Canal water reflects the uniform massive trunks of three Lombardy poplars, their crowns reaching skyward as if searching the heavens for God.[41]

Shock waves of the Great Depression dislodged the French tradition and hit Utah especially hard. The Beehive State, in 1933, had the nation's fourth highest rate of unemployment. Annual per capital income dropped nearly 50 percent. Police manned highway checkpoints to turn back migrant labor. Shack towns of tar-paper shanties—Hoovervilles, they were called—sprouted wherever the lines of shivering homeless quietly waited for bread. For the arts, nationwide, the trauma forced introspection. In the prose of John Dos Passos, in the protest of Woody Guthrie, in the murals of John Stuart Curry and Thomas Hart Benton, and in the bleak photography of Dorothea Lange, the despair stirred realism and a prideful rebuke of European ideals. "If we are to have anything that can be called a vital American art," wrote Maynard Dixon, a powerful presence in Utah, "it must come this way; not by the obedient repetition of European formulas, but through the ability and courage of our artists to take the life and the material of their own country and of these express their aspirations." Regionalist Edward Hopper concurred. "We are not French," said Hopper, "and any attempt to be so is to

Figure 7. Irrigation water reflects Lombardy poplars in Philip Barkdull's *Designed Landscape: Symphony in Colour* (1930). (Springville Museum of Art, Utah)

deny our inheritance and to try to impose upon ourselves a character that can be nothing but a veneer."[42]

A stoic man in a soft hat and suspenders—his trademark, a shirt-pocketed sprig of sagebrush—probably did as much as any Great Depression painter to document the dislocation in a mix of vernacular styles. LeConte Stewart of Davis County, Utah, in a career spanning seven decades, rarely strayed far from his cottage in Kaysville where a narrow strip of farmland hugged the eastern shore of the Great Salt Lake. Stewart's grayish purples and blues savored the serenity of the scrub vegetation, its pageantry but also, said a critic, "the sorrow of men who have trekked across [them] to die."[43] Sagebrush, his sprig of solace, was also his eau de cologne. "As a youngster in Richfield and Glenwood, where I was born," Stewart explained, "I stubbed bare toes over sage and prickly pear chasing cows over the sun-baked hillsides. The smell of the soil and pungent odor of sage got into my blood."[44]

In 1903, when the artist was twelve, heart failure claimed his mother. One by one three of his four siblings died soon after. In 1913 his father was visibly grieved when the young man spent six hundred dollars in savings to respond to a magazine ad for the Art Student League in New York. "I'd rather [paint] than eat," Stewart had insisted. A year later he was back in Kaysville, suffering from chronic bronchitis. He taught school. He lettered signs. He married. In 1917, when called overseas for his Mormon mission, he painted Edenic murals in a temple near Honolulu. More mural projects for the church in Canada and Arizona led to one-man shows in Ogden. In the 1920s he painted orchards and barns in a bold vibrating style of muted colors called tonal impressionism. But the subject matter darkened with the anguish of the Great Depression. Stark paintings of stricken Utah—of clutter and abandonment, of gas stations, hotels, frozen mills, and derelict homesteads—were praised and elsewhere denounced as "negative" and "ugly" but "down-to-earth" and "true."[45] Stewart's House by the Railroad Tracks (1935) featured an autumn field with a yellow house, its paint blackened by soot (fig. 8). Ogden, Becker's Brewing (1933) and Cannery (1937) showed factories without factory workers (fig. 9). The Smiths', the Jones', and the Browns' (1936) depicted a row of shabby housing in a field of telephone poles (fig. 10).

In the 1930s, like no other American time, the art world was drawn to these homely places and consumed by the plight of the poor. Stewart paralleled the journey of other American masters—Grant Wood of Iowa was one, Hopper of New York was another—who gravitated toward the commonplace and aggressively realistic in a movement that came to be called American

TOP: Figure 8. Steel and telephone poles frame a blackened farmhouse in LeConte Stewart's *House by the Railroad Tracks* (1935). (Private collection) BOTTOM: Figure 9. Empty factories and storefronts were hallmarks of LeConte Stewart's American scene realism. *Pictured:* Ogden, Becker's Brewing (1933). (Private collection)

Figure 10. Houses, wires, and poles line a Salt Lake rail corridor in LeConte Stewart's *The Smiths', the Jones', and the Browns'* (1936). (Springville Museum of Art, Utah)

scene regionalism. Stewart painted so many thousands of Utah landscapes that his work has been hard to label. Some saw introspection, where others found defiance. Either way, the best of his work made sobering comment on Babylon's encounter with Zion. In *Private Car* (1937), for example, he depicted hobos on moving boxcars. One stood in cocky pose as if the train were his private car. In *Death Curve at Roy, Utah* (about 1936), the glare of garish neon broke the vastness of a menacing night. Neither painting was a polemic, yet they signaled a cultural change. In the kingdom of agrarian virtue, where technology was divinely ordained, progress had ceased to be progress. Machines ran amok in the garden. Beautification had derailed in blight.[46]

It has been said that no one ever really recovered from the despair of the Great Depression. Stewart, in 1938, turned inward like the vanishing streams. That summer he accepted a teaching post at the University of Utah, and there for the next eighteen years his studies of the Mormon landscape retreated to autumn colors and snow-blanketed silos and barns. In 1985 Stewart, age ninety-four and still tracking backward, winced at the Sheetrock and plywood advancing toward Davis County. "This town used to be full of old barns," Stewart lamented. "Everything that I find that's good to [paint] they tear down."[47]

Framing Armageddon

Now chaos, now garden, the desert emerged in the Christian view of creation as emptiness transformed. Deserts ever since have begged the obvious question: empty of what? Certainly, in the gap between Colorado and California, the emptiness has seldom been empty of food. Native peoples found more than they could harvest (but sometimes more than they could preserve and store) in the Basin's nutritional balance of beans, roots, bulbs, fish, bison, game birds, grasshoppers, and other sources of protein.[48] Empty, then, of what? "Of everything and nothing," wrote literary critic John Beck in an essay on cultural landscapes.[49] Seemingly vast, the desert bred hope and fear and uninhibited experimentation. Chaotic, it must be ordered. Empty, it must be filled.

The imperative to fill and confine what appeared to be empty and endless crowded the metaphorical desert with parables and morality tales. According to Catrin Gersdoft, a scholar from the Baltic Sea who writes about vacant places, the most American of those stories emerged from the need for a tabula rasa where history could be scripted anew. Gersdoft, writing in 2009, found four basic story lines: first was the Jeffersonian narrative of the West as a *garden* of boundless abundance; second, a *wilderness* story of the desert as spiritual refuge; third, a West-meets-East parable of *Orientalism* in which aridity was contrasted against wet Victorian landscapes; and fourth, a story of *otherness* (or "heterotopia," as French theorist Michel Foucault defined it) where Americans have constructed a sandbox for cultural experimentation, where bombs and sightings of flying saucers are apocalyptic harbingers of doom.[50] Often in their visual idealizations the stories were deterministic. In railroad and mining promotions, in parables of self-reliance and landscapes of dreams turned to dust during the trauma of the Great Depression, the stories aggrandized machines. Historians of technology, stressing complexity, have mostly come to reject stories that purport to compact human encounters with deserts or trace them like a chain reaction to a single powder-keg spark. Metaphors, nevertheless, thrive where legend and folklore diverge from the empirical structure of history books.[51]

And so it has always been in North America's largest desert where heat and flatness conspire with stereotypes and idealizations to aggrandize and distort. Only the artist or true believer stands far enough back to contain the hallucination. Only at a mythic distance from specific events in unique locations is it possible to see the machine—or capitalism, or aridity, or God, or any single factor—as history's overpowering force. Closer inspection reveals the confusion of social and cultural factors that set machines in motion, shaping historical change.

Whether the things we make make us, or vice versa, there is no denying that machines, as metaphors and metaphysics, filter the ways Americans have come to perceive the boundaries of vacant space. In Nevada, especially, where the West still appears to the East as formless and empty, iconography provokes fatalism. Photographer Edward Weston was one of the first to double back on the tradition of Ansell Adams, where humanity's trespass was screened from Sierra Club calendar art. Weston, in 1937, posed a steam shovel's hungry claw above Reno's Truckee Basin as if to devour the romantic sublime. Postmodernists, ever since, have reconstructed the idea of the West with landscapes of exploitation, with billboards, graffiti, and strip malls; with bomb craters and shrapnel; with open-pit cyanide mining at places such as Battle Mountain and an ancient homeland contaminated at Yucca Mountain's

Figure 11. Gus Bundy's action photos of horse-meat hunters shocked Congress and prompted a ban on mechanical roundups. *Pictured:* Bundy's *Horse and Truck* (1951). (Photo courtesy of the Gus Bundy family and Special Collections Department, University of Nevada–Reno Library)

Figure 12. The ravage of missile testing inspired Richard Misrach's study of northern Nevada. *Pictured: Bomb Crater and Destroyed Convoy, Bravo 20, Nevada* (1986). (Richard Misrach, courtesy Fraenkel Gallery, San Francisco)

nuclear dump. Manifest Destiny is here rescripted to mean an attack—literally, in the case of weapons testing—on negative space that confounds.[52]

Often in the iconography of the pulverized desert the apocalypse rained down from above. In 1951, for example, Nevada photographer Gus Bundy used a hidden camera to document the aerial roundup of tens of thousands of wild mustangs. *Life* eventually published Bundy's secretive photos of horses being herded with planes, stampeded with shotguns, slaughtered for horse meat, and hauled off the playas in trucks (fig. 11). Brutality again shot down from the sky in Richard Misrach's *Bravo 20* study of a northern Nevada bomb-cratered artillery range (fig. 12). Published in 1990, *Bravo 20* included architectural drawings that taunted Congress with a sardonic proposal for a new national park. Misrach's plans showed a tourist-friendly walk-in bomb crater with interpretive signage that categorized species of bombs. Northwest of Las Vegas, meanwhile, Armageddon inspired suburbanite Robert Beckmann to illustrate the suburban potential of a sixteen-kiloton nuclear bomb.

Figure 13. Nevada's Robert Beckmann isolated frames of Pentagon footage that showed the effects of a nuclear testing on a two-story suburban house. *Pictured: Test House—First Light* (2008), adapted from Beckmann's 1993 *Body of a House* exhibition. (Robert Beckmann)

Beckmann's 1993 mixed-media series isolated eight frames from 2.3 seconds of Pentagon footage showing a house obliterated from the dummy "doomtown" suburban sector of the US Department of Energy's Nevada Test Site (fig. 13). Another Beckmann photo-acrylic showed an orange-white cloud of radiation mushrooming above the lucky 7-7-7 of a slot-machine's fatal jackpot. The obvious metaphor is atomic war as the ultimate gamble. More subtle is the postmodern critique of blank Nevada as a tranquilizing abstraction for the numbing of horrific events.[53]

What the postmodernists have in common with their Great Basin predecessors is the trope of the machine in desolation as the fulcrum of irrevocable change. That story line says more about geography than technology. It reveals the nonplace of the unknowable desert as terra incognita where myth shades perception and heat refracts a mirage.

NOTES

1. Walt Whitman, *Leaves of Grass* (New York: G. P. Putnam's Sons, 1897), 47, 316, 319. For archival confusion over "last spike" photographs, see William D. Pattison, "The Pacific Railroad Rediscovered," *Geographical Review* 52, no. 1 (1962): 33–36; Richard Lowry, "Iron Frames: Reconstructing the Landscape Views of A. J. Russell's Photography," *Nineteenth-Century Contexts* 13 (Spring 1989): 41–66; G. Ferris Cronkhite, "Walt Whitman and the Locomotive," *American Quarterly* 6, no. 2 (1954): 164–72; "East and West," *New York Times*, May 11, 1869; Edward Sabin, *Building the Pacific Railroad* (Philadelphia: Lippincott, 1919), 175; and Michael W. Johnson, "Rendezvous at Promontory: A New Look at the Golden Spike Ceremony," *Utah Historical Quarterly* 72, no. 1 (2004): 47–69.

2. John C. Frémont, *The Exploring Expedition to the Rocky Mountains, Oregon, and California* (Buffalo, NY: Derby, 1850), 298; Dan Carpenter quoted in Richard V. Francaviglia, *Believing in Place: A Spiritual Geography of the Great Basin* (Reno: University of Nevada Press, 2003), 8; Mark Twain, *Roughing It* (1871; reprint, New York: Harper & Brothers, 1913), 127; Owen Wister, "Lin McLean," *Sunset* 20 (November 1907–April 1908): 572. William Smythe challenged Wister's view of Nevada in *The Conquest of Arid America* (New York: Macmillan, 1905), 214. See also Elizabeth Raymond, "When the Desert Won't Bloom: Environmental Limitation and the Great Basin," in *Many Wests: Place, Culture, and Regional Identity*, edited by David M. Wrobel and Michael C. Steiner (Lawrence: University Press of Kansas, 2007), 71–92; and Stephen Trimble, *The Sagebrush Ocean: A Natural History of the Great Basin* (1989; reprint, Reno: University of Nevada Press, 1999), vi.

3. Walter Prescott Webb, "The Frontier Machine," in *Roundup: A Nebraska Reader*, edited by Virginia Faulkner (Lincoln: University of Nebraska Press, 1957), 14. Walter Prescott Webb's great work, published in 1931, was about the semidesert of the near-West tallgrass prairie on the eastern side of the Rockies. In 1957, in a controversial essay published in *Harper's*, the analysis migrated west to the continent's "desert heart." Although Webb's main fascination was climate, he was Marxian in his view that factory mechanization would leap beyond social control. See George O'Har, "Where the Buffalo Roam: Walter Prescott Webb's *The Great Plains*," *Technology and Culture* 47 (January 2006): 156–63; and Walter Prescott Webb, "The American West, Perpetual Mirage," *Harper's*, May 1957, 25–31.

4. Smythe, *Conquest of Arid America*, 220; Leo Marx, *The Machine in the Garden: Technology and the Pastoral Ideal in America* (New York: Oxford University Press, 1964), 344.

5. Debate over the root cause of expansionism, whether myth or machines, capitalism or culture, has been a dominate theme of western historical writing since Frederick Jackson Turner's 1893 frontier thesis. William Truettner uses art to

understand the debate in *The West as America: Reinterpreting Images of the Frontier* (Washington, DC: Smithsonian Institution Press, 1991), 27–53.

6. William Shaw, "'The Handmill Gives You the Feudal Lord': Marx's Technological Determinism," *History and Theory* 18, no. 2 (1979): 155–76. For the argument that Marxist determinism was more economic than technological, see Bruce Bimber, "Three Faces of Technological Determinism," in *Does Technology Drive History? The Dilemma of Technological Determinism*, edited by Merritt Roe Smith and Leo Marx (Cambridge: MIT Press, 1994), 89–99.

7. Lewis Mumford, *Art and Technics* (New York: Columbia University Press, 1952), 11–12.

8. Albert Deane Richardson, *Beyond the Mississippi: From the Great River to the Great Ocean, Life and Adventure on the Prairies, Mountains, and Pacific Coast* (Hartford, CT: American Publishing, 1867), 567.

9. George A. Crofutt, *Crofutt's New Overland Tourist and Pacific Coast Guide* (Chicago: Overland, 1879), 300; Joshua C. Taylor, *America as Art* (Washington, DC: Smithsonian Institution Press, 1976), 145–46; J. Valerie Fifier, *American Progress: The Growth of the Transport, Tourist, and Information Industries in the Nineteenth-Century West, Seen Through the Life and Times of George A. Crofutt, Pioneer and Publicist of the Transcontinental Age* (Guilford, CT: Globe Pequot Press, 1988), 201–5; Harry T. Peters, *Currier & Ives, Printmakers to the American People* (New York: Doubleday, 1976), 114. See also Patricia Hills, "Picturing Progress in the Era of Westward Expansion," in *West as America*, edited by Truettner, 127–36.

10. Anne F. Hyde, "Cultural Filters: The Significance of Perception in the History of the American West," *Western Historical Quarterly* 24, no. 3 (1993): 353.

11. Martha A. Sandweiss, *Print the Legend: Photography and the American West* (New Haven, CT: Yale University Press, 2002), 285, 296. See also Solomon N. Carvalho, *Incidents of Travel and Adventure in the Far West* (New York: Derby & Jackson, 1856), 124.

12. The most complete biographical treatment is James D. Horan, *Timothy O'Sullivan: America's Forgotten Photographer* (Garden City, NY: Doubleday, 1966). See also Rosalind Krauss, "Photography's Discursive Spaces: Landscape/View," *Art Journal* 42, no. 4 (1982): 311–19.

13. James Gregory Moore, *King of the 40th Parallel: Discovery in the American West* (Stanford, CA: Stanford University Press, 2006), 218.

14. On the evolving complexities of scientific mapping, see William Goetzmann, *Exploration and Empire*, edited by Francis Parkman Prize (New York: History Book Club, 2006), 333–51. See also Robert Wilson, *The Explorer King: Adventure, Science, and the Great Diamond Hoax* (New York: Simon and Schuster, 2006), 235–54; and Richard V. Francaviglia, *Mapping and Imagination in the Great Basin: A Cartographic History* (Reno: University of Nevada Press, 2005), 126–30.

15. King summarized in "Catastrophism and the Evolution," *American Naturalist* 11 (August 1877): 449–70. See also Goetzmann, *Exploration and Empire*, 465.

16. Alan Trachtenberg, *Reading American Photographs: Images as History, Mathew Brady to Walker Evans* (New York: Hill and Wang, 1989), 132.

17. William H. Goetzmann and William N. Goetzmann, *West of the Imagination* (New York: W. W. Norton, 1986), 200.

18. Toby Jurovics et al., *Framing the West: The Survey Photographs of Timothy O'Sullivan* (Washington, DC: Library of Congress and Smithsonian American Art Museum, 2010), 16–23. For a discussion of interpretive bias, see also how Joel Snyder and Josh Ellenbogen consider panoramic views in *American Survey Photographs by Bell and O'Sullivan* (Chicago: David and Alfred Smart Museum of Art, University of Chicago, 2006).

19. Trachtenberg, *Reading American Photographs*, 144, 146.

20. Robert Adams, *Why People Photograph* (New York: Aperture, 1994), 150, quoted in Jurovics et al., *Framing the West*, 23. See also Rick Dingus, *The Photographic Artifacts of Timothy O'Sullivan* (Albuquerque: University of New Mexico Press, 1982), 60–63.

21. Eugene P. Moehring, *Urbanism and Empire in the Far West, 1840–1890* (Reno: University of Nevada Press, 1890), 83–166. See also Leonard J. Arrington, "The Deseret Telegraph: A Church-Owned Public Utility," *Journal of Economic History* 11, no. 2 (1951): 117–39.

22. Bradley W. Richards, *The Savage View: Charles Savage, Pioneer Mormon Photographer* (Nevada City, CA: Carl Mautz, 1995), 56. For Savage and A. A. Hart, see also Weston Naef and James Wood, *Era of Exploration: The Rise of Landscape Photography in the American West, 1860–1885* (New York: Metropolitan Museum of Art, 1975), 43–49. George Kraus related the camera-shy Chinese story in *High Road to Promontory: The Building of the Central Pacific (Now the Southern Pacific) Across the High Sierra* (Palo Alto, CA: American West Publishing, 1969), 273. Edson T. Strobridge of the Central Pacific Railroad Photographic History Museum dismisses the story as "nothing more than the ramblings of an old man who thought it was funny to make fun of the Chinese."

23. Trachtenberg, *Reading American Photographs*, xiv.

24. A. J. Russell, preface to *Great West Illustrated* (New York: Union Pacific Railroad, 1869), iii.

25. Samuel Bowles, *Our New West* (Hartford, CT: Hartford Publishing, 1869), 68. See also Ferdinand V. Hayden, *Sun Pictures of Rocky Mountain Scenery* (New York: Julius Bien, 1870), 123; and Susan Danly, "Andrew Joseph Russell's *The Great West Illustrated*," in *The Railroad in American Art: Representations of Technological Change*, edited by Susan Danly and Leo Marx (Cambridge: MIT Press, 1988), 93–112. For the painterly sublime aesthetics of Russell's photography, see Barbara

Novak, *Nature and Culture: American Landscape and Painting, 1825–1875* (New York: Oxford University Press, 1980), 177–79; and David E. Nye, *American Technological Sublime* (Cambridge, MA: MIT Press, 1994), 72–76.

26. Ronald W. Walker's "Introduction to the Illinois Edition" of Leonard J. Arrington, *The Great Basin Kingdom: An Economic History of the Latter-day Saints, 1830–1900* (Urbana: University of Illinois Press, 2004), xi; Francaviglia, *Believing in Place*, xiv. For Mormon culture as inward looking, see Ken Verdonia's 1995 interview with church historian Leonard Arrington in the online companion to the University of Utah's *Promontory*, a historical documentary concerning the joining of rails, http://www.kued.org/productions/promontory.

27. Marx, *Machine in the Garden*, 215, 226. See also Mark Fiege, *Irrigated Eden: The Making of an Agricultural Landscape in the American West* (Seattle: University of Washington Press, 1999), 144, 171–72.

28. Jared Farmer, *On Zion's Mount: Mormons, Indians, and the American Landscape* (Cambridge, MA: Harvard University Press, 2008), 45, 47. For Brigham Young's observation, see Richard H. Jackson, "Mormon Perception and Settlement," *Annals of the Association of American Geographers* 68, no. 3 (1978): 328, 331; and Ronald K. Esplin, "'A Place Prepared': Joseph, Brigham, and the Quest for Promised Refuge in the West," in *Window of Faith: Latter-day Saint Perspectives on World History*, edited by Roy A. Prete (Provo, UT: Religious Studies Center, Brigham Young University, 2005), 71–97.

29. Farmer, *On Zion's Mount*, 108; Tissandier quoted in Will South and Dean L. May, *Images of the Great South Lake* (Salt Lake City: Utah Museum of Fine Arts, 1996), 31.

30. Thomas K. Hafen, "City of Saints, City of Sinners: The Development of Salt Lake City as a Tourist Attraction, 1869–1900," *Western Historical Quarterly* 28 (Autumn 1997): 355.

31. Orson F. Whitney, *History of Utah* (Salt Lake City: G. Q. Cannon, 1892), 1:325. For context, see also Richard H. Jackson, "Righteousness and Environmental Change: The Mormons and the Environment," in *Essays on the American West, 1973–1974*, edited by Thomas G. Alexander (Provo, UT: Brigham Young University, 1975), 23.

32. The artist's full name was Carl Christian Anton Christensen. See Richard L. Jensen and Richard O. Oman, *C. C. A. Christensen, 1831–1912: Mormon Immigrant Artist* (Salt Lake City: Church of Jesus Christ of Latter-day Saints, 1984), 47, passim. See also Vern G. Swanson et al., *Utah Art, Utah Artist* (Layton, UT: Gibbs Smith, 2001), 8–9.

33. Donna L. Poulton of the Utah Museum of Fine Arts, Vern G. Swanson of the Springfield Museum of Art, and gallery owner David Erickon of Salt Lake City schooled the author in Mormon pioneer art. Swanson's Springfield Museum

has posted biographies of pioneer artists at http://sma.nebo.edu. See also Robert S. Olpin, Ann W. Orton, and Thomas F. Rugh, *Painters of the Wasatch Mountains* (Layton, UT: Gibbs Smith, 2005), 25. For Danquart Weggeland, see Andrew Jenson, *Latter-day Saint Biographical Encyclopedia* (Salt Lake City: Deseret News Press, 1941), 2:272–75. For church patronage, see James L. Haseltine, "Mormons and the Visual Arts," *Dialogue: A Journal of Mormon Thought* 1, no. 2 (1966): 17–29.

34. Richard V. Francaviglia, *The Mormon Landscape: Existence, Creation, and Perception of a Unique Image in the American West* (New York: AMS Press, 1978), 81.

35. P. Nibley, *Brigham Young, the Man and His Work* (Salt Lake City: Deseret News Press, 1937), 181. For the Enlightenment roots of the Puritan-LDS "recovery" narrative, see Carolyn Merchant, *Earthcare: Women and the Environment* (New York: Routledge, 1995), 33.

36. Wallace Stegner, *Mormon Country* (New York: Duel, Sloan, and Pearce, 1942), 27. See also Terryle L. Givens, *People of Paradox: A History of Mormon Culture* (New York: Oxford University Press, 2007), 107, 241–47.

37. Stegner, *Mormon Country*, 24; Mark Leone quoted in Arnold R. Alanen and Robert Z. Melinck, *Preserving Cultural Landscapes in America* (Baltimore: Johns Hopkins University Press, 2000), 174.

38. Richard V. Francaviglia, "Mormon Central-Hall Houses in the American West," *Annals of the Association of American Geographers* 61, no. 1 (1971): 65–71. See also L. Nelson, *The Mormon Village: A Pattern and Technique of Land Settlement* (Salt Lake City: University of Utah Press, 1952); D. W. Meing, "The Mormon Cultural Region," *Annals of the Association of American Geographers* 55, no. 2 (1965): 191–220; and Richard H. Jackson and Robert L. Layton, "The Mormon Village: An Analysis of a Settlement Type," *Professional Geographer* 28, no. 2 (1976): 136–41.

39. Donald Worster, *The Wealth of Nature: Environmental History and the Ecological Imagination* (New York: Oxford University Press, 1993), 119; Smythe, *Conquest of Arid America*, 327, 330–31.

40. Fiege, *Irrigated Eden*, 171–73. See also Worster, *Wealth of Nature*, 120; and Carlos A. Schwantes and James P. Ronda, *The West the Railroads Made* (Seattle: University of Washington Press, 2008), xix.

41. Richard G. Oman and Robert O. Davis, *Images of Faith: Art of the Latter-day Saints* (Salt Lake: Deseret Book, 1995), 41–69; Linda Jones Gibbs, *Harvesting the Light: The Paris Art Mission and Beginnings of Utah Impressionism* (Salt Lake City: Church of Jesus Christ of Latter-day Saints, 1987); "John Hafen: Art as Visual Poetry," *Dialogue: A Journal of Mormon Thought* 23, no. 4 (1990): 183–84.

42. Donald J. Hagerty, *The Art of Maynard Dixon* (Layton, UT: Gibbs Smith, 2010), 111; Dixon and Hopper quoted in Donna Poulsen, "Looking Inward: LeConte Stewart's Depression Era Art," typewritten draft of an exhibition essay for

the Utah Museum of Fine Art (2012). See also Morris Dickstein, *Dancing in the Dark: A Cultural History of the Great Depression* (New York: W. W. Norton, 2009); Leonard J. Arrington, "The Sagebrush Resurrection: New Deal Expenditures in the Western States, 1933–1939," *Pacific Historical Review* 52 (February 1983): 1–16; and Duane Damon, *Headin' for Better Times: The Arts of the Great Depression* (Minneapolis: Twentieth Century Books, 2002), 14.

43. Donna L. Poulsen and Vern G. Swanson, *Painters of Utah's Canyons and Deserts* (Layton, UT: Gibbs Smith, 2009), 92. See also Wallace Stegner, "The Power of Homely Detail," *American Heritage* 36, no. 5 (1985): 62.

44. Poulsen, "Looking Inward," 92. See also Glen M. Leonard, *A History of Davis County* (Salt Lake: Utah State Historical Society, 1999), 96.

45. Robert O. Davis, *LeConte Stewart: The Spirit of the Landscape* (Salt Lake City: Church of Jesus Christ of the Latter-day Saints, 1985), 5, 9–11, 35.

46. Glen Warchol, "Iconic Utah Painter LeConte Stewart's Work Spotlighted in Two Exhibits," *Salt Lake Tribune*, July 26, 2011. See also Ehren Clark, "Spirit of an Era: LeConte Stewart's Depression Era Paintings," *15 Bytes: Utah's Art Magazine*, September 2011, 1, 5.

47. Stegner, "Power of Homely Detail," 65.

48. Peter Farb, *Man's Rise to Civilization: The Cultural Ascent of the Indians of North America* (New York: E. P. Dutton, 1978), 25–28.

49. John Beck, "Without Form and Void: The American Desert as Trope and Terrain," *Nepantla: Views from South* 2, no. 1 (2001): 64.

50. Catrin Gersdorf, *The Poetics and Politics of the Desert: Landscape and the Construction of America* (Amsterdam: Rodopi, 2009), 88.

51. Reinhard Rürup, "Historians and Modern Technology: Reflections on the Development and Current Problems of the History of Technology," *Technology and Culture* 15, no. 2 (1974): 161–93. For distinctions between "macro" and "micro" levels of deterministic storytelling, see Thomas J. Misa, "Retrieving Sociotechnical Change from Technological Determinism," in *Does Technology Drive History?*, edited by Smith and Marx, 115–41. For desert fables as metaphysical truth, see William A. Wilson, *What's True in Mormon History? The Contribution of Folklore to Mormon Studies*, Leonard J. Arrington Mormon History Series, no. 13 (Salt Lake City: University of Utah Press, 2008), 7, http://www.google.com/search?tbo=p&tbm=bks&q=bibliogroup:%22Leonard+J.+Arrington+Mormon+history+lecture+series%22&source=gbs_metadata_r&cad=6.

52. Since the 1963 publication of Eliot Porter's requiem to Glen Canyon in *The Place No One Knew*, hundreds of large-format photography books have documented the desert in environmental distress. See, for example, William Jenkins, *New Topographics: Photographs of a Man-Altered Landscape* (Rochester, NY: International Museum of Photography, 1975); and Mike Davis, "Dead West: Ecocide

in Marlboro Country," in *Over the Edge: Remapping the American West,* edited by Valerie J. Matsumoto and Blake Allmendinger (Berkeley: University of California Press, 1992), 341–45.

53. Richard Misrach with Myriam Weisang Misrach, *Bravo 20: The Bombing of the American West* (Baltimore: Johns Hopkins University Press, 1990), xiv, 94–110. For Gus Bundy, see David Cruise and Alison Griffiths, *Wild Horse Annie and the Last of the Mustangs: The Life of Velma Johnston* (New York: Simon and Schuster, 2010), 120–22. For Robert Beckmann, see William Fox, *Mapping the Empty: Eight Arts and Nevada* (Reno: University of Nevada Press, 1999), 86–100.

Urban Places/Empty Spaces

Big and Small Governments in the Great Basin

STEPHANIE L. WITT

BIG AND SMALL GOVERNMENTS, mostly small, govern the Great Basin Desert. The biggest, the US federal government, has a regional presence that permeates even the remotest corners of the Basin, largely because of the massive tracts of federally owned land and infrastructure spread throughout the region. State, county, and municipal governments are sprinkled here and there, often within the gaps and corridors left by the federal presence.[1] The biggest local governments are the four cities that sit on the rim: Boise, Idaho; Salt Lake City, Utah; and Reno and Las Vegas, Nevada. Although they occupy a tiny proportion of the Basin's land area, they account for the vast majority of the population and economic activity. The big and small governments maintain an uneasy and sometimes hostile relationship with one another that makes the politics of the Great Basin often contentious and sometimes dysfunctional.

These tensions are exacerbated by the extreme reliance of the small governments on the resources and policies of their larger brethren, and nowhere are these conflicts exhibited more often than over land use and management. The hostile relationship that occasionally flares up with federal agencies goes back many decades, but conflicts arise as well between rural counties and their states and metropolitan centers over the allocation of state revenues, local option taxation authority, and the taxes paid by rural citizens who shop in urban retail centers.

There is a startling contrast between the four cities of the rim and the thinly populated stretches of the desert. These rapidly growing urbanized areas face problems involving the provision of urban services and amenities, air quality, water supply and water pollution, and traffic congestion and sprawl. However, because they overrepresent nonurban interests, the state legislatures of Idaho and Nevada see little reason to help their larger cities address their quite unique problems. For example, in Idaho the state legislature has refused to authorize local option taxes for its cities in spite of a four-decade effort on the part of the Association of Idaho Cities to seek that power.[2] In Nevada the legislature resorted to taking locally collected taxes in Clark and Washoe Counties, where Las Vegas and Reno are located, respectively, to balance the state budget, a practice stopped by the Nevada Supreme Court only in 2011. By using its two largest metropolitan areas to fix the state's chronic fiscal shortage, the state has left urban governments worse off than if they had been neglected altogether.

Urban policy problems are pressing because the metropolitan areas of the Great Basin have been experiencing explosive growth for several decades. According to the US Census Bureau, Nevada was the fastest-growing state in the first decade of the twenty-first century; in only ten years its population increased by 35.1 percent, from 2 million to 2.7 million. This rapid growth netted the state of Nevada a fourth congressional seat in the 2012 election. In the same period Utah added 23.8 percent to its population, and Idaho 21 percent. No major cities are located in California and Oregon's portions of the Great Basin Desert.

The Basin is gaining population almost entirely because of the burgeoning cities and towns on its rim. In the past half century the Boise, Reno, and Las Vegas metropolitan areas have been, for varying periods of time, on the top-ten list of the fastest-growing metropolitan regions in the United States, with the Salt Lake area not far behind. By the 2010 census Salt Lake's Metropolitan Statistical Area had reached 1,124,197, but adding the interlinked corridor of development reaching north to the Ogden MSA and south through the Provo MSA brought the figure to 2,198,191. In 2010 Salt Lake City accounted for only 17 percent of its own MSA's population and just 8 percent of the urban population spread along the Wasatch Range, but during the day Salt Lake City's population doubles by some estimates as commuters come into the city for work.[3] By the 2010 census, the Boise MSA had mushroomed to 616,561, and Reno's MSA reached 425,417. Clark County, the seat of the Las Vegas metropolitan area, reached 1,951,269.

The nonurbanized portions of the Great Basin states reveal entirely different trajectories. Esmeralda, Lander, Mineral, and Pershing Counties, all in Nevada, lost population in the 2000–2010 period, and another four Nevada counties had growth rates of less than 6 percent. Put differently, the other nine counties in Nevada account for virtually all of the state's population increase. This pattern of development results in sharply defined boundaries between the urban from the nonurban and establishes the contours of a divided politics not only in Nevada, but throughout most of the Basin.

Public Lands and the Urban Nature of the Great Basin Desert

A vast expanse of federally owned public lands makes up the majority of the three states of Idaho, Utah, and Nevada, yet the Great Basin has a highly urbanized settlement pattern. Federally owned public lands constitute 70.6 percent of the region, leaving just under 30 percent of the region's landmass for settlement, agriculture, and commercial and industrial uses.[4] This constraint imposes a relatively dense settlement pattern that is at odds with most people's images of an empty desert landscape. As table 1 shows, there are 1,387 people per square mile in Salt Lake County (which contains Salt Lake City), 373 people per square mile in Ada County (Boise), 247 in Clark County (Las Vegas), and 67 in Washoe County (Reno). Except for Reno these urban densities exceed the US national average, which was 87.4 people per square mile in 2010.

Because these public lands are protected from settlement, urban development is forced into relatively small areas, resulting in populations per square mile in the urban counties that rival those of any urban area in the United States. In Nevada, for example, 87 percent of the state's population lives in Clark and Washoe Counties, home to the cities of Las Vegas and Reno. Across the Basin as a whole, 82.7 percent of the population lives in eleven of the sixty-two counties. The constraint imposed by public lands is illustrated by the fact that Clark County's nearly 2 million residents are squeezed into approximately 5 percent of the county's land area.

The parts of the Great Basin Desert classified as "urban" have higher population densities than the national average, but does this make the region *urban*? The US Census Bureau has defined *urban* with great precision, and by its definition the Basin is the most highly urbanized bioregion in the United States. Of course, this statistic carries little weight with people living in the Basin because they are so keenly aware that there are vast stretches of mostly unoccupied desert outside their doorstep. This is different from most

TABLE 1
People per Square Mile in Counties with Major cities of the Great Basin

County	2010 Population	Square Miles	People/Square Mile
Clark (Las Vegas)	1,951,269	7,891.43	247.30
Washoe (Reno)	421,407	6,302.37	66.90
Ada (Boise)	392, 365	1,052.58	372.80
Salt Lake (SLC)	1,029,655	742.28	1,387.10
Utah (SLC)	545,307	1,998.33	272.88

of the nation, where land is freely available for settlement. In the American tradition, rural landscapes have generally been represented in paintings and photographs as bucolic scenes of farms and small towns. By contrast, in most of the Great Basin *rural* in this sense is rare. Most of the Basin is not rural; it is, instead, almost *empty*.

When referring to the nonurban parts of the Basin, *frontier,* despite its historical connotations, may be a more accurate term than *rural.* The National Center for Frontier Communities (NCFC) developed a consensus definition of *frontier* based upon a matrix that includes persons per square mile, distance in miles to services or markets, and travel time in minutes to services or markets.[5] Table 2 lists the counties in the Basin that would be considered frontier counties by three alternative criteria: those with fewer than 2 persons per square mile, those containing fewer than 6 persons per square mile, and those designated as frontier using the matrix developed by the National Center for Frontier Communities. Counties that would be considered "frontier counties" under all three definitions are shaded. Table 2 displays the 2010 population, the square miles covered by each county, and the county's population density. By this definition, thirty-nine of the sixty-two, or 63 percent, of the counties in the Great Basin are "frontier counties." Fourteen of the sixty-two counties contain fewer than 2 persons per square mile, which has historically served as the population threshold for "frontier." Twenty-seven of the sixty-two counties would be considered frontier counties under the more generous definition of fewer than 6 persons per square mile. Five basin counties have population densities under 1 person per square mile. The county with the lowest population density is Esmeralda, in Nevada, with 0.2 persons per square mile. The county with the highest population density that is still considered "frontier" (measured by travel time to markets) is Lyon County, Nevada, with nearly 52,000 residents and a density of 26.1 persons per square mile.

The data from table 2 illustrate just how few people inhabit the more rural parts of the region and highlight the sharp contrast in population and population densities between the Basin's urbanized and frontier communities. These differences create political tensions not only in the Basin as a whole, but also between the big and small governments located in each of these separate universes. The composition of the Boise MSA illustrates this well. The MSA, as designated by the US Census Bureau, includes Ada, Canyon, Gem, Owyhee, and Boise Counties. Ada County, where Boise is located, has 364.6 persons per square mile, but Owyhee County, with which it shares a

TABLE 2
Frontier Counties in the Great Basin Desert

County	State	2010 Population	Square Miles	Density	Fewer than 6 people/ square mile?	Fewer than 2 people/ square mile?	NCFC
Inyo	California	18,546	10,192	1.8	Y	Y	Y
Mono	California	14,202	3,044	4.7	Y	N	Y
Bear Lake	Idaho	5,986	971	6.2	N	N	Y
Caribou	Idaho	6,963	1,766	3.9	Y	N	Y
Cassia	Idaho	22,952	2,567	8.9	N	N	Y
Clark	Idaho	982	1,765	0.6	Y	Y	Y
Elmore	Idaho	27,038	3,078	8.8	N	N	Y
Gooding	Idaho	15,464	731	21.2	N	N	Y
Lincoln	Idaho	5,208	1,206	4.3	Y	N	Y
Oneida	Idaho	4,286	1,200	3.6	Y	N	Y
Owyhee	Idaho	11,526	7,678	1.5	Y	Y	Y
Power	Idaho	7,817	1,406	5.6	Y	N	Y
Churchill	Nevada	24,877	4,929	5.0	Y	N	Y
Elko	Nevada	48,818	17,182	2.8	Y	N	Y
Esmeralda	Nevada	783	3,589	0.2	Y	Y	Y
Eureka	Nevada	1,987	4,176	0.5	Y	Y	Y
Humboldt	Nevada	16,528	9,648	1.7	Y	Y	Y
Lander	Nevada	5,775	5,494	1.1	Y	Y	Y
Lincoln	Nevada	5,345	10,635	0.5	Y	Y	Y
Lyon	Nevada	51,980	1,994	26.1	N	N	Y
Mineral	Nevada	4,772	3,757	1.3	Y	Y	Y
Nye	Nevada	43,946	18,147	2.4	Y	N	Y
Pershing	Nevada	6,753	6,009	1.1	Y	Y	Y
Storey	Nevada	4,010	264	15.2	N	N	Y
White Pine	Nevada	10,030	8,877	1.1	Y	Y	Y
Harney	Oregon	7,422	10,135	0.7	Y	Y	Y
Lake	Oregon	7,895	8,136	1.0	Y	Y	Y
Malheur	Oregon	31,313	9,888	3.2	Y	N	Y
Beaver	Utah	6,629	2,590	2.6	Y	N	Y
Box Elder	Utah	49,975	5,724	8.7	N	N	Y
Iron	Utah	46,163	3,298	14.0	N	N	Y
Juab	Utah	10,246	3,392	3.0	Y	N	Y
Millard	Utah	12,503	6,590	1.9	Y	Y	Y
Morgan	Utah	9,469	609	15.5	N	N	Y
Piute	Utah	1,556	758	2.1	Y	N	Y
Rich	Utah	2,264	1,029	2.2	Y	N	Y
Sanpete	Utah	27,822	1,588	17.5	N	N	Y
Sevier	Utah	20,802	1,910	10.9	N	N	Y
Tooele	Utah	58,218	6,946	8.4	N	N	Y

SOURCES: National Association of Counties and National Center for Frontier Communities; http://www.naco.org/ Counties/Pages/FindACounty.aspx; http://www.frontierus.org/2000census.php.
NOTE: Counties that meet all three "frontier" criteria are shaded.

border, has a population of 1.5 persons per square mile and is considered a frontier county by the NCFC.[6] Ada County's Highway District (a countywide district) manages 417 stoplights, but Owyhee County has exactly none. Thus, despite the fact that the two counties share a border within the same metropolitan area, the perspective of their citizens on regional issues is likely to differ substantially.

The one perspective that frontier and urban counties often do share is resentment toward the government that is bigger than any of them. Like much of the arid West, agriculture, urban development, and even, to some extent, ranching are dependent on federally funded dam and irrigation projects that provide water. Large metropolitan areas would not be possible without these federal resources. The vision and tenacity of early private-sector attempts to marshal the water of the Boise River, and their ultimate failure, were immortalized in Wallace Stegner's novel *Angle of Repose*. A small sign commemorates the former home site of Mary Hallock Foote and her husband, Arthur, upon whom Stegner based his novel. It is located several hundred yards below the federally financed Lucky Peak Dam and is several miles downriver from Arrowrock Dam, another sizable federal structure. Foote and private investors were unable to do what the federal government could: finance a large dam and irrigation canal system. This reality was recognized by John Wesley Powell's report on the "arid lands." He noted, "Small streams can be taken out [for irrigation] and distributed by individual enterprise, but cooperative labor or aggregated capital must be employed in taking out the larger streams."[7] The federal government has been the "cooperative labor" in building dams near each of the four cities on the Great Basin's edge.

A Tradition of Populism

The populist impulse to give the "little people" voice is deeply embedded in the western political tradition. In Idaho's first presidential election, in 1892, for example, the Populist Party candidate, James B. Weaver, received the state's Electoral College votes. Like elsewhere, western populism was motivated by resentment toward big business and finance capital, but the reality was that big business continued to call the shots in public policy making. In Nevada mining interests dominated the state's politics, and when Nevada later moved to a tourist-centered gambling economy, large gaming companies wielded outsize influence.[8] Utah went a different route because the political influence of railroad and mining interests was moderated by the dominance of the Church of Jesus Christ of Latter-day Saints.

The enduring legacy of populism is probably found not in its ability to curb the influence of powerful interests, but in its ability to reduce the scope of government. The initiative, referendum, and recall elections are typically found mostly in the West. The initiative was designed to reduce the influence of special interests, but it has often not worked that way because "the costs of initiative campaigns guarantee special interest dollars. . . . [H]ard issues are technical and are concerned with means rather than policy ends."[9] Many of the most restrictive property tax limitations under which local governments labor are the result of voter-approved initiatives. In addition, candidates running for office regularly sound the theme of limited government. It is no surprise that the Basin generated several Tea Party endorsed candidates in the 2010 electoral cycle, or that some of them were successful (for example, Idaho's Republican congressman Raul Labrador and Utah's Republican US senator Mike Lee).

Perhaps the most consequential and most well-known initiative was California's Proposition 13, which passed in 1978. The tax revolt quickly spread to other western states, and in fact became a national phenomenon. In Idaho the California law energized what had been a tepid initiative campaign to limit local property taxes, and in the wake of Prop 13 organizers succeeded in securing enough signatures to put a similarly worded initiative on the November general election ballot. The initiative passed handily but ran up against a problem: given that the constitutional language in Idaho's version of Prop 13 conflicted with provisions in Idaho's state constitution, implementation of the law was not possible, and it was later repealed. Part of the bargain that led to repeal was that legislators imposed a cap on property tax increases and mandated reappraisal programs throughout the state. The effect on its largest city was quickly felt:

> The property tax limitation law hard hit Boise. With its heavy reliance on the property tax for its operating budget, especially police and fire departments, it had to make painful personnel cuts. In the early 1990s, the city did not have as many public safety employees as it did in 1978, the year prior to the passage of the 1 percent initiative. From fiscal years 1979 to 1990, the city increased in population by 25 percent and the taxable value of its property increased by over 100 percent, but the number of municipal employees essentially remained the same.[10]

Prop 13 also had an impact in Nevada. Voters approved a property tax limitation measure, but under the Nevada Constitution such measures have to be approved by the voters twice before they become law. Before a second vote could be taken, however, the Nevada Legislature passed legislation that reduced property taxes by 27 percent, repealed sales tax on food (which was later approved by a referendum), and froze state funding, including for higher education. This legislation reduced political pressures somewhat, and in the 1980 general election, the property measure that voters had approved overwhelmingly in 1978 went down in defeat.[11]

Of course, the initiative process can be used to curb spending by states as much as it can limit local governments. In Nevada a 1996 initiative imposed the requirement of a two-thirds vote of the legislature in order to raise or impose new taxes. This supermajority requirement is what prompted the Nevada Assembly to approve additional county tax authority in 2011. Someone had to raise revenues to pay for services, and the state felt it could not. As one state newspaper described it in this headline: "Counties, State Argue: 'You Raise Taxes.' 'No, You Do It.'"[12]

In many cases, voter initiatives have crippled the ability of state and local governments to provide services to rapidly growing populations. However, the fact that the urban electorate accounts for so many votes gives local officials in urban areas a potential means of achieving some measure of autonomy from state legislatures. In this way the initiative may be used as it was originally intended—as a safety valve to circumvent unresponsive legislators. In Idaho this potential is especially important because state officials have traditionally been indifferent to or hostile to urban interests. For nearly forty years Boise and other cities have been seeking local option taxing authority, but they have been frustrated by a legislature that does not trust local officials to keep taxes low. Finally, Idaho city officials and chambers of commerce are planning to place on the 2014 general election ballot an initiative to give Idaho cities the taxation authority they have sought for so long.

Government Capacity and Policy Problems in the Great Basin

A half century of rapid population growth has challenged each of the four cities of the rim to face growth pressures with limited financial tools, to counteract local skepticism about land use planning that makes regional cooperation difficult, and to deal with state legislators beholden to rural interests. The "big governments" of Boise, Salt Lake City, Reno, and Las Vegas dominate their states in population and in economic importance, yet they are limited by state legislatures skeptical toward urban interests and by property tax limitations passed by a population eager to use the initiative process.

The Idaho Legislature has taken, at best, a skeptical and, at worst, a hostile attitude toward its cities. A chief example of this is the long-fought battle to extend local option taxation to cities in Idaho. Local governments can only adopt taxes that are authorized either by the state constitution or by state statute. A local option tax would allow Idaho cities to adopt a sales tax that would be added on to the state sales tax. Once authorized by the state, local option taxes require voter approval. Forms of local option taxes are in use throughout the western United States, but Idaho has thus far authorized only a limited resort city local option tax.[13]

One widely discussed local option tax would be used to expand mass transit options in the Boise metropolitan area. In 2008 the Idaho Legislature considered a bill that would have authorized local taxation authority for this purpose, but it would have required a two-thirds voter-approval level and limited the tax to only one county at a time, thereby eliminating a metropolitan-area solution to mass transit funding or any other metro-wide issue.[14] Even this legislation failed.

Legislative hostility toward urban interests was also evident in attempts to limit or eliminate urban renewal agencies in Idaho and their ability to use tax increment financing for redevelopment projects. Legislative scrutiny of urban renewal has extended over several sessions, including a suggestion by Boise's mayor that the urban renewal district be used to fund a downtown streetcar project. A quick look at the 2012 Association of Idaho Cities legislative issues reveals the defensive posture cities have adopted relative to the Idaho Legislature: "*protect* revenue sharing, highway distribution accounts and state liquor account revenues; *preserve* urban renewal authority; *preserve* municipal annexation authority."[15]

Perhaps the most overtly hostile act a state legislature can take against its local governments is to "take" the locally collected taxes for state purposes. This occurred in California and Nevada in recent years.[16] In Nevada the state took more than $102 million from Clark County to balance the state's budget deficit in 2009 and 2010. The state also took revenue from Washoe, the other urbanized county in Nevada. Local governments sued, and the Nevada Supreme Court determined that this practice must stop because the moneys were collected for a different purpose. Clark County is now suing to have the $102 million returned. It is unlikely, however, that the state will voluntarily return the funds. As the Nevada League of Cities' website notes, "Why does the state feel so secure constantly taking as it pleases and thumbing its nose at the county and other local governments? Because it's an asymmetrical negotiation—state government has all the power."[17]

Governing Across the Cultural Divide

The big and small governments within the Great Basin sometimes seem to operate in parallel universes. They regard one another with a wary eye, and sometimes they become involved in active conflicts. Frontier counties resist federal land management decisions impacting the public lands within their borders. In Nevada and Idaho urbanized counties and cities deal with unfriendly or indifferent legislatures that provide few resources but sometimes encroach on their local taxing and policy-making authority. Drawing on the tradition of populism in the Basin, citizens tired of escalating property values turn to the initiative process to vent their frustrations and limit the region's governments' powers. The resulting limitations present the region's state and local governments with an unusual challenge.

The divide between the urbanized and the outback counties arises from the fact that the policy issues they face are very different. Mass transit, urban renewal, and regional planning are significant concerns for the people living in urban areas, whereas endangered species designations, grazing allotments, and federal payments in lieu of taxes attract the attention of people living in frontier communities. State legislatures try to balance competing claims while also trying to address their own problems. The mixture of perspectives and conflicting interests makes up a constantly simmering stew.

NOTES

1. There are, of course, other governments in the Great Basin Desert, such as special districts including school districts, tribal governments, and regional bodies addressing planning or service delivery.

2. Idaho city officials were successful in gaining for "resort cities" local sales, liquor, and hotel-motel taxation authority in the late 1970s.

3. Ralph Becker, "Mayor's Budget Address 2013," http://www.slcgov.com/mayor -becker-fiscal-year-2013-budget-address-recommended-budget.

4. This percentage is calculated using the definition of the Great Basin Desert as defined by Grayson and utilizing county-level statistics on public lands as provided by the US Census Bureau.

5. National Center for Frontier Communities, "Definition of Frontier," http://www.frontierus.org.

6. Boise County is also considered a frontier county by the NCFC but falls outside of our definition of the Great Basin Desert.

7. John Wesley Powell, "Report of the Lands in the Arid Region," excerpted in *Seeing Things Whole: The Essential John Wesley Powell,* edited by William deBuys (Washington, DC: Island Press, 2001), 167.

8. Lenore Bushnell, "Nevada: The Tourist State," in *Politics in the American West,* edited by Frank H. Jonas (Salt Lake City: University of Utah Press, 1969), 233.

9. Ronald J. Hrebenar and Robert C. Benedict, "Political Parties, Elections, and Campaigns, II: Evaluation and Trends," in *Politics and Public Policy in the Contemporary American West,* edited by Clive S. Thomas (Albuquerque: University of New Mexico Press, 1991), 136.

10. James B. Weatherby and Stephanie L. Witt, *The Urban West: Managing Growth and Decline* (Westport, CT: Praeger, 1994), 29.

11. Michael Archer, *A Man of His Word: The Life and Times of Nevada's Senator William J. Raggio* (Ashland, OR: Hellgate Press, 2011), 318, 317.

12. Nevada State Constitution, Article 4, Section 18.2; David McGrath Schwartz, "Counties, State Argue: 'You Raise Taxes.' 'No, You Do It,'" *Las Vegas Sun,* March 13, 2011, http://www.lasveassun.com.

13. Stephanie L. Witt and James B. Weatherby, *Urban West Revisited* (Boise, ID: Boise State University, 2012), 94.

14. "Local Option Worth a Shot," *Idaho Press-Tribune* (Nampa), September 18, 2011.

15. Dustin Hurst, "House Mulls Repeal of Idaho's Urban Renewal Law," February 24, 2012, http://www.idahoreporter.com; Association of Idaho Cities, "2012 AIC Legislative Issues," in *2012 Legislative Manual* (Boise, ID: Association of Idaho Cities, 2012), 2 (emphasis added).

16. In 2010 California voters approved Proposition 22 that limited the state's ability to "divert" local tax revenues for state budget needs.

17. "Money Fight," *Las Vegas Review-Journal,* June 17, 2012, http://www.lvrj.com/opinion/money-fight-159340375.html; Nevada League of Cities and Municipalities, "It's Time Local Government Stop Asking the State for Permission to Act," July 27, 2012, http://www.nvleague.org/news/local-government-stop-asking.

Go Away Closer

The Collision of Culture and Governance

STEPHANIE L. WITT AND BRIAN LAURENT

THE RELATIONSHIP BETWEEN CITIZENS AND GOVERNMENT in the Great Basin is riddled with paradox. Resistance to government is a habit of mind so deep that it has become a leading marker of a distinctive culture within the Basin even within the context of the popular celebration of attributes such as rugged individualism and self-reliance throughout the American West. In the Great Basin a complex public infrastructure composed of county, state, and federal governments supports human activities of every kind, but all but the smallest of them are viewed with suspicion. Especially in the desert outback, counties have evolved as the popular expression of the Jeffersonian ideal of government closest to the people, and they have been used as blunt instruments to contest federal, and sometimes state, authority. The region's counties have been embroiled in a sometimes acrimonious relationship with federal land management agencies and state legislatures for some time, yet they are heavily dependent upon both. A major source of friction is that counties do not possess the resources to provide adequate government services over vast, thinly populated geographic areas, yet local officials resent the larger governments on which they depend. This dependence fosters a "go away closer" dynamic fraught with tension and turmoil.

Because the vast majority of the region's landmass is untaxable federal land (70.6 percent) and population is thinly distributed,[1] county governments in the Great Basin find it difficult or impossible to generate enough revenues from the property tax and other local sources to pay for the services demanded by their citizens or mandated by state constitutions and statutes. County governments in the Great Basin find themselves caught in the middle. Their nominal jurisdiction encompasses all land within their borders, including federal land; they are administrative arms of the state; and their powers and structures are specified in state constitutions and statutes.[2] Federal reimbursements from grazing, mining, forestry, or other uses are critically important to county budgets, but the counties have little influence and no control over the federal land management practices that affect the volume of revenues generated by those activities. This circumstance is a perfect prescription for a perpetually troubled relationship, one made more difficult because of the distinctive political culture nurtured by the history and geography of the Great Basin.

The Basin's desolate and challenging natural environment has given rise to an exaggerated version of the western cultural tradition that emphasizes self-sufficiency and resistance to government. The harsh environment of the desert moved nineteenth-century newspaper editor Samuel Bowles to describe it as "a region whose uses are unimaginable, unless to hold the rest of the globe together, or to teach patience to travelers, or to keep close-locked in its mountain ranges those mineral treasurers that the world did not need or was not ready for until now." In his book *Basin and Range*, writer John McPhee quotes a Lovelock, Nevada, resident to the effect that "the entire history of Nevada is one of plant life, animal life and human life adapting to very difficult conditions. People here are the most individualistic you can find. . . . They want to live free from government interference. They don't fit into a structured way of life. This area was settled by people who shun progress. Their way of life would be totally unattractive to most, but they chose it. They have chosen conditions that would be considered intolerable elsewhere."[3]

Hulse notes that "Nevadans and their predecessors have shaped a special type of society, one which has adapted to a harsh environment." It seems that there has always been a resistance to control or influence from powerful forces far away. The early miners resented the control exerted by the mine owners and banks in San Francisco. Local entrepreneurs resented taking orders from the Utah capital, and in 1861 they sought statehood to avoid it.[4] Resistance to governmental authority was deeply embedded in the history and mythology of the mining town. Franklin Buck is quoted as describing his Nevada mining town this way: "You are right in thinking that we live here just as we please. If we want a hot whiskey toddy we have it. If we choose to lay abed late, we do so. We come and go and nobody wonders. . . . [W]e are free from all fashions and conventionalities of society." Nevadans were skeptical of the need for a state government from the beginning. As the argument over whether to seek statehood raged, a newspaper editor opined, "The Humboldt world is deadset against engaging to help support any more lunkheads till times get better. . . . If we have a state government we'll have more fat-headed officers to support." Bowers notes the irony that despite this deep-seated antagonism toward government, it is largely (only?)

through a massive governmental presence that most of the Great Basin was developed at all. "It is doubtful that any other state in the Union has been so dependent for its existence and survival on the federal government; yet Nevadans are among the most vociferous critics of the federal government and the first to tout themselves as 'rugged individualists' who pulled themselves up by their own bootstraps. Nevada came into existence as a state as a result of the federal government's nurturing; it has grown and prospered as a result of vast federal investment in dams, roads, military bases and industrial complexes."[5]

The Sagebrush Rebellions of the 1970s and 1990s were rooted in county-level opposition to federal land management policies. Frustration over federal policy led county and state officials to call for state or local control over the vast stretches of public lands in the Great Basin. In particular, environmental legislation and new rules governing the administration of federal lands enraged county officials. At stake were financial concerns linked to the receipt of federal reimbursements that relied heavily upon federal management practices. Tighter environmental regulations steadily reduced federal paybacks to the counties. Wilderness designation and other regulations limiting access to public lands angered local residents who had grown used to unrestricted rights to hunting, fishing, and recreational access. The successive Sagebrush Rebellions and the County Supremacy movement grew out of the tensions arising from a collision of cultures, one rooted in the national environmental movement and the other in local cultural attitudes. County governments and the federal government represented these two opposing forces. In order to understand how these tensions play out, the overwhelming presence and importance of federal lands in the Great Basin must be understood.

The Federal Presence and Local Government

The federal presence in the Great Basin Desert is hard to miss. There is no county in Nevada that does not contain significant federal landholdings, and "no other state among the contiguous forty eight has a greater part of its territory under the direct control of the federal government."[6] Federal lands make up 70.6 percent of the Great Basin Desert, but as the data in table 1 show, for many counties the proportion is much higher: in six of them federal holdings cover more than 90 percent of the land area. The federal lands in the region include those managed by the Bureau of Land Management (BLM), the US Forest Service, the US Fish and Wildlife Service (USFWS), the

TABLE 1
Top Federal Land Counties in Great Basin Desert Region

State	County	PILT Payment, 2011	Federal Land (acres)	PILT per acre	Federal Land (square mile)	Total Land Area (square mile)	Federal land (%)
NV	Esmeralda	$97,198	2,247,850	$0.04	3,512	3,589	97.9
NV	Clark	$3,134,374	4,809,896	$0.65	7,515	7,911	95.0
NV	Lander	$814,050	3,333,331	$0.24	5,208	5,494	94.8
NV	Lincoln	$774,488	6,410,564	$0.12	10,017	10,635	94.2
NV	White Pine	$1,118,972	5,196,845	$0.22	8,120	8,877	91.5
CA	Mono	$1,052,328	1,760,296	$0.60	2,750	3,044	90.4
CA	Inyo	$1,610,415	5,503,611	$0.29	8,599	10,192	84.4
NV	Eureka	$288,663	2,156,889	$0.13	3,370	4,176	80.7
NV	Mineral	$639,682	1,940,455	$0.33	3,032	3,757	80.7

SOURCE: US Department of Interior, http://www.nbc.gov/pilt/pilt/search.cfm.

National Park Service, the Bureau of Reclamation, the US Army, US Air Force, the US Navy (naval air station), the US Department of Energy, and the Bureau of Indian Affairs.

In the twentieth century an assortment of federal activities located on public lands exerted a huge impact on local environments. Federal lands in Nevada have been used for "ammunition depots, air bases, livestock management, bombing ranges and the training ground for fighter-plane pilots, atomic testing, rocket development, the home base of hundreds of intercontinental missiles . . . and the deposit of high-level nuclear waste."[7] The federal presence has also been felt in Idaho in the Idaho National Laboratory, national landmarks, publicly owned rangeland and forests, and bombing ranges and air bases. Similarly, Utah hosts federal defense installations, national forests, and several national parks and monuments.

For a long time residents of the Great Basin not only tolerated but generally welcomed new projects because they brought jobs and economic activity. This began to change markedly in the 1960s, especially in Nevada. Resentment toward the federal government was fueled by the extreme dependence of local governments upon federal activities. Since Congress had made federally owned lands exempt from taxation, state and local governments could find little land to tax. The problem was that most states utilize county governments as administrative arms of the state, which guarantees that a network of services such as roads, courts, voting and elections, and law enforcement jails must extend into even the remotest areas. The mismatch between resources and responsibilities puts counties in a bind.

The relationship between the federal government and Great Basin counties has been shaped by the evolving financial arrangements between federal agencies and counties. Several federal statutes govern the distribution of federal payments to counties. The Twenty-Five Percent Fund Act of 1908 (the National Forest Revenue Act) allocated one-fourth of the federal revenues received from logging in national forests to the states and counties where the timber harvests took place. In 1976 Congress passed the Payment in Lieu of Taxes Act to compensate for losses from property taxes in counties even where there were no timber revenues. This legislation included virtually all federal holdings, including national forests, parks, and wildlife refuges and public lands managed by the BLM and other agencies. The Secure Rural Schools Act and Community Self-Determination Act of 2000 (which was renewed in 2008) implemented a revised formula for federal payments that took into account the acreage of federal holdings in states and counties, the level of previous payments (to compensate for declining harvests), and the per capital income of state or local residents. Despite these changes, because transfers to counties from the federal government was still affected by the revenues generated by timber harvests and resource extraction industries such as mining, county governments continued to be greatly concerned about extraction-based policies on federal lands.

The federal government's policy approach to public lands and in the West can be divided into three major periods.[8] The first begins at the nation's founding and goes to 1890, when the national government's main concerns were resource development and methods of transferring public lands to private ownership. The second period, which lasted from approximately 1890 through 1940, was characterized by conservation of natural resources on the public lands through the creation of the US Forest Service and the National Park Service and the passage of the Taylor Grazing Act. The third period, which stretched from approximately 1940 to 1980, emphasized the *preservation* of natural resources. Most of the twenty-two major environmental statutes passed in this forty-year period were enacted within a few years in the 1960s and 1970s; these included landmark laws such as the Clean Air Act, the Clean Drinking Water Act, and the National Environmental Policy Act.

Recently, changes in federal land management policy have reduced the amount of money received by counties throughout the West because the original statutes and policies that developed the financial relationship between counties and the federal government were supplanted by a new generation of environmental laws and policies. The focus of federal land management policy changed from resource extraction (timber, range, and minerals) to fish and wildlife, watershed health, and conservation.⁹ This change in policy emphasis has exerted a direct and negative impact on county government budgets and the stability of communities that have relied upon long-ago established uses. The Idaho Association of Counties summarizes the impact of this change in policy: "Protection of the environment has increased in importance in the decision-making process at all levels of government. Idaho's county officials, representing the concerns of their constituents, are keenly aware of the rich heritage, the beauty, and the natural resources of their local environment. However, the environmental and socioeconomic issues must be considered to achieve a solution, which balances a high degree of environmental protection with the preservation and enhancement of local communities."¹⁰

Respondents to a 2011 survey of county commissioners in the Intermountain West indicated that federal payments to their counties continue to be very important to their budgets.¹¹ In response to a question about the importance of federal payments, only 4 percent of commissioners indicated that federal payments were "somewhat" or "extremely unimportant," while 87 percent of the respondents indicated that federal payments were "extremely" or "somewhat important." The reasons for these responses are also reflected in an e-mail exchange with a rural Oregon County judge (similar to a commissioner): "Through many efforts the success of PILT [payment in lieu of taxes] being appropriated [by the federal government] at 100% has filled the gap for county government. The real problem is that the loss of local control for the use of natural resources, grazing, timber and a little mining has resulted in severe job loss, now eventually population decline and because of the state school funding formula we have are seeing very difficult funding for our schools."

The impact of PILT payments on county budgets varies, of course, depending upon the structure of the local economy and the amount of the PILT payment. In some Nevada counties (Humboldt, for example), PILT payments are equal to 10 percent of the county general fund revenue. This may explain why eight of the nine county commissioners from Nevada who answered the survey indicated the PILT payments were "extremely important" to their county's budget (the ninth respondent indicated the payments were "somewhat important").

County and Federal Land Management Agency Conflict

County officials seek ways to be involved in the planning and decision-making processes undertaken by federal land management agencies. The Sagebrush Rebellion, which began in 1979 in Nevada, focused western states' concerns over a variety of federal land management policy. The Sagebrush Rebellion collection at the University of Nevada describes it this way: "The Sagebrush Rebellion was a general attitude reflecting the feeling that federal policies affecting the west were made in ignorance of conditions and concerns in the west, that those policies were made for a so-called national constituency without regard for western problems, that this 'colonial' treatment was going to get worse as the west was called upon to satisfy the national's energy needs, and federal administration displayed outright animosity toward the west."[12]

In the 1990s county officials began passing a series of ordinances asserting supremacy over the federal lands within their borders. The "County Supremacy" ordinances, also referred to as "Wise Use" ordinances, were oriented around multiple uses of public lands, drawing upon Gifford Pinchot's early-twentieth-century definition of conservation as "the wise use of resources."[13] Estimates of the number of counties that passed these ordinances varied widely from 150 to 500 counties nationwide. Surveys of intermountain county commissioners in the mid-1990s indicated that commissioners from rural counties with high percentages of federal lands were much more likely to indicate that they had poor relationships with federal agencies than were commissioners from urban counties.[14]

The frustrations over the conflicts with federal land management agencies have been institutionalized in the gathering of funds to support counties with natural resource policy and litigation costs.[15] The Western Interstate Region caucus of the National Association of Counties listed the following as their top priorities in 2012, reflecting the importance of the county-federal relationship and financial arrangements:

- educating lawmakers and the public about the unique policy challenges facing western counties
- maintaining mandatory funding for Payments in Lieu of Taxes (PILT) and Secure Rural Schools
- regulatory relief
- economic recovery
- opposing the top down federal land use decisions[16]

The conflict and negotiation between western states, counties, and the federal government continue today. In 2010 the Bureau of Land Management announced an initiative to inventory BLM lands to identify and protect wilderness-quality land. Wilderness designation would preclude roads, permanent structures, and activities such as logging, mining, and vehicular traffic.[17] Western governors immediately announced their opposition to the 2010 BLM initiatives. They feared, above all else, that additional wilderness designation would interfere with potential energy development on BLM land. Idaho's governor said that he saw federal designation as a "job killer." The Public Lands Committee of the Idaho Association of Counties passed a resolution opposing the BLM wilderness planning effort.[18] The Nevada Association of Counties also passed a resolution opposing the BLM initiative.

Officials from the BLM assert that the initiatives have been mischaracterized, pointing out that 677,000 acres of the land being discussed is reserved for solar energy development.[19] But the fight over additional wilderness designation is predicted to continue through the 2016 presidential election.[20] Congress eventually voted to withhold all funds for the wilderness lands inventory from BLM, but Interior Secretary Ken Salazar has suggested that the BLM will continue to find ways to work with "Congress, the States, tribes and local communities" to identify potential lands for protection under the Wilderness Act."[21]

Another example of federal-county conflict over the management of public lands can be found in recent resistance to changes to the Deer Flat National Refuge in Canyon County, Idaho. President Theodore Roosevelt created the Deer Flat National Wildlife Refuge in 1909. In 1937 a series of islands located in the Snake River to the south of Lake Lowell were added to the Deer Flat Refuge. The refuge was initially created as a Bureau of Reclamation irrigation project as part of the reservoir system tied to dams along the Boise River in 1909. The reservoir created by the diversion of water from the Boise River via the New York canal was named Lake Lowell. Lake Lowell "is now one of the largest off-stream reservoirs in the American west, with the capacity to irrigate over 200,000 acres of land."[22] Agriculture has flourished in the irrigated farmland in Canyon County, where Lake Lowell is located. According to Canyon County officials, 84 percent of the county is currently in agricultural use.[23]

Over the years the Deer Flat Refuge became a popular fishing and boating recreation site. In 2011 the US Fish and Wildlife Service proposed a comprehensive conservation plan that would reduce boating on Lake Lowell in order to minimize the impact on wildlife and fish. The draft management plan would also prohibit dogs, bikes, and horses in the area. Vigorous opposition to these proposed changes has come from both the county and the state governments. As related in a newspaper account, "Canyon County Commission Chairman David Ferdinand said he is 'outraged' and that refuge managers are not taking recreational needs and the lake's economic impact on the county seriously."[24] In a September 2011 conversation Canyon County commissioners noted that forty-seven hundred boaters claimed Lake Lowell as their "home lake" in state registration processes and estimated the economic impact of recreational boating in Canyon County to be many millions of dollars a year. They also took issue with the USFWS assertions that additional restrictions on boating are necessary for the protection of wildlife in the refuge, noting that "we have 100 years of history to prove wildlife are thriving" in the refuge under current practice. Commissioners expressed a fear that the public may lose access to Lake Lowell altogether and pointed to recent conflicts in which refuge staff have closed gates or limited access to various areas around the lake.

In a May 2011 letter to the Deer Flat National Wildlife Refuge manager, Idaho governor Butch Otter wrote: "Make no mistake: the responsibility and jurisdiction to manage fish and resident wildlife belong to the state of Idaho. The U.S. Fish and Wildlife Service must recognize that all Idaho wildlife is the property of the state of Idaho (Idaho State Code 36-103) and must not create a competing management scheme."[25]

Otter's letter also noted that the original purpose of the man-made reservoir was irrigation. The conflict over the Deer Flat Refuge highlights fights over sovereignty: who owns the land, the wildlife, and the water: the US government, the state of Idaho, or Canyon County? The Deer Flat Refuge also illustrates conflicts over who should decide on the uses of such a natural resource. Do federal land management agencies need to take into account existing local uses such as boating when considering practices that will protect wildlife and natural settings?

The controversy over the Deer Flat National Wildlife Refuge illustrates that there are a multitude of opportunities for conflict:

- land underneath the reservoir: US Bureau of Reclamation
- water in Lake Lowell: Boise Board of Control, irrigation water users

- wildlife that live in the refuge: US Fish and Wildlife Service and/or Idaho Fish and Game
- roads, docks, and parks surrounding Lake Lowell: Canyon County

All of these agencies and governments have distinctive missions and cultures that lead them to different priorities in regard to their approach to the Deer Flat National Wildlife Refuge:

- US Bureau of Reclamation: "to manage, develop, and protect water and related resources in an environmentally and economically sound manner in the interest of the American public." (http://www.usbr.gov/main/about/mission.html)
- Boise Board of Control: irrigation operating entity for 160,000 acres in five irrigation districts in southern Idaho and eastern Oregon. "The Boise Project furnishes a full irrigation water supply to about 224,000 acres and a supplemental supply to some 173,000 acres under special and Warren Act contracts. The irrigable lands are in southwestern Idaho and eastern Oregon." (http://www.usbr.gov/projects/Project.jsp?proj_Name=Boise+Project)
- US Fish and Wildlife Service: "The U.S. Fish and Wildlife Service's mission is, working with others, to conserve, protect and enhance fish, wildlife, and plants and their habitats for the continuing benefit of the American people." (http://www.fws.gov/who/)
- Canyon County, Idaho: a political and administrative division of the state of Idaho.
- Idaho Department of Fish and Game: "All wildlife, including all wild animals, wild birds, and fish, within the state of Idaho, is hereby declared to be the property of the state of Idaho. It shall be preserved, protected, perpetuated, and managed. It shall be only captured or taken at such times or places, under such conditions, or by such means, or in such manner, as will preserve, protect, and perpetuate such wildlife, and provide for the citizens of this state and, as by law permitted to others, continued supplies of such wildlife for hunting, fishing and trapping." (http://fishandgame.idaho.gov /public/about/commission/?getPage=186)

These kinds of multijurisdictional battles are taking place in many parts of the Great Basin. Battles between governments at all levels are endemic because the authority of governments is ambiguous or overlapping and because they have different missions and answer to different constituencies. The "right" answer to jurisdiction is sometimes clearly established—as when counties attempt to abrogate federal authority—but sometimes there is no answer but negotiation. The challenge of reaching compromise is daunting because so many constituencies are represented at the table.

County Commissioner Attitudes Toward Federal Agencies

County commissioners from the Intermountain West counties were asked to assess their county's current working relationship with various federal agencies. The question posed was: "How would you describe your county's working relationship with the following agencies? The agencies included the Army Corps of Engineers, Bureau of Land Management, Bureau of Reclamation, Fish and Wildlife Service, Forest Service, and National Park Service. The Bureau of Land Management, in spite of its prominent role in recent discussions over additional wilderness land designation, is the only federal agency for which more than 60 percent of respondents indicated that the working relationship with counties is "good."[26] Just under 60 percent of respondents indicated that their county's working relationship with the Forest Service was good, while under 50 percent said that their county's working relationship with the Army Corps of Engineers was "good." The National Park Service was the federal agency for which the lowest percentage of responding commissioners indicated they had a "good" working relationship (20 percent). And the Park Service was also the agency that the largest percentage of commissioners chose as "not applicable" in describing their working relationship (40 percent). County commissioner respondents to our survey focused on the lack of understanding of county issues and poor communication when asked to offer comments regarding why their working relationship with federal agencies was "poor." The following is a sampling of their comments:

- "They [federal agencies] have their own agenda, not concerned for our citizen's wishes."
- "They [federal agencies] are nonresponsive and heavy handed."
- "They [federal agencies] have no true consideration for the needs of the county."
- "They do not understand rural America."

Other comments focused on the poor working relationship between counties and the federal government and the challenges of working with a large bureaucracy.

- "Red tape."
- "Over regulation, little or no communication, bureaucrats with agendas."
- "Lack of coordination of plans and policies."
- "Difficulty in permitting and slow response time when urgent issues arrive."
- "Federal policies tend to be one-size-fits-all. Unworkable in our area given other federal oversight of some of our resources."
- "Poor leadership and employees being moved around, here today, gone tomorrow."

The relationship between counties and the federal government is not uniform across the region. A fall 2010 survey of Idaho county commissioners found that *none* of the respondents indicated that their county's working relationship with federal agencies was "easy,"[27] and approximately 25 percent of Idaho respondents indicated that the county's working relationship with federal agencies was "somewhat easy." In that same survey only 5 percent of respondents said the county's working relationship with federal agencies was "very difficult," approximately 17 percent said the working relationship was "difficult," and 35 percent thought the working relationship was "somewhat difficult." These responses are interesting because they show a clear split, but in general the attitudes are not as negative as one might expect from the large amount of press generated when conflicts break out. Getting along is not news.

Counties and the State

Ambivalence to a higher level of government is also evident in the relationship of counties with their state governments. Counties are, in one sense, administrative arms of their states and thus subject to the rules imposed by state legislatures. States and counties share responsibility for many services, yet when push comes to shove, counties are virtually at the mercy of the states. County officials find themselves on the receiving end of state-mandated directives and at the mercy of state-enacted tax authorities. These dynamics can lead to resentment and frustration.

County commissioners from the intermountain states reported much better working relationships with state government agencies than with federal agencies. For example, slightly more than 70 percent of respondents indicated that they had a good working relationship with the state department of agriculture. More than 50 percent of respondents indicated that they had a good working relationship with state departments of fish and game, health and welfare, public safety, transportation, and water resources. The highest proportion of respondents, 17 percent, reported a "poor" working relationship with the state department of environmental quality (DEQ). Overall, the working relationships between state executive branch agencies and counties are perceived to be stronger by county commissioners than those between counties and federal agencies.

When asked why the working relationships between state and county governments was sometimes poor, county commissioners expressed the same frustration that they had expressed about the level of communication and understanding with federal agencies:

- "Communications."
- "They are just trying to keep their jobs and forget about what is best for the land and rural America."
- "They just do not want to work with us."
- "Do not have a good vision."
- "Lack of understanding."

There were also complaints related to state agency bureaucracy, including a few related to a lack of capacity in state government agencies:

- "Too many rules and regulations."
- "Excessive regulation, too much oversight."
- "Trouble with the permitting process."
- "I put poor on the environmental because they are the biggest bottleneck for any kind of development in our county."
- "Corrections dept does not take responsibility for the housing and care of state inmates in a timely fashion, thus creating a burden on county resources."
- "DEQ has way too much say versus what is law."
- "Not enough personnel to enforce regulations."
- "Inefficient state practices and management."

County officials in Nevada are sensitive to the controlling force of the state government in their lives. Nearly all commissioners or managers started off their interviews by stating, "This is a Dillon's Rule state." This choice of words pointed to the relatively tight control that the State of Nevada holds over its counties. This manifests mostly in the delegation of responsibilities to counties and constraints upon county taxation authorities. The state has mandated county-level sales taxes, including transient room taxes and car rental taxes, with specifications in the statute about how the collected funds will be spent at the local level. In one case the State of Nevada mandated that Clark County collect a 2 percent local sales tax on transient rooms (hotel). The state further directed that the county return a fraction of a percent of the money collected to the state tourism promotion bureau and that the remainder be placed in the Clark County School District's capital fund. In sum, the state legislature forced a particular county to create a tax and then give the proceeds of that tax to another local governmental entity. This unusual arrangement was a product of the nearly impossible task of keeping up with population growth in Clark County. Growth was so rapid for a period of time that the Clark County School District was building one elementary school a month. According to a commissioner interviewed by the author, the legislature saw the additional sales tax as a way to fund the needed school buildings.

County officials in Idaho also struggle with their relationship with the State of Idaho. The Idaho Association of Counties has unsuccessfully sought local option taxation authority for many years, a tax authority the state legislature has been unwilling to grant to either counties or cities.[28] During the 2012 legislative session, counties and the state fought over whether the state or the county would have control over the siting and regulation of natural gas drilling. This was originally left to the discretion of county governments in Idaho, but the state was under pressure from the natural gas industry to provide one set of rules statewide. In a sign that relations between the state legislature and the counties had deteriorated significantly, one commissioner noted with shock to the author that a legislative leader had dismissed the counties as "just another interest group" in his meeting with county officials at the county association conference. A judge from a rural Oregon county explained his frustration with state-imposed tax limitations in an e-mail in response to this statement: "One of the things I'm writing about is the difficulties that counties in the Great Basin Desert region face in providing services and government over such vast distances with small tax bases (due to large public lands areas) and with states shedding responsibility for services to counties. Do you find that to be an accurate way of understanding your county?"

> Yes I believe your statement to be broadly accurate. I say broadly because it does describe the situation that Oregon counties face. My problem with the statement is that it does not take into account the desire and ability of rural

folks to be successful if left alone to handle their own needs and desires. *For instance when this county could set its own property taxes to fill the need of our local schools we voted each year for a base tax two and a half times bigger than what today's rate is. In other words "we the people" made the decisions on how to be governed (and how to pay for it) at least partially because of the small tax base.* That concept works in rural America I believe. (emphasis added)

Perhaps the best indicator that the state-county relationship is troubled in Nevada is the fact that the state has taken locally collected property tax revenue to help balance the state budget in recent years. This resulted in a lawsuit in which local governments asserted that the state could not divert these taxes in this way. The Nevada Supreme Court agreed, and the governor and legislature halted plans to continue the practice in 2012.[29] Clark County officials reported that they had more than $100 million diverted from their local tax collections to the state coffers at a time when their own revenues were plummeting due to the housing crisis. As one phrased it, "We're swimming in the same revenue stream and they [the state] made our revenue problems worse." Another commissioner remarked that the legislature resorted to taking local revenues when the legislature could not muster the two-thirds vote necessary to raise taxes at the state level and that it was easier to take the local taxes.

An urban county commissioner in Nevada observed that the state has found "lots of ways to skim funds off of certain local budgets" and that it "didn't use to matter" when growth fueled local tax base growth. Now, however, county officials grouse about tense relationships between the state and counties and note that the state has "dumped state responsibilities on counties." Commissioners report that there are a lot of things being pushed down from the state level that have added to the burden of keeping county budgets and services intact. One rural Nevada county noted that presentence investigations, environmental health inspections, Medicaid cost shares, child protective services, and probation and parole had all been pushed down wholly or in part from the state to the county—adding an additional $300,000 to their budget (an approximately 2 percent additional cost to their general fund). At the same time counties throughout the Great Basin have been forced to cut their budgets in recent years.

Local Economies and Governmental Capacity

Great Basin counties are locked into property tax limitations and local option tax rules designed and imposed by state legislatures increasingly worried about balancing their own budgets. Their limited financial tools are constrained even more by the presence of so much untaxed federal land, leaving counties dependent on PILT as a partial replacement of their tax base. The financial capacity of Great Basin counties is threatened further when state governments push more of the cost for mandated services down to the county level. These structural characteristics create a multitude of problems, but it is worth noting that counties in the Great Basin have always struggled to build the capacity to govern. Limited resources and instability have been the rule for a long time.

One measure of the resource limitations of county governments in the Basin is the number of counties that have had more than one county seat. In an earlier time it was not unusual for communities in newly formed western counties to compete for the privilege of being named the seat of government.[30] Hulse notes that "in the early local history of Nevada, the most frequent intra-county controversies were waged over which town(s) should have the honors and privileges that the county seat bestowed." Ten of Nevada's current seventeen counties have had more than one county seat, and five of those counties have had three or more county seats. Five of the county seat moves resulted from redrawn county boundaries. In Oregon's Great Basin counties the legislature designated temporary county seats at the time it created the counties, which resulted in a series of votes and fights over the site of a permanent seat. In Harney County, for example, Harney City residents filed a petition in a three-year fight that "claimed that some of Burns' citizens had made bribes with the promises of money and employment, had intimidated school children to vote, had furnished whiskey to voters and had circulated fraudulent ballots to 'careless, illiterate and hasty voters.'"[31]

Many of the changes in the location of county seats have been linked to the rapid rise and fall of mining communities. Many of those present ghost towns were once thriving county seats, but are now listed in directories of ghost towns (see table 2). The desert landscape is dotted with the remains of communities that grew up on the basis of mineral extraction or marginal agriculture. The county courthouse was the place to register mineral claims and water and land rights, vote, and seek help from the sheriff, among other things.[32] The discovery of valuable ore deposits would create a boomtown,

TABLE 2
Great Basin Desert Counties and Former County Seats

County	Names of Former County Seats
Churchill, NV	Bucklands (turned out to be in Lyons County), La Plata[a] (1864), Stillwater[a] (1868)
Douglas, NV	Genoa, Minden (1915)
Elmore, ID	Rocky Bar[a]
Esmeralda, NV	Aurora[a] founded in 1860, once had population of 10,000. Was uncertain if in NV or CA. Was at one time the county seat of both Mono County, CA, and Esmeralda, NV. Goldfield, Hawthorne[a] (now in Mineral County)
Humboldt, NV	Unionville[a] (now in Pershing County)
Lander, NV	Jacobs Springs, Austin[a]
Lincoln, NV	Crystal Springs,[a] Hiko[a]
Lyon, NV	Dayton[a]
Morgan, UT	Peterson
Nye, NV	Belmont[a]
Oneida, ID	Soda Springs
Owyhee, ID	Ruby City,[a] Silver City[a]
Piute, UT	Circleville
Rich, UT	St. Charles (turned out to be in Idaho)
Washoe, NV	Washoe City[a]
White Pine, NV	Hamilton[a]

SOURCE: Idaho Association of Counties, Nevada Association of Counties, Utah Association of Counties, Harney County, and Ghosttowns.com.
[a]Denotes community now listed in "ghost town" listings.

and it would disappear as soon as the ore played out. Mining has been and continues to be an important part of the Nevada and Great Basin economy. The Great Basin has some of the richest silver deposits ever discovered but also some of the shallowest. In his seminal work on the basin and range region, McPhee notes that "mining and milling towns developed and died in less than a decade." McPhee notes that during the approximately thirty years of the silver boom, "there were more communities in Nevada than there are now."[33] This is why many former county seats no longer even exist as living communities: La Plata, Stillwater, Genoa, Aurora, Hawthorne, Unionville, Austin, Crystal Springs, Hiko, Dayton, Ione, Belmont, Washoe City, Silver City, Ruby City, Rocky Bar, and Hamilton are among the former county seats now listed in directories of ghost towns. In at least three cases, fire destroyed the courthouse in once populous county seats, prompting the move to another, still viable, place.

Most county seat moves took place between statehood and 1910; the only county seat change in the last half of the twentieth century was in Lander County, Nevada, in 1979, when the seat of government was moved from

Austin to Battle Mountain. Even so, maintaining the institutions of county government, complete with a full set of elected row, or constitutional, officers, can prove to be difficult and costly, especially in rural counties with small or declining populations. In recognition of the difficulty of funding and finding volunteers to stand for office, Nevada and Utah statutes allow counties to combine elected offices upon approval of the voters, and Oregon retains the county court structure in several rural counties. Eight of the seventeen Nevada counties have chosen to combine the clerk and treasurer positions, and one county has combined the clerk and recorder positions. More than half of the counties in the state of Nevada have opted to combine elected row officers, although Lander County, with only around five thousand residents, and White Pine County, with around nine thousand residents, still elect a full slate of county officials.

In Utah ten of the eighteen counties that fall within the Great Basin have combined the clerk and auditor positions, Piute County combines the treasurer and recorder positions, and Sanpete as well as Weber, Iron, and Juab Counties combine the recorder and surveyor positions. Box Elder County recently (2010) reverted back to the full slate of elected positions after previously combining posts. Two of Oregon's three Great Basin counties have the somewhat unusual "county court" structure, in which voters elect a county judge and two commissioners. The county judge is the chief administrative officer of the county and is a full-time employee, while the commissioners are part-time. The judicial function of the county judge includes probate matters and, in some counties, juvenile court.

The challenge of providing services in remote places has produced some backlash against new residents and their demands for services. Some rural counties have gone to great pains to advise potential new residents that they should lower their expectations about what services to expect. Several counties, presumably fed up with complaints and questions from new or prospective residents, have posted a document called *Code of the West* on their web pages. The *Code of the West* is a seven-page statement admonishing residents to expect low service levels, including areas without electricity, unpaved roads, and a lack of water or sewer services, and to anticipate farmers who run noisy machines all night, stinky animals that wander open range, wild animals that might hurt children, and pesticides. Interestingly, the document ends with the "sincere hope that this information can help you enjoy your decision to reside in the county. The intent is not to dissuade you, but to inform you."[34] A similar version also appears on the websites of at least

TABLE 3
Great Basin Desert Counties Under 10,000 in Population by Percentage
of Employment in Government

County	2010 Population	Percentage of Employment in Government, 2011 (federal, state, and local combined)
Bear Lake (ID)	5,986	18.0
Beaver (UT)	6,629	20.0
Caribou (ID)	6,993	17.0
Clark (ID)	948	27.0
Esmeralda (NV)	783	31.8
Eureka (NV)	1,987	4.3
Harney (OR)	7,422	26.0
Lake (OR)	7,089	28.0
Lander (NV)	5,775	15.6
Lincoln (NV)	5,345	50.8
Lincoln (ID)	5,208	21.0
Mineral (NV)	4,772	35.2
Morgan (UT)	9,469	21.0
Oneida (ID)	4,286	17.0
Pershing (NV)	6,753	38.3
Piute (UT)	1,556	32.0
Power (ID)	7,817	18.0
Rich (UT)	2,264	21.0
Storey (NV)	4,010	6.5
Regional average (counties under 10,000 only)		23.61

SOURCE: US Census.

fifteen other counties in the West, including those maintained by Pershing and Esmeralda Counties in Nevada. The frustration with newcomers and their expectations was expressed in an interview with one rural county commissioner, who noted that people were buying land sight unseen over the Internet, only to be shocked upon arriving to find that there were no roads or that access to their property turned out to be across a bone-dry playa.

The collision of culture and governance is also evident in the fact that in spite of the region's reputation for resistance to government, public jobs make up a sizable percentage of the employment in some of the more remote counties (see table 3). In tiny Esmeralda County, Nevada (2010 population 783), 29.6 percent of the jobs are in local government, and 2.2 percent are in federal agencies. Similarly, in Mineral County, Nevada (2010 population 4,772), local government constitutes 29.7 percent of employment in the county, and federal jobs account for 4.9 percent. Lincoln County, Nevada, has the highest percentage of jobs in the government sector, at 50.8 percent. Table 4 displays the Great Basin counties with fewer than 10,000 people

(2010) by the percentage of jobs in government in 2011. The average percentage of jobs in Great Basin Desert counties under 10,000 in population is 23.61 percent (2011). By contrast, the Great Basin's largest county, Clark County, Nevada, has 14.4 percent of its jobs in the government sector. In Ada County, Idaho, home to the state capital of Boise, 15 percent of its job force work in the public sector.

Resolving the Paradox

The collision between a culture of resistance and the need for governance has many consequences in the Great Basin. Counties are struggling to provide services over vast geographic distances covered mostly by public lands, but they face severe fiscal and capacity constraints. Sometimes fighting absentee federal "landlords" over environmental management, other times fighting state legislatures trying to balance their own budgets, counties are often at the nexus of several forces. In spite of their resistance to government, the region is driven by the fiscal and policy presence of governments, both large and small, and this circumstance creates a "go away closer" paradox that would be familiar to any parent with a teenager in the house. The fact that counties in the Great Basin continue to be dependent on the federal government and at the mercy of the states virtually guarantees that the tense relation will persist.

NOTES

1. This number is calculated by estimating which counties are within the Great Basin Desert as described in "The Last Urban Frontier" of this volume and then calculating the percentage of federal lands in each county.

2. In Nevada voters elect county commissioners, sheriff, treasurer, clerk, assessor, recorder, district attorney, and public administrator. The number of county commissioners ranges from three to five to seven, with the size determined by the local electorate. All of the county elected positions are partisan, and the state imposes a term limit of twelve years. Interestingly, other county elected officials are exempt from this limitation. In Oregon two of the three Great Basin counties (Harney and Malheur) are governed by a county structure in which voters elect a nonpartisan county judge who serves as administrator, plus two commissioners. Lake County utilizes a three-member county commission. Also elected are the district attorney, treasurer, clerk/recorder, sheriff, justice of the peace, and assessor/tax collector. In Idaho all counties utilize the three-member county commissioner structure and also elect the sheriff, prosecuting attorney, clerk, treasurer, assessor, and

coroner. All of the Idaho county elected officials run in partisan elections. Utah counties may elect to change their form of government to an expanded commission, a county executive and council, or a council-manager form of government.

3. Michael S. Durham, *Desert Between the Mountains: Mormons, Miners, Padres, Mountain Men, and the Opening of the Great Basin, 1772–1869* (New York: Henry Holt, 1997), 8; John McPhee, *Basin and Range* (New York: Farrar, Straus, and Giroux, 1980), 227.

4. James W. Hulse, *The Silver State: Nevada's Heritage Reinterpreted*, 3rd ed. (Reno: University of Nevada Press, 2004), 2. The resentment toward San Francisco is recounted in Michael W. Bowers, *The Sagebrush State: Nevada's History, Government, and Politics*, 3rd ed. (Reno: University of Nevada Press, 2006), 22. The desire to avoid governance from Utah is described in Hulse, *Silver State*, 68.

5. Buck quoted in W. Paul Reeve, *Making Space on the Western Frontier: Mormons, Miners, and Southern Paiutes* (Urbana: University of Illinois Press, 2007), 118; newspaper editor quoted in Durham, *Desert Between the Mountains*, 287; Bowers, *Sagebrush State*, 133–34.

6. Hulse, *Silver State*, 13.

7. James W. Hulse, *The Silver State: Nevada's Heritage Reinterpreted*, 3rd ed. (Reno: University of Nevada Press, 2004), 14.

8. The discussion of the evolution of environmental policy follows that of Christopher McGrory Klyza and David Sousa, *American Environmental Policy, 1990–2006: Beyond Gridlock* (Cambridge, MA: MIT Press, 2008).

9. Adams and Gaid, "Federal Land Management," 3.

10. Idaho Association of Counties, *Idaho Public Lands: Facts and Figures* (Boise: Idaho Association of Counties, 2010), 5 (emphasis added).

11. This survey was conducted in the spring of 2010. Surveys were sent to county commissioners in Idaho, Utah, Colorado, Nevada, Arizona, and New Mexico. Results were obtained from 105 commissioners (approximately 25 percent of commissioners) and 50 percent of counties. The survey includes counties that are outside of the Great Basin Desert.

12. "Questions and Answers" on the "Sagebrush Rebellion" fact sheet, folder 4, Guide to the Records of Sagebrush Rebellion, Collection no. 85-04 (University of Nevada, Reno, Special Collections), http://knowledgecenter.unr.edu/specoll/mss /85-04.html.

13. R. McGreggor Cawley, *Federal Land, Western Anger: The Sagebrush Rebellion and Environmental Politics* (Lawrence: University Press of Kansas, 1993), 166.

14. Stephanie L. Witt and Leslie R. Alm, "County Government and the Public Lands: A Review of the County Supremacy Movement in Four Western States," in *Public Lands Management in the West: Citizens, Interest Groups, and Values*, edited by Brent S. Steel (Westport, CT: Praeger, 1997), 95–110.

15. Idaho Association of Counties, *Idaho Public Lands*, 10.

16. Ryan Yates, "NACO Western Interstate Region Sets Priorities," *County Commentary* (Idaho Association of Counties) (November–December 2011): 7.

17. Wilderness Society, "What Is Wilderness" (2011), http://www.wilderness.org.au/articles/what-wilderness.

18. "Idaho Gov. Butch Otter: BLM Wild Lands Inventory Is a 'Job Killer,'" *Idaho Statesman*, March 2, 1011, http://www.idahostatesman.com; Jon Cantamessa, *Public Lands Report (Mid-Winter Conference 2011)* (Boise: Idaho Association of Counties, 2011), http://www.idcounties.org.

19. Patrick O'Grady, "BLM Segregates Arizona Land for Potential Solar Zones," *Phoenix Business Journal*, June 30, 2011, http://www.bizjournals.com/phoenix/blog/business/2011/06/blm-segregates-arizona-land-for.html?ed=2011-06-30s=articleduana=edupup.

20. "Idaho Gov. Butch Otter."

21. Rocky Barker, "Salazar Offers Alternative to 'Wild Lands Inventory,'" *Idaho Statesman Blog: Letters from the West*, June 1, 2011, http://www.idahostatesman.com.

22. U.S. Fish & Wildlife Service Deer Flat National Wildlife Refuge, "Refuge History," http://www.fws.gov/deerflat/visit/history.html.

23. "Agribusiness: Why Is Canyon County Right for You?," http://www.canyon.co.org/Agribusiness.

24. Kristen Rodine, "Recreation Restrictions Loom for Lake Lowell," *Idaho Statesman*, May 8, 2011, http://www.idahostatesman.com.

25. Governor Butch Otter, letter to Jennifer Brown-Scott, July 29, 2011.

26. Responses were condensed from "extremely good" and "somewhat good" to "good" as well as "extremely poor" and "somewhat poor" to "poor."

27. This survey was sent to all Idaho county commissioners in the fall of 2010. Responses were obtained from 22 of the 132 commissioners for a response rate of 17 percent.

28. The state of Idaho does allow the adoption of a "resort city" local option tax on hotels, but it is not available to counties.

29. Ed Vogel and Benjamin Spillman, "Gov. Sandoval Changes Course, Will Support Extension of Taxes," *Las Vegas Review-Journal*, http://www.lvrj.com.

30. Henry F. Mason, "County Seat Controversies in Southwestern Kansas," *Kansas Historical Quarterly* 2, no. 1 (1933): 45–65.

31. Hulse, *Silver State*, 258; Kathleen M. Weidenhold, *Exploring Oregon's Historic Courthouses* (Corvallis: Oregon State University Press, 1998).

32. Hulse, *Silver State*, 259.

33. McPhee, *Basin and Range*, 161, 158.

34. *Esmeralda County and the Code of the West*, 7, http://www.accessesmeralda.com.

A Crucible for Populist Resistance

Tracing the Roots of the Sagebrush Rebellion

CHRISTOPHER A. SIMON

THE COUNTY SUPREMACY and Wise Use movements are frequently identified as right-wing populist crusades that sprang up at the beginning of the 1980s in rural counties in western states, although a similar brand of populist resistance has also occurred in states east of the Mississippi.[1] Animus directed at federal land and natural resource managers has ranged from county-level "custom and culture" ordinances to county land use policies to symbolic efforts to forcefully evict federal land use administrators from counties. In some cases federal officials have been physically threatened or even arrested by local authorities.[2] Because so much is at stake in land use decisions in the West and in the Great Basin, it is a conflict with deep roots.

The impression that the Sagebrush Rebellion is a recent phenomenon is not accurate. Political scientist Sandra Davis has referred to the recent resistance movements as the fifth Sagebrush Rebellion;[3] similar movements were provoked by conflicts over water policy in the 1880s, forest management preservation policies of the 1890s, grazing-fee policies in the 1920s–1940s, and fights over range management in the 1960s. Across time a common theme is resistance to evolving federal statutes and administrative rules that regulate access to public lands or regulatory barriers to the access of natural resources by economic interests (or both), such as grazing, timber harvesting, water withdrawals, and mining. The fact that a variety of interests benefit from the unrestricted use of public lands virtually guarantees that conflict will break out from time to time even if the particular catalyst might change.

The Wise Use and Country Supremacy movements have both been energized by a deep resentment of federal ownership and management policies, but the movements differ significantly. Wise Use has focused primarily on particular features of land management policy, while the County Supremacy movement has gone beyond policy disputes and questioned the legitimacy of federal landownership entirely. Wise Use has been more restricted and more specific in its intent because it has been based on client-based and entrepreneurial politics in which local users contest regulations that limit their activities. By contrast, the County Supremacy movement reflects a broad-based interest-group politics that ties material benefit to abstract ideological claims.[4]

The roots of conflict go back a long way, but they were kept in check by the *distributive* land use policies of the Homestead Act of 1862 and related policies that encouraged the movement west.[5] After a century of uneven management of natural resources and numerous attempts at meaningful reform, national public land management and natural resource policy shifted to a more *regulatory* stance. Access to public lands for cattle grazing, timber harvesting, and hard mineral extraction faced new restrictions and limitations. The 1960s and 1970s witnessed the passage of a series of laws significantly altering the way public lands and their ecosystems would be preserved. Native species protection, habitat preservation, and multiple-use policy meant that the priorities and values of a remarkably diverse group of interests would be taken into account. Local users, such as ranchers, have found that their historic prerogatives have come into question, large mining and industrial firms have increased their activities but also met more resistance, and environmental groups of many stripes have also entered the arena.[6] As a result, bitter conflict has become the norm.

Conflicts have become more intense for other reasons as well. Highly concentrated economies are particularly vulnerable to changes in social values and policies. Rural counties often rely on low economic hurdles to gaining access to public lands. The resources available on public lands have underwritten the economic development of many rural areas. Without easy access to these resources, many rural communities in the West would likely not have developed at all. Resource extraction was, and often still remains, critical to community and economic development in the West and in the Great Basin; thus, a lot is at stake when federal policy changes.

Because local needs are specific and easily amplified, the County Supremacy and Wise Use movements have tended to favor radically decentralized, bottom-up land use policy. In what Sagebrush Rebels tend to perceive as the West's "golden age" of the mid- to late nineteenth century, the generally distributive public land and natural resource policies were often created and implemented in an atmosphere of clientelist politics dominated by local ranchers, miners, timber harvesters, and other users. Conversely, the national environmental movement has been motivated by an interest in protecting and preserving public lands for a broad spectrum of users, and most of them are not local. The drive for a national, top-down regulatory regime to advance environmental goals has created an enduring climate of conflict.

The Historical Context

While rooted in very different philosophies of governance, private property rights and public land management in the American West share a common origin in the form of the Homestead Act of 1862. Over a period of roughly a century, the US government distributed a large portion of its landholdings west of the Mississippi River to prospective farmers and ranchers eager to make their fortunes. The act and the expansionist sentiment it expressed have exerted an enduring influence on land use policy in the American West.

As a policy innovation the Homestead Act can be traced to a series of legislation proposals in the 1850s, but for a variety of reasons the homestead bills introduced in Congress failed to become law. Northern industrialists were concerned that homesteading would lead to a reduction in the supply of workers in factories and raise the cost of labor. In the South political and economic interests feared that homesteading would lead to an increase in the number of "free" states. What broke the logjam is that the southern states left the Union in 1861. Soon after, homestead policy quickly became a high priority for President Abraham Lincoln's domestic agenda.

The Homestead Act "offered 160 acres of free public land to settlers who would build a home on it and farm it for at least five years. Anyone 21 years old who was either a citizen or declared the intention to become one could stake a claim."[7] After the initial five-year period had elapsed, the homesteader was offered the opportunity to purchase the land from the federal government for $1.25 per acre. Over the next century approximately four million individuals made claims for more than a quarter-billion acres of free public land—land that would become private property under the terms of the act.

The lands not claimed or which were designated public lands or forests, military reservations, or Indian reservations remained under the control of the federal government. Unlike the eastern and midwestern states, when the western territories came into the Union they contained huge tracts of unclaimed public land, and the federal government's assertion of ownership stimulated little opposition or comment. When the United States admitted newly created western states, it required that the states include an Enabling Clause. The newly admitted western states would recognize federal landownership in the state and would not challenge it in the future. The Homestead Act provided a path forward for converting the more valued portions of the public lands to private ownership. Meanwhile, Indian reservations tended to shrink, and land judged to have little economic benefit was later designated for national parks, beginning with Yellowstone National Park in 1872 and Yosemite in 1890.[8]

A Republican-controlled Congress approved the General Mining Act of 1872, which was intended to have broader reach than the Lode Mining Act of 1866 and the Placer Mining Act of 1870. The act governed the extraction of "hard-rock or metallic minerals such as gold, silver, lead, tin, copper, nickel, molybdenum, uranium, and others," but did not apply to three commodities that would later become extremely valuable—coal, oil, and gas.[9] The Mining Act essentially codified the informal practice of staking mining claims on federal lands and thereby appropriating the ore for private use.[10] Central to the law is the issue of the "prudent man rule." Essentially, the "prudent man rule" states that a mining claim's validity rests on the ability of a claimant to demonstrate that there is a market for the metals extracted and that extraction is profitable.[11] The Mining Act represented a distributive policy that would not be challenged until late in the twentieth century.

Although it has been amended over the years, the Mining Act of 1872 still governs the process of staking a mining claim on public lands. With the passage of the Mineral Leasing Act of 1920, the secretary of the interior was tasked with offering leases, on the basis of competitive bids, for the extraction of petroleum and gas from public lands. In addition and for the first time, presidential directive and Department of Interior policies often limited access to public lands by withdrawing them from lease consideration,[12] "'in the interests of conservation.'"[13]

In the years following the passage of the Homestead Act, public lands not homesteaded and not used for other recognized purposes were often used for the unregulated grazing of privately owned livestock. The native grasses were a free source of forage for ranchers, although the feedstock was often sparse on arid and semiarid land. The federal government did little or nothing to regulate the use of public lands for these purposes because it was generally assumed that the vast majority of this land would be privatized eventually through homesteading; therefore, "any money spent on land management would be lost."[14] By the 1880s a "tragedy of the commons" developed when rangeland became massively overgrazed.[15]

The Taylor Grazing Act of 1934 can be regarded as an attempt at regulation, but in actuality the main policy goal was the efficient use of public land for distributive purposes—that is, grazing.[16] The Bureau of Land

Management in 1946 attempted to consolidate the complex patchwork of public land use laws that had grown up over time, and it did not take long before the bureau's attempt to systematize administrative rules and processes ran into resistance. The newly created BLM began to focus on a more broadly defined constituency, although agency capture at the local level by agrarian interests was common.[17] Overgrazing issues persisted, and a focus on distributive policy constituencies generally trumped environmental concerns and recreational uses.

A series of public laws were passed in the 1940s and early 1950s that changed the distributive nature of mineral policy on public lands. The Mineral Materials Act of 1947 allowed for the extraction of products such as sand and gravel, which were not considered hard rock valuable minerals, as had been defined in the 1872 law.[18] Multiple mineral extraction on tracts of public land was offered guidance in 30 USC 12, and surface mining extraction was clarified by 30 USC §611.

The incremental accrual of regulations ran up against the sweeping demands of the environment movement of the 1960s, when concerns about mining and other activities on public lands were introduced into the national policy discourse.[19] Clearly, a general cultural shift now emphasized the virtues of preserving natural environments,[20] and the Wilderness Act of 1964 incorporates such sentiments. Gifford Pinchot's founding philosophy for the US Forest Service (USFS), which was enshrined in the Weeks Act of 1911, had focused on the distributive policy of the sale of timber resources for commercial use. For a century timber companies had made substantial profit off the sale of timber products harvested on public lands, but there was little incentive, or expectation, that they would restore the lost wildlife habitat. In an era of rising environmentalism, however, such a single-minded emphasis on exploitation could no longer be sustained, and by the 1970s old policies such as these came under sustained attack.

The National Environmental Policy Act (NEPA) was passed by Congress and signed by President Nixon on January 1, 1970. NEPA fundamentally changed the politics of federal land management. According to Hofman, in the pre-NEPA BLM, "a problem of complacency" had developed. BLM managers were insufficiently concerned with the "complexity in environmental systems. . . . [I]t [was] clear that BLM had a lot to learn about all of the interrelated factors in the environment."[21] NEPA serves as landmark legislation in the land management revolution, moving from a century-long clientele-based distributive policy environment to a new regulatory regime.

The Endangered Species Act (ESA) of 1973 took the transformation of public land management policy one step further. Land and natural resource policy would be contested in the national interest-group policy political system. The listing of endangered species such as the Great Northern Spotted Owl in 1988 set off a firestorm of protest against federal land management in Oregon, where many timber-dependent counties feared the loss of their economic base. Such concerns spilled over into regulations governing other uses, such as grazing, but the economic impacts were uneven and often negligible. Sagebrush Rebels were prone to alarmist exaggeration. For instance, Lewandrowski and Ingram found that 0.2 percent of the gross domestic product was affected by environmental restrictions on grazing.[22]

The creation of the Environmental Protection Agency in 1970 was a landmark moment in regulatory politics. The EPA is an independent regulatory agency tasked primarily with enforcement of environmental protection statutes. As an independent agency, it is to a large degree insulated from political pressure. The passage of laws such as the Clean Water Act (1970, amended 1977), the Clean Air Act (1977), the Endangered Species Act (1973), and other laws serves as the basis of a complex regulatory regime presiding over public land use, environmental quality, and natural resources. EPA rules are enforced by the agency itself as well as other public land management agencies, such as the BLM. The agency has effectively institutionalized the regulatory politics surrounding public land and natural resource management. Its ability to establish and enforce rules is subject to public hearing and is subject to challenge in the federal court system; however, the costs of challenging EPA rules are quite high and often require legal representation in administrative hearings or in federal courts.

The Federal Land Policy Management Act of 1976 signaled a policy shift that decisively and explicitly moved public lands management away from distributive policy and toward a regulatory orientation. With the passage of FLPMA, the homesteading policies of the federal government, which extended back to the Northwest Ordinance Act of 1787, came to an end. Lands retained by the federal government would remain in the public domain, although land swaps sometimes occurred as a result of laws such as the Southern Nevada Public Land Management Act (1998). The policy shift had dramatic consequences because regulation significantly altered the political, social, and economic model upon which generations of landowners had come to rely.

From a regulatory standpoint, the policy required that land use management focus on multiple uses of public lands. Regulatory policy associated with earlier land management acts focused significant attention on managing resources so that resource extraction could continue. Historically, the primary purpose of forest management had been to ensure the continued supply of timber for harvest. BLM management policies were intended to protect rangeland from overgrazing or from noxious plants that might reduce the quality of forage for grazing. FLPMA, however, focused attention on nonextraction uses of public lands—for example, recreation. Additionally, the protection of native species on public lands focused greater attention on preserving nature for its own sake and for protection of the biosphere, rather than cultivating it for human purposes.

Changes in federal laws altered the culture and personnel of federal land management and natural resource agencies. In the 1970s and 1980s future generations of land and natural resource managers were trained in a rapidly evolving political and educational environment. Environmental protection and preservation of native species became a central issue in the curriculum of natural resource and forest management professors and their students. Beginning in the 1960s environmental science and policy studies courses and degree fields became more common, focusing on the use of regulatory policy to manage public lands and natural resources. A division developed between a materialist-focused emphasis based on a supply-side economic argument for the managed *use* of natural resources and a postmaterialist emphasis on the preservation of public lands and resources. The new generation of land use and natural resource managers emerging from the regulatory-focused educational experiences were more likely to accept the regulatory approach to public land and natural resource management. These far-reaching institutional changes virtually guaranteed that federal land management and environmental agencies would clash regularly with the interests that profited by exploiting the resources found on public lands.

The Great Basin: Fertile Ground for Resistance

Nowhere in the West does the federal government own as high a percentage of land as in the Great Basin. Seventy percent of the land in the Great Basin, and 83 percent in the state of Nevada and 65 percent in Utah, is owned by the federal government. Idaho, at 62 percent, is the only other western state where half or more of the land area is public. Federal agencies administer 53 percent of the land in Oregon, although about three-fourths of the proportions of the state located in the Basin are federal. Federal ownership

of so much available land area would naturally lead to resentment, but conflicts over water, land, and other resources have provided fertile ground
for a political culture built on distrust.[23] Resistance to federal authority is a
recurring theme of politics throughout the West, but conflicts have tended
to take on an especially bitter tone in the Great Basin. For a long time the
Basin has been "ground zero" for a frontal assault on federal authority. The
State of Nevada unsuccessfully contested federal control in the courts during
the 1960s, and by the end of the 1970s the resistance that had begun in the
Great Basin had morphed into a broad coalition of state and local officials,
developers, and industrial interests throughout the West. Public officials and
private interests in the western states pressed the view that Washington was
sacrificing development on the altar of environment, and in doing so it "displayed outright animosity toward the west."[24]

The federal government poses a unique target for anger or annoyance in
rural counties of the Great Basin. In most counties the federal government
owns most of the land (more than 90 percent in some cases), but it does
not pay property taxes on its landholdings. Nevertheless, federal dollars find
their way into state, county, and city coffers through several avenues. In addition to a variety of federal grants available, the federal government contrib-
utes moneys in the form of "payment in lieu of taxes."[25] For some counties,
PILT payments constitute the main source of revenue.

Federal policy makers manage the use of and access to the public lands
they control, and from the local perspective federal decisions are unpredictable and potentially devastating for local economies. For example, the
Taylor Grazing Act (1934) established guidelines for grazing leases and reg-
ulates acceptable grazing activities with the intention of "preventing overgrazing and social deterioration, to provide orderly use, improvement, and
development to stabilize the livestock industry dependent upon the public
range, and other purposes."[26] Kehmeier and his colleagues found that the
grazing demand on USFS forest land was highly elastic, so the agency has no
choice but to be an active manager.[27] Adjusting grazing fees is a very effective
method of preventing overgrazing. Claims granted to private users for grazing, mining, energy exploration, or site development are subject to revoca-
tion. Federal policy also determines the fees, royalty rates, and other rents
charged for certain uses of public lands. Those rents can be changed regardless of local input and allotments.

In a 1977 article J. B. Wycoff concluded that rural communities that
relied heavily on grazing or mineral extraction from public lands were

highly vulnerable to land use policy changes. The sudden decline in a major industry—such as livestock grazing or mining—had a strong ripple effect on other industries in the community. In many cases the loss of the major public land-related industry had the effect of eliminating other sectors of the local economy that had made the community independent and economically sustainable. In a study of public land management in Nevada, Christopher A. Simon and John B. Dobra found that many counties in the state had highly concentrated economies and were vulnerable to changes in federal land management.[28]

While agency culture and public policy have evolved toward a more environmentalist position, the counties and clientele served by these agencies may not have changed quite as rapidly.[29] Two central factors frequently used to explain the County Supremacy and Wise Use movements are economic conditions and social and cultural conditions in counties and local communities.[30] The counties that propose or pass County Supremacy or Wise Use initiatives are often extraction-based communities facing a steep decline in their socioeconomic base, which is perceived to be largely a function of federal public lands and natural resource policy.

It should occasion no surprise that counties that are the most affected by federal regulations have provided much of the support for County Supremacy and Wise Use initiatives. Research by Stephanie Witt and Leslie Alm on counties in four states marking the boundaries of the Great Basin confirms that counties that are highly dependent on public lands for resource extraction are more likely to pass or consider County Supremacy and Wise Use initiatives than are other counties.[31] These counties are highly sensitive to any movement away from distributive land and natural resource policies, regardless of the elasticity of demand for public lands and natural resource use.[32]

In addition, these communities tend to be subject to "boom-bust" cycles. Extractive industries such as ranching, timber, and mining are often especially sensitive to periods of national or regional economic decline. Regulatory policies that move local economies away from resource extraction and toward such activities as recreation and ecotourism often lead to lower-paying service-industry jobs that do not bring local prosperity or fit into local cultural assumptions and community identity.

The demands of local industries also shape federal-local conflict. Logging corporations are keenly interested in maintaining ready access, often via unpaved roads, to dwindling timber stands auctioned by the US Forest

Service to logging firms. Mining enterprises operating on public lands or that involve transecting public lands are also impacted by road-access restrictions.[33] Additionally, access to blocs of privately owned land often used for ranching purposes that has become "stranded"—in other words, surrounded by public lands—is a source of tension in areas where the federal government owns most of the land area. During the 1990s the Clinton administration's "roadless wilderness" policy impacted timber harvesting and public access along Jarbridge Road in northeastern Nevada.[34] Local residents responded with bulldozers and shovels to open the road, and federal administrators were flooded with threats if they did not withdraw. Over the years this episode has become the occasion for an annual road project involving dozens of volunteers, and it has become a symbol of resistance that resonates far beyond Nevada.

In the Great Basin and elsewhere, Wise Use advocates believe that government agencies are "captured" by well-organized environmental interests operating at the national level.[35] Federal land and natural resource agencies, therefore, are often caught in the middle of a struggle between two disparate views of land and natural resource management. However, interviews with local government officials in Nevada reveal a more nuanced understanding. Although some federal employees are accused of holding a bias favoring environmental concerns over local interests, for the most part federal land managers are thought to be aware of and sympathetic to local concerns, and there is an understanding that they face statutory and administrative limitations that limit what they are able to do.[36] In effect, these federal administrators are themselves accepted into the local community, and that is an important element in defusing the volatile conflicts occasioned by an overwhelming reliance upon federal decisions.

The Battle Lines

Despite the movement toward a federal environmental regime, County Supremacy and Wise Use advocates have been reinvigorated in their effort to increase their influence in public land and natural resource management. In considerable measure they have been encouraged by the increasing activities of powerful interests with stakes in western land use policy; in this sense clientele-oriented politics has been resurrected.[37] Resource extraction–dependent counties perceive an opportunity to contest environmental restrictions on fossil energy development. Simultaneously, renewable energy advocates remain largely silent about the impact of green energy systems on native species. Fossil energy developers remain mute as well, having been offered, for quite some time, a quiet pass by the Environmental Protection Agency on the impact of hydraulic fracturing used in the extraction of shale oil. The new EPA carbon dioxide emissions rule,[38] however, is likely to have a significant impact on fossil energy development on public and private lands, and any future decisions regarding water use in hydraulic fracturing should be carefully watched.[39] In either case, should the rules impact energy development on public lands, it is likely that a sixth Sagebrush Rebellion will be upon us. The situation is not entirely new to US land, natural resource, environmental, and energy policy. In the wake of the 1973 oil embargo and the spike in petroleum prices, the fossil energy industry began to consider potential energy resources on public lands[40]—during the same period when US policy makers were pursuing landmark environmental, natural resource, and public land policy agenda.

In addition to a powerful array of interest groups, there is a very broad base of popular support for the latest iteration of the Sagebrush Rebellion. The Wise Use and County Supremacy movements have been associated with economic decline, rising tax rates, unemployment, racism, nativism, anti-Semitism, and antienvironmentalism.[41] The federal government's emphasis on the environment has provided a way to distill these diverse motivations, and global environmental protection has become a particular target.[42] The marriage of popular support and interest-group politics has produced a powerful alliance. The group called People for the West promotes the "Wise Use" of public lands throughout the West as well as elsewhere. The group "has 75 chapters among 11 Western states—as well as a new chapter in Missouri—and 20,000 activists on its membership rolls."[43]

A well-organized group such as People for the West attracts the attention of government leaders on the national stage. The Wise Use movement has supported former secretary of the interior Gale Norton, former US senator Dirk Kempthorne (R-ID), and other officeholders. The Republican Party has been an ally in their cause. Although the movement also claims support from some "key Democrats" in Congress, "'Since the Democrats got into power our income has doubled,' said [Ron Arnold], executive vice president of the Center for the Defense of Free Enterprise in Spokane, Washington."[44] GOP leaders have offered vocal support for the positions of local grazing and mining interests in gaining or maintaining ready access to public lands for private commercial purposes.[45]

Huck found that the Wise Use movement was initiated in 1988 by Ron

Arnold and Alan Gottleib, "who run the Center for the Defense of Free Enterprise." Other key organizations involved in the Wise Use Movement are the Defenders of Property Rights and the National Federal Lands Conference. The groups tend to draw on particular economic and social and cultural themes and ideas. From an economic standpoint, the organizations involved in promoting the Wise Use movement appeal to libertarians who share a strong commitment to limited government regulation and free enterprise. These elements fit easily with nativism, racial supremacy, and anticommunism. Some groups have been linked to the militia movement, which Huck refers to as a "lunatic fringe" tied to such groups as the John Birch Society and Lyndon LaRouche and the Unification Church.[46]

Antigreen ideology attempts to link environmentalism with communism. Greens are referred to as "watermelons . . . green on the outside, red on the inside." The antigreen message has been effective for County Supremacy and Wise Use advocates, who claim "success" in defeating the ratification of the Rio Treaty by the United States.[47] In writings and interviews, Wise Use advocates reject all aspects of the environmental movement; for them, there is no room for compromise. Ron Arnold, a leader in the Center for the Defense of Free Enterprise, believes that "the environmental movement must be destroyed because it holds a dark vision of mankind as spreading like a cancer on Earth. [Arnold] believes the environmental movement has an antihuman agenda that ultimately includes the destruction of civilization and the eradication of human beings."[48]

The property rights dimension to the Wise Use movement tends to focus on the rights of ranchers to access the public lands for grazing. A determined and highly vocal advocate for the Wise Use movement, the late Wayne Hage, presented one of the most widely circulated arguments on behalf of grazing interests. In his book *Storm over Rangelands,* Hage argued that ranchers who hold grazing permits have established a property right to the use of their grazing allotments. Multiple-use policies place grazing rights on equal status with recreation, wildlife preservation, and other dimensions of public land management—an approach that Hage and his allies found deeply objectionable. Hage argued that water rights in the West are governed by the doctrine of prior appropriation, which is a "Congressionally recognized property right" and served as a "'beneficial use'" in grazing.[49] From Hage's point of view, grazing rights can be bought or sold by the holder of a grazing permit, as would be the case with other property exchanges.

There is, however, a clear argument against Hage's perspective. As Abelson points out, the term *right* is misused by ranching interests. Abelson points to the Taylor Grazing Act (1934), which specifically states that there are no rights attaching to grazing permits, and no subsequent act has changed that fact. Beyond statutory history, there is clear evidence that the courts do not accept the property rights argument. In *Acton v. U.S.* (1968), *U.S. v. Fuller* (1971), and *White Sands Ranchers v. U.S.* (1988), the courts established clear precedent for the principle that grazing permit holders are not entitled to compensation for the loss of grazing permits. Compensation would be required only if there were a property right attached to the permit.[50]

The foundation of the property right argument is built around historic patterns of livestock grazing on public lands. Ranchers have come to rely on the use of public lands for feeding their cattle and maintaining a sustainable and profitable ranching business. Ranchers often express their concerns about the impact of grazing fees and permit costs on the economics of cattle ranching. Per animal unit costs (AUM; that is, a cow and her calf) of grazing on public lands have risen, while the price of beef has fluctuated. When the price of beef increases relative to the cost of raising livestock for meat, then per AUM costs are less likely to impact profit margins.[51] The price of beef declined in the 1970s and early 1980s before spiking in the late 1980s, but in the following decade the price of beef declined significantly.[52] Casual analysis indicates that these price fluctuations paralleled Sagebrush Rebellion activity and the related rural outcry over grazing fees.

Going to the Wall over Rights

As previously mentioned, when the United States admitted western states to the Union, it required that the states include an Enabling Clause in which the state would recognize federal landownership in the state and not challenge that ownership. This principle created a clear difference between the terms of statehood that had been offered to the original thirteen states, which entered the Union on a condition of sovereignty. County Supremacy advocates have seized on this historical difference to assert that federal landownership violates the principle of "equal footing"; in addition, they claim, federal ownership goes beyond the powers enumerated in Article 1, Section 8, Clause 17, of the Constitution, which grants the federal government the power to erect military facilities and other "needful Buildings," but does not specify any other uses.

A formal argument for this position has been advanced by Dan Kemmis in his book *This Sovereign Land.* Kemmis contests federal ownership on the principle that his is a "rational approach" not directly related to the Wise Use movement.[53] Kemmis advances the argument that the conditions placed on statehood for the original thirteen states were systematically different from the terms offered to western states when they were admitted to the Union. He contests the legitimacy of the Enabling Acts written into state constitutions on the ground that the granting of statehood should be equal for all the states. Once a state comes into existence, according to Kemmis, federal claims are relinquished, and land within the state no longer falls under federal jurisdiction.

Conable contests such legal arguments. He points to the fact that states admitted following the Northwest Ordinance Act contained federal land at the time of admission, and therefore these states were admitted with "equal footing," since equal footing does not mean that the state would not contain federal lands. In response, County Supremacy activists cite nineteenth-century Supreme Court decisions dealing with equal-footing issues. In *Pollard v. Hagen* (1845), the Court focused on the issue of state ownership of navigable waterways. The champions of County Supremacy extrapolate from the Court decision, arguing that federal land—dry land or waterways—impedes on equal footing.[54] They have not found support in the courts for this position.

In 1994 the State of Nevada gave hope to County Supremacy advocates when the state passed legislation claiming that it held title to the public lands in the state. The counties took things to a new level of conflict when the county administrator in Nye County, Nevada, bulldozed open a road on federal lands, claiming that the county government had control of public lands within its borders. In the case *U.S. v. Nye County, Nevada* (1996), a US District Court decision invalidated the Nye County argument and reaffirmed the unconstitutionality of State of Nevada legislation regarding its claim of title of federal lands within its borders. The US District Court for Nevada reaffirmed the power of the federal law under the Supremacy Clause. The long history of losses in the courts has led Conable to conclude that state and local advocates for County Supremacy are "wasting money and time in their attempts to gain control of federal lands through county initiatives and the courts."[55]

Conclusion

From a statutory perspective, the 1990s marked a major shift in environmental and natural resource policy that stoked the Sagebrush Rebellion of the 1990s and again in the early twenty-first century. Despite resistance and protest, federal regulatory policy has remained largely intact, although the politics of land and natural resource management began to shift toward a "third way" form of sustainability. President Clinton's Executive Order 12132 opened the door to a higher level of local input into federal land management rule making. Additionally, the priorities of economic and energy development began to override environmental protection in regulatory policy and politics.

Over the past twenty years, a series of distributive policies have signaled a shift toward a new era of client-oriented politics. Although some of the former clients, namely, ranchers, have fallen from favor, a new set of clients has replaced them. The shift in clientele is associated with the "greening" of public land and environmental policy. Increasingly, environmental policy has moved beyond simple regulation and preservation of public lands and protection of native species. The public lands debate is now central to the greening of society at large and the promotion of sustainable development. Recent laws affecting public lands are driven by competing economic interests such as energy and mining, environmental preservation, and domestic and internationally focused ecotourism. Increasingly, development of every kind has become the handmaiden of environmental protection.

A major shift in energy policy occurred with the passage of the Energy Policy Act (EPAct) of 1992. The policy placed an increased emphasis on renewable energy development. The "clean energy" movement is closely tied to international global warming policy initiatives. The reduction in the use of coal and petroleum as energy sources is a critical part of reducing harmful emissions into the environment.

While the acreage required is fairly minimal, the placement of renewable energy systems on public lands raises some important issues. First, environmental interest groups, such as the Sierra Club, are often muted in the debate about the use of public lands they once fought to preserve. Endangered species, such as various species of desert toads, are not afforded ESA protections in part due to interest-group politics. Second, ranchers and other inhabitants of western counties face declining water tables due to the high demand for water resources used in thermal electric renewable energy systems and in mining. Attempts to bring a wide spectrum of interests into the policy-making process often fall short because of the increasingly single-minded efforts to identify sources of renewable and fossil energy.[56]

Laws such as the Energy Policy Act of 2005 increased access to public lands for shale oil and natural gas development. Fossil energy development has brought an economic boon to many counties in the West and a concomitant rise in populations and standards of living. Viewed collectively, the renewable energy policies have created a new form of clientele politics that offers benefits to both "greens" and "browns." The revolutionary entrepreneurial politics of the 1960s and 1970s—policies that fueled the counterrevolution known as the Sagebrush Rebellion—may be eroded by current policy trends.

As Hofman has noted, the current policy environment has potentially long-term implications for land and natural resource decision making.[57] A year before the EPAct of 2005, Martin and Steelman established that the current "multiple use" doctrine has changed agency culture by moving it away from a "preservation oriented view to manage public lands." In the wake of the EPAct of 2005, the preservationist perspective is further constrained by a multiple-use paradigm emphasizing a larger role for extractive industries on public lands—one that ties fossil energy development to national security. The alliance between energy and security is growing in strength. Domestic energy development on public lands is seen as a path to energy independence, and it is thus framed both in populist terms ("Drill, baby, drill!") and as an example of "majoritarian politics": namely, an issue with widely distributed costs and widely distributed benefits. Defined in this way the public lands issue in the West has been, if not openly embraced, at least tolerated by the "green" Obama administration.[58] If such an accommodation of diverse interests proves durable, much of the anger that has sustained the Sagebrush Rebellion for so long may be temporarily assuaged.

NOTES

1. Brad Knickerbocker, "Counter Movement Backs Wise Use," *Christian Science Monitor*, January 12, 1993, 11.

2. Kim A. O'Connell, "County Threatens NPS with Arrest at Grand Canyon," *National Parks* 70, nos. 1–2 (1996): 1.

3. Sandra K. Davis, *Western Public Lands and Environmental Politics* (Boulder, CO: Westview Press, 1997).

4. James Q. Wilson, *Bureaucracy: What Government Agencies Do and Why They Do It* (New York: Basic Books, 1989).

5. Fergus Bordewich, "How the West Was Really Won," *Wall Street Journal*, May 18, 2012. Bordewich's analysis leaves out the impact of nineteenth-century land use

policy on Native Americans and Hispanics. Much of the American West was ceded to the United States as a result of its military victory over Mexico in 1848. In many ways one could argue that the Homestead Act was *redistributive* to the degree that it took land from the Native Americans and Mexican landholders and gave the land to US claimants or the US government. See also Theodore J. Lowi, "Four Systems of Policy, Politics, and Choice," *Public Administration Review* 32, no. 4 (1972): 298–310.

6. See Erika Allen Wolters and Brent Steel, "Cheatgrass Empire: Public Lands as a Contested Resource," in this volume.

7. Bordewich, "How the West Was Really Won," A15.

8. Thomas R. Cox, "The 'Worthless Lands' Thesis: Another Perspective," *Journal of Forest History* 27, no. 3 (1983): 144–45. See also Alfred Runte, *National Parks: The American Experience*, 3rd ed. (Lincoln: University of Nebraska Press, 1997).

9. Carl J. Mayer, "The 1872 Mining Law: Historical Origin of the Discovery Rule," *University of Chicago Law Review* 53, no. 2 (1986): 625.

10. Bancroft G. Davis, "Fifty Years of Mining Law," *Harvard Law Review* 50, no. 6 (1937): 897–908.

11. Mayer, "1872 Mining Law," 624–53.

12. Davis, "Fifty Years of Mining Law."

13. Thomas J. Teisberg, "Federal Management of Energy and Mineral Resources on the Public Lands," *Bell Journal of Economics* 11, no. 2 (1980): 451.

14. Joseph Ross, "FLPMA Turns 30: The Bureau of Land Management Also Celebrates Its 60th Birthday," *Rangelands* 28, no. 5 (2006): 16.

15. Gareth Hardin, "The Tragedy of the Commons," *Science* 162 (1968): 1243–48.

16. Ross, "FLPMA Turns 30," 17.

17. Leigh Raymond, "Localism in Environmental Policy: New Insights from an Old Case," *Policy Sciences* 35, no. 2 (2002): 180.

18. G. O. Virtue, "Public Ownership of Mineral Lands in the United States," *Journal of Political Economy* 3, no. 2 (1895): 202.

19. In his book *The Population Bomb* (1968), Paul Ehrlich argued that resources were being rapidly diminished. In the same year, Gareth Hardin published his now famous "Tragedy of the Commons" article in which he argued that public goods were misallocated and managed, requiring greater government regulation of their use and distribution. Finally, Rachel Carson published *Silent Spring* (1968), which documented the misuse of resources and environmental degradation.

20. Carroll Ann Hodges, "Mineral Resources, Environmental Issues, and Land Use," *Science* 268, no. 5215 (1995): 2005, 2008.

21. Ronald D. Hofman, "Implementation of the National Environmental Policy Act," *Publius* 2, no. 2 (1972): 120.

22. *Northern Spotted Owl v. Hodel*, 716 F. Supp. 479 W.D. Wash. (1988); Jan

Lewandrowski and Kevin Ingram, "Restricted Grazing on Federal Lands in the West to Protect Threatened and Endangered Species: Ranch and Livestock Sector Impacts," *Review of Agricultural Economics* 24, no. 1 (2002): 78–107.

23. For a definitive historical treatment, see Charles F. Wilkinson, *Crossing the Next Meridian: Land, Water, and the Future of the West* (Washington, DC: Island Press, 1992).

24. "Questions and Answers" on the "Sagebrush Rebellion" fact sheet, folder 4, Guide to the Records of Sagebrush Rebellion, Collection no. 85-04 (University of Nevada, Reno, Special Collections), http://knowledgecenter.unr.edu/specoll /mss/85-04.html.

25. Don Seastone, "Revenue Sharing or Payments in Lieu of Taxes on Federal Lands?," *Land Economics* 47, no. 1 (1971): 373–81.

26. Virgil Hurlburt, "The Taylor Grazing Act," *Journal of Land and Public Utility Economics* 11, no. 2 (1935): 203–4.

27. Paul N. Kehmeier et al., "Demand for Forest Service Grazing in Colorado," *Journal of Range Management* 40, no. 6 (1987): 560–64.

28. J. B. Wycoff, "Problems of Public Lands in the West," *Western Journal of Agricultural Economics* 2 (December 1971): 11–20; Christopher A. Simon and John Dobra, "Local Government Perspectives of Federal Land Management in Nevada," *Land Use Policy* 20 (2003): 275–90.

29. Ingrid M. Martin and Toddi A. Steelman, "Multiple Methods to Understand Agency Values and Objectives: Lessons for Public Land Management," *Policy Sciences* 37, no. 1 (2004): 37–69.

30. Christopher A. Simon, "The Oregon County Supremacy Movement and Public Lands in Oregon," in *Public Lands Management in the West: Citizens, Interest Groups, and Values,* edited by Brent S. Steel (Westport, CT: Praeger, 1997), 111–28.

31. Stephanie Witt and Leslie Alm, "County Government and the Public Lands: A Review of the County Supremacy Movement in Four Western States," in ibid., 95–110.

32. Kehmeier et al., "Demand for Forest Service Grazing."

33. Knickerbocker, "Counter Movement Backs Wise Use."

34. Valarie Richardson, "'Wise Use' Drive Fights Environmentalists: Grass-Roots Groups Spread Across West to Defend Human, Business Interests," *Washington Times,* January 20, 1993, A16.

35. Linda Kanamine, "Group Challenges Eco-Establishment," *USA Today,* October 19, 1994, A2.

36. Simon and Dobra, "Local Government Perspectives."

37. John Lancaster, "Western Industries Fuel Grass-Roots Drive for 'Wise-Use' of Resources," *Washington Post,* May 16, 1991, A3.

38. Tom Tiernan, "Appropriators Concerned That EPA Will Expand Scope of Fracking Study," *Inside Energy with Federal Lands,* May 21, 2012, 1.

39. Pam Hunter, "'Fracking' Rule Sparks Debate," *Engineering News-Record* 267, no. 16 (2011): 6; Lauren O'Neill, "Greens, Industry Both Shellacking Middle-Ground BLM Fracking Rule," *Natural Gas Week*, May 14, 2012, 1.

40. Carlisle F. Runge, "Energy Exploration on Wilderness: 'Privatization' and Public Lands Management," *Land Economics* 60, no. 1 (1984): 56–68.

41. Simon, "Oregon County Supremacy Movement," 188–219.

42. Kim A. O'Connell, "Groups Foster Alarm About U.N. Park Takeover," *National Parks* 70, nos. 7–8 (1996): 26–28.

43. Richardson, "'Wise Use' Drive Fights Environmentalists.".

44. Valarie Richardson, "Grassroots Groups Re-package Themselves," *Washington Times*, January 27, 1995, F2; Richardson, "'Wise Use' Drive Fights Environmentalists."

45. O'Connell, "County Threatens NPA with Arrest at Grand Canyon," 1.

46. Peter Huck, "Environment: War on the Range," *Guardian*, November 22, 1995, T6.

47. Ross, "FLPMA Turns 30."

48. Katherine Long, "A Grinch Who Loathes Green Groups: 'Our Goal Is to Destroy the Environmental Movement,' Says Affable Ron Arnold, a Champion of Wise Use," *Toronto Star*, December 21, 1991, D6.

49. Wayne Hage, *Storm over Rangelands* (Bellevue, WA: Free Enterprise Press, 1990); David Abelson, "Water Rights and Grazing Permits: Transforming Public Lands into Private Lands," *Colorado Law Review* 65 (1993–94): 407–26.

50. Ibid.

51. James M. Jackson, "A Comment on the Wilderness Debate: A Rancher's View," *Natural Resources Journal* 29 (1989): 844–48.

52. Dillon M. Feuz and Paul A. Burgener, "Historical Cattle and Beef Prices, Seasonal Patterns, and Futures Basis for Nebraska, 1960–2004" (University of Nebraska, Cooperative Extension Institute of Agricultural and Natural Resources Panhandle Research and Extension Center, April 2005), 1–37.

53. Daniel Kemmis, *This Sovereign Land: A New Vision for Governing the West* (Washington, DC: Island Press, 2002).

54. Paul Conable, "Equal Footing, County Supremacy, and the Western Public Lands," *Environmental Law* 26 (1996): 1270–71, 1279–84.

55. Ibid., 1286.

56. Christopher A. Simon, "Cultural Constraints on Wind and Solar Energy in the US Context," *Comparative Technology Transfer and Society* 7, no. 3 (2009): 251–69.

57. Hofman, "National Environmental Policy Act."

58. Martin and Steelman, "Multiple Methods to Understand Agency Values"; Irwin Stelzer, "Oil Production Surges Under 'Green' Obama," *Sunday Times*, April 1, 2012, 6.

The Sagebrush Empire

The Fragile Desert

Managing the Great Basin's Environmental Crisis

JESSICA L. DESHAZO AND ZACHARY A. SMITH

TOWARD THE END OF THE LAST ICE AGE, about fifteen thousand years ago, the lakes covering virtually all of present-day Nevada and parts of Utah, California, Oregon, and Idaho dried up, leaving behind what we now call the Great Basin. The Great Basin is a harsh environment. Summers are hot with little precipitation, and winters are cold. It is considered a cold desert. Most of the precipitation comes in the form of snow, and the winds in the summer dry out much of the moisture that is left in the soil. Nonetheless, more than two hundred bird, seventy mammal, and four hundred plant species are found in the Basin. Changing conditions on the land, largely due to human contact and climate change, have significantly impacted the natural environment.

Sagebrush ecosystems, which constitute most of the Great Basin, are some of the most endangered ecosystems in the United States. The invasions of cheatgrass (*Bromustectorum*) and other nonnative species such as red brome (*Bromusrubrum*) and medusahead (*Taenatherum caput-medusa*), and the expansion of piñon-juniper stands have changed the pattern, frequency, and intensity of wildfire in the Basin. Climate changes will continue to impact water resources throughout the desert. The sources of surface water in the Basin are fully appropriated, and like many mountainous areas around the world snowpack is melting earlier, meaning that the availability of water to wildlife is decreasing. Climate change and rapid urban and suburban growth have increased demands for natural resources, notably water. All of these factors have changed the face and future of the Great Basin.[1]

Prior to the settlement of the Great Basin by Europeans, the Native Americans in the Basin were primarily hunters and gatherers. They hunted small game (rabbits, mice, lizards, and the like), and they had little or no environmental impact. These early inhabitants lived primarily in the foothills of the surrounding mountains and moved their settlements several times a year as food and water availability varied with the seasons. Pioneer Mormons arrived in the Great Basin in 1847, and there was immediate conflict with the indigenous population over resource use. Like the Native Americans, the Mormons knew the best places to settle were in the foothills, where they would have a steady supply of water. By 1860 it was clear that this was a conflict that the Native Americans would not win—and this marks the beginning of human impacts that would lead to the degradation of the Great Basin environment.[2]

The Basin has experienced many invasions, migrations, and disruptions that have impacted the region's environmental and natural resources. Beginning in the 1980s and lasting until about 2007, the influx of residents from California and other parts of the country transformed parts of the Basin from a rural to a semirural region as ranches were subdivided into minifarms and subdivisions in the outlying parts of the rim cities.[3]

In this chapter we will focus on the changes that have occurred during the middle of the twentieth century to today. We will pay particular attention to the desert's flora and fauna—the invasion of exotic species and what that has meant for ecological stability. This includes cattle grazing and the presence of feral horses and burros. In addition, we will examine the water budget and the threats that the appropriation of water, notably by Las Vegas, have for parts of the Basin. We will also discuss energy development and mining in and the relationship of these activities to the pollution of air and water. Finally, we will provide an analysis of what we think will be necessary to create a future that protects the Basin's ecosystem.

Endangered Species

Historical analysis shows that invasion of species, disruption of natural systems, and climate change have contributed to alterations of flora and fauna as well as a 50 percent decline in many natural resources throughout the region over the past one hundred years.[4] As the editors of a special edition of the journal *Restoration Ecology* noted, "Maintenance and restoration of the Great Basin's native species and ecosystems is daunting. Current trends suggest that extensive losses of native plant and animal communities will continue unless new, holistic landscape strategies are effectively designed and implemented."[5]

Similar observations have been made by many ecologists who study the Great Basin.[6] Unfortunately, there is little evidence that the strategies to ameliorate environment damage are being put into place. Overgrazing by cattle has resulted in the loss of surface cover necessary to protect native plants and support animals. Since the Great Basin covers parts of several states, it is difficult to identify the numbers of endangered species within the Basin itself. For example, Oregon is home to thirty-seven endangered animal species, but many of these animals are not in any of the parts of Oregon outside the Basin. Nevada, the one state located almost entirely within the Basin, has twenty-six endangered animal species and eight endangered plant species. The loss of species in the Great Basin can be attributed primarily to the invasion of exotic species, both plant and animal. Unless native species are maintained, it will be impossible to ensure the resilience of the Basin's ecosystems.

Grazing

Ranching, grazing, and public land use are at the core of environmental stewardship in the Great Basin. Historically, grazing was poorly regulated or unregulated. The native grasslands that covered the Basin one hundred years ago are now largely gone due to many decades of overgrazing. It is unclear where the term originated, but many refer to natural resource management, like the public lands in the Great Basin, as being beholden to the "Lords of Yesteryear."[7] This refers to the notion that natural resource management decisions and practices are governed by the norms and the laws developed more than a century ago. In the context of grazing and the public lands, this is translated to open grazing, limited government interference, and low grazing fees.

These practices are often in conflict with sound land management principles as we understand them today. Grazing science has come to better understand how many cattle can be put on what types of land to maintain the sustainability of the land.[8] Too often in the past, grazing decisions have suffered from a common pool problem—ranchers may not own the land, but they hold the grazing permits, and therefore feel this gives them a right to pretty much do as they please. Today the Bureau of Land Management, the primary landholder in the Basin, understands the abilities of the land better than it did in decades past, and the bureau seeks to limit grazing to fit what it deems best management practices. In Nevada 69 percent of BLM-administered land is under grazing allotments, and the figure for the Great Basin portions of California is 81 percent. Although not all of the land within allotments is actively grazed at any given time, it does mean that the land is available for grazing.[9]

The overwhelming majority of grazing permit holders understand the limits of the land and follow the requirements of their grazing permits.

Some, however, adhere to the Lords of Yesteryear and resent federal inter-ference with their grazing "right." This leads to conflicts between ranch-ers and federal agencies over land management practices. For example, in southern Nevada a dispute has been going on for more than twenty years between the BLM and a local rancher, Cliven Bundy. For all of that period Bundy has been violating various federal regulations and administrative rul-ings but refuses to remove his cattle from lands to which he has no current right to graze. Bundy "does not accept federal jurisdiction over his various ranching rights."[10] There have been other cases like this, and at times the BLM took the step of removing cattle that were grazing illegally. In April 2014, when BLM personnel tried to remove Bundy's cattle, dozens of armed sup-porters showed up at the ranch, and to avoid a violent confrontation the BLM withdrew. The tensions that followed represented an antifederal attitude that goes back a long way, but there were divisions within the ranks. The Nevada Cattlemen's Association issued a statement opposing Bundy's approach, and the matter has subsequently gone to the courts.[11]

It should be noted that these disputes and the differences in land manage-ment philosophy they represent do not go to the question of the amount or level of grazing fees levied by the federal government. Critics of what are called the Lords of Yesteryear often maintain that the low grazing fees inher-ited from the past need to be raised. Their argument is that the fees do not represent the true cost of managing federal lands, and therefore they amount to a federal subsidy of the cattle industry in the West. The current grazing fee, $1.35 per animal unit month, has not been increased since 1978. A report by the Government Accountability Office found that the BLM would need to charge $7.64 per animal unit month to simply recover the government's administrative costs of regulating grazing.[12]

Exotic and Invasive Species

Cattle are not the only source of ecological change within the Great Basin. Exotic and invasive species are altering the environment in unprecedented ways. Invasive species not only displace native species but also alter natural ecological processes and destroy local ecosystems. Cheatgrass, piñon-juniper woodlands, and wild horses and burros are among the most damaging of these plant and animal species.

Cheatgrass

There are a number of exotic plant species in the Great Basin, but cheatgrass in particular has caused the greatest disturbance.[13] Cheatgrass was introduced into the Basin in the late nineteenth century by settlers who brought their cattle with them. Cheatgrass has no biological predators in North America and can completely displace the native grasses in any ecosystem it invades. There are places in the Basin where cheatgrass has completely replaced all native plant species. Moving through such areas one finds oneself immersed in a sea of yellow and orange as far as the eye can see. This invasion and replacement has taken place on approximately 20,000 square kilometers of the desert. Cheatgrass, which can grow from a few inches up to a couple of feet in height, is fast growing and can cross-pollinate, which gives it a reproductive advantage over other species of plants. Because it germinates in the autumn, it is growing by late winter and early spring.[14] This means it gets a head start on native grasses and is able to outcompete them for resources. None of this would matter much if cheatgrass provided good fodder for animals, but this is not the case. During the spring when this annual is young and green, it provides forage to livestock and other animals, but when it dries out during the hot summer its seed spurs can damage the lips, mouths, and eyes of grazing animals.

When cheatgrass dries out, it becomes a serious fire hazard—burning hot and fast.[15] On flat terrain with wind speeds of twenty miles per hour, a typical cheatgrass fire can generate flames up to eight feet in height and travel more than four miles per hour.[16] Compounding its fire threat is the fact that it becomes flammable earlier and continues to be susceptible to wildfires later than most native perennials. In addition to its role in facilitating intense and fast-moving wildfires, cheatgrass also reestablishes itself faster than native species on fire-damaged lands.[17]

Piñon-Juniper Woodlands

Piñon-juniper woodlands cover about 18 percent of the Great Basin.[18] Piñons and most junipers are invasive but not exotic species in the Basin. Junipers have been referred to as a "Green Glacier" because they have recently been encroaching into grasslands.[19] Piñon-juniper woodlands decrease water yields and spring flows because they use most of the moisture in the soil. Researchers have argued that the Green Glacier is creating a twenty-first-century ecological crisis similar to that of the Dust Bowl.[20] As piñon-juniper tree stands spread and become denser, they invade grassland and sagebrush ecosystems. As the stands of piñon-juniper thicken, the understory becomes sparser. The decrease in understory can lead to soil erosion as grasses and shrubs that are needed to hold the soil in place die off. The spread of piñon-juniper stands is depleting the ecosystem habitats of diverse species. One, the sage grouse, is expected to be added to the endangered species list soon due to loss of habitat by piñon-juniper. These birds cannot survive in areas where sagebrush is absent.[21]

It is estimated that since 1860, the area and density of trees have increased from three- to tenfold due to fire exclusion, overgrazing, favorable climate, and recovery from settlement-era harvesting. The spread of piñon and juniper tree stands increases the risk of severe wildfires, and, at low to midelevations, this problem is compounded by cheatgrass invasion. Land managers across the Great Basin are using fire and other methods to increase the ecological resilience of sagebrush ecosystems and decrease the risk of high-severity fires.[22]

Wild Horses and Burros

Like cheatgrass, wild horses and burros are an exotic, invasive species capable of causing severe damage to native ecosystems. Even so, they are protected by federal legislation. The preface to the Wild Free-Roaming Horses and Burros Act of 1971 enshrined horses and burros as living symbols of the American West:

> Congress finds and declares that wild free-roaming horses and burros are living symbols of the historic and pioneer spirit of the West; that they contribute to the diversity of life forms within the Nation and enrich the lives of the American people; and that these horses and burros are fast disappearing from the American scene. It is the policy of Congress that wild free-roaming horses and burros shall be protected from capture, branding, harassment, or death; and to accomplish this they are to be considered in the area where presently found, as an integral part of the natural system of the public lands.[23]

As it turns out these exotic species are not as "fast disappearing from the American scene" as members of Congress thought. In fact, if unchecked the herds of wild horses and burros in the Great Basin would, within a few years, strip the land of the cover necessary to sustain their numbers and result in starvation and die-off of the herds.[24] In the context of the management of wild horses and burros, the Lords of Yesteryear notion has been turned on its head. Although these animals clearly represent yesteryear, they are generally not welcomed by the nonurban inhabitants of the Basin. Having no natural predators, their numbers expand, and they compete with cattle and indigenous wildlife for feed and water. As one resource manager told the authors in the course of conducting this research, "These are an invasive species that do as much damage as any—I call them Cheatgrass on four legs."[25]

To manage herd numbers, the BLM surveys herds and habitats to determine which herds are at risk of overgrazing in their area or at risk for running out of water. Based on these surveys, horses and burros are gathered each year for sale or adoption. Another method of managing the population is limiting the fertility of the animals and thus their reproduction. The BLM estimates that the herds reproduce at a rate of 20 percent annually. Currently, the Great Basin can support roughly 26,500 wild horses and burros. There are an estimated 37,300 in the region, which is more than 10,000 more than the ecosystem can support. The BLM attempts to balance managing the resilience of the land with the size of the herds. Their slogan is "healthy herds on healthy rangelands."[26] Range managers whom the authors contacted were nearly unanimous in their approval of the efforts the BLM undertakes to manage wild horses and burros.

Not everyone agrees. Wildlife managers employ a term, the *Bambi Syndrome*, to refer to the popular impulse to protect animals that are detrimental to the environment. Critics often claim that BLM management is aimed at the complete destruction of herds. For example, the International Society for the Protection of Mustangs and Burros, which calls wild horses the "last living symbols of the American West," writes on its web page: "BLM's constant removals of wild horses have contributed to the destruction of the herds' social structures." The Hidden Valley Wild Horse Protection Fund notes: "Our governments have turned their backs on the beautiful creatures and failed to execute their responsibilities for care." Save Our Wild Horses, a group located in Washington, DC, writes on its web page, "We are once again facing the total destruction of our wild horse and burros by the very agency that is supposed to protect them, the Bureau of Land Management."[27]

As anyone who has seen a band of horses running wild on the range can attest, there is no question that the existence of wild horses and burros in the Great Basin adds to the region's lure and mystique. Equally, there is little question that a failure to manage their numbers would lead to the compromised ecosystems and harm to the animals themselves. As with other issues facing the delicate ecology of the Great Basin desert, the difficulty is in finding a balance.

Air Quality

Air quality in the Great Basin is generally good. The air in the region around the Great Basin National Park was described in a 2009 report by the US Government Accountability Office as "some of the best air quality and visibility in the United States."[28] This is less true in the rim cities, where particulate matter and ozone pollution have occasionally risen above federal standards. Particulate matter blows from the desert and from agricultural land as well as from the smoke from wildfires. Ozone occurs when sunlight interacts with the pollutants emitted by motor vehicles as well as some other emission sources associated with urban areas. Three of the rim cities, Boise, Reno, and Las Vegas, all have relatively good air quality most of the year, although all suffer from particulate and ozone pollution at times.[29] The Salt Lake City urban region's air-quality problems are more severe, in part because of urban sprawl along the Wasatch Front and because it is a major metropolitan area with a full complement of urban activities (including two refineries and a copper smelter). Especially in winter, carbon dioxide levels can be severe, and every year there are several days in the Salt Lake Valley when the air quality is "unhealthy" and people are encouraged to stay indoors. During a period in the winter of 2011, four of the five most polluted air locations in the United States were found in the Salt Lake Valley.[30]

Although it is not inevitable, as urbanization continues in the rim cities we can expect air quality to decline. In 2004 and 2006 proposals were made to build two coal-fired power plants in the central parts of the Basin near the city of Ely, Nevada. The burning of coal is a leading cause of air pollution all over the world. Carbon dioxide, sulfur dioxide, particulate matter, nitrogen oxide, carbon monoxide, hydrocarbons, volatile organic compounds (which form ozone), mercury, arsenic, lead, and other toxic heavy metals are all released into the air by burning coal. This list includes all the six criteria pollutants the Environmental Protection Agency (EPA) established as measures of national air-quality standards, as required by the requirements of the Clean Air Act. By 2009 plans for both coal-fired plants had been dropped, due largely to environmental concerns, regulatory problems, and economic uncertainties.[31] Still, as urban populations grow in and near the Basin, the need for electric power will continue to increase.

Like much of the Great Basin, the small towns of the eastern Sierra Nevada suffer from particulate-matter pollution. This is exacerbated in the southern portion of the eastern Sierra by dust that is blown up by the dry Owens Lake bed. Until 1914 the water that flowed off the eastern Sierra terminated in Owens Lake. At the turn of the century, the City of Los Angeles bought the water rights in Owens Valley and drained the lake dry. Under court order the city is undergoing a number of mitigation measures to keep the dust down. These include laying gravel, periodic flooding, and planting shrubbery. Legal disputes over these mitigation measures between the Los Angeles and the Great Basin Air Quality Management District are ongoing.[32] In addition, the eastern Sierra region occasionally suffers ozone problems primarily from pollutants blown into the area from the Central Valley of California.[33]

Mining

Mining in the Great Basin mostly occurs in Nevada. There are twenty-four metal mine locations, twenty-four industrial mineral mine locations, six oil fields, and twelve geothermal power plants in the state.[34] Utah has more than seven hundred individual mines in its portion of the Great Basin. Critics argue that current mining law, which was developed more than a century ago, constitutes a subsidy to the industry and that state tax policy reflects this giveaway mentality. From 2000 to 2007 the gold extracted and sold in Nevada was worth $25.5 billion from which the industry paid the State of Nevada $125.3 million in taxes. "That's about a half a percent in state taxes. A pittance."[35]

Hard rock mining, primarily although not exclusively for gold, generates mountains of hazardous waste. Gold mining in the Great Basin makes up 11 percent of the world's gold mining and 74 percent in the United States.[36] According to the Center for Biological Diversity, hard rock mining "releases more toxic substances . . . than any other industry in the United States."[37] Mining accounts for more than 95 percent of the toxic chemical pollution in Nevada, and in 1998 the state was listed at the top of the EPA's Toxic Release Inventory because it emitted 1.3 billion pounds of toxic materials into the environment. Arsenic, lead, and mercury are the most common forms of toxic chemical pollution.[38] During the gold mining and extraction process, gold ore is heated, which releases mercury into the air. A single mine in Nevada reported eighty thousand pounds of mercury, of which nine thousand pounds were emitted directly into the atmosphere.[39] This airborne mercury can travel great distances and often ends up in rivers and lakes. In the water bacteria can transform the mercury into methyl mercury, which is soluble. This soluble methyl mercury ends up in fish and is then transferred to humans when the fish is eaten. Even in small quantities mercury is extremely poisonous for the human body. When mercury reaches a sufficient level in the human body, it becomes extremely poisonous.

Mining is also extremely thirsty, and it therefore can affect the quality and quantity of both ground- and surface water. One mine in the Carlin Trend area of Nevada pumps sixty thousand gallons per minute of groundwater. The water from open-pit mines that are being dewatered is either redistributed by infiltration, reinjection, irrigation of agricultural lands, or surface discharge into the Humboldt River or its tributary channels. Only a small portion of the water is used for mining practices.[40] Overall, the water quality is good and could be used as drinking water with some treatment. However, in some of the test areas, arsenic is naturally high.[41]

Water

Many small towns in the Great Basin rely on water systems with a variety of supply and quality problems. For most communities groundwater is the primary source of water, and qualities vary from area to area. For example, the small community of Keeler, California (in Inyo County), has a water system that is polluted with arsenic and other substances, so much so that the water in their municipal system is not even good for watering plants. As a result residents buy bottled water from nearby Lone Pine. Another example is the Elko County, Nevada, bedroom community of Spring Creek. Spring Creek sank a well that has a slightly elevated arsenic level. As a result residents of the area are forced to pay water bills that reach more than $100 each month to bring the water up to drinking-water standards, even if their homes do not receive water from that particular well.

Climate change will have a negative impact on the amount of water available in the Basin. In this semiarid region, more precipitation will come in the form of rain than snow, and the snowpack will melt faster under warming conditions. The Great Basin has already been experiencing snowmelt weeks earlier than in recent decades.[42] The drier regions of the Basin will experience decreased groundwater recharge, thus decreasing the longevity of groundwater resources.

Due to the region's growing population, water use is being converted from agricultural to urban use. Las Vegas is certain to have a more immediate and dramatic impact on the Great Basin's water than the other three rim cities.

More than a quarter century ago the Southern Nevada Water Authority (SNWA) planned to build a pipeline to secure Great Basin groundwater. The Nevada state engineer approved up to 86,988 acre-feet to be pumped from four valleys located near the Utah border (Spring, Dry Lake, Delamar, and Cave) each year.[43] The exact amount would depend upon staged pumping in the area that will provide the pipeline with the most water, Spring Valley. A worst-case scenario for the total cost of the pipeline is $7.3 billion, which would require a rate increase for water users from an average $36 to $90 per month.[44]

For years controversy has swirled over the potential environmental impacts of a pipeline. Most people who live in the affected area believe that massive groundwater pumping will create another Owens Valley. Environmental groups point to even broader effects. Predictably, the Southern Nevada Water Authority and the Nevada state engineer have argued that the amount of pumping involved will have a negligible impact on the environment.

Native American tribes have been fighting the pipeline for years. The chairman of the Confederated Tribes of the Goshiute Reservation has been quoted as saying, "We oppose the SNWA pipeline project because it will cause permanent environmental damage to tribal aboriginal lands and will destroy tribal sacred sites including the Swamp Cedars Massacre site."[45] An interesting aspect of the protests against the pipeline is that ranchers, Native Americans, business owners, and environmentalists have been standing in solidarity to oppose it. Ranchers oppose the pipeline because the SNWA has been purchasing ranches in the Snake and Spring Valleys to obtain their water rights to build the pipeline.

The Snake Valley borders the Great Basin National Park on the east. The park, located more than three hundred miles from Las Vegas, could be harmed because Spring Valley forms its western boundary. "Spring Valley's groundwater is hydrologically linked to the park's historic Lehman Cave and 45 wild caves that support several species of bats. . . . The caves include many rare formations and is one of the most popular visitor destinations in the park."[46] Also, air quality could be negatively impacted due to increased dust emissions that result from drawing down the water table.

The controversy over the pipeline came to an unexpected turning point in April 2013 when the governor of Utah announced that he would not sign an agreement that had been hammered out with the SNWA that would have allowed it to withdraw water from the aquifer shared by the two states. A few months later, in December, a Nevada state judge ruled that the State of

Nevada had failed to show that the amount of water the state planned to withdraw from the valleys of eastern Nevada could be replenished by natural snowmelt. The judge's decision came after more than five years of complicated political maneuvering involving governments at all levels. The conflict between southern Nevada and eastern Nevada was reflected in the refusal by the White Pine County Commission, which sought to reduce the volume of water that could be pumped by the SNWA, refused an offer from the water authority to compensate the county for any economic losses that pumping might bring and asked that an independent authority be created to monitor the effects of pumping. In the end the county commission's opposition became moot because the SNWA bought up several ranches—with their water rights—in the county. At the state level, a growing water war between Utah and Nevada was kept barely in check by behind-the-scenes bargaining managed by Harry Reid, Nevada's senior senator and the Senate majority leader. A deal emerged that would have exchanged support for a bill to facilitate the SNWA's pipeline plans in exchange for legislation that would "sell some federal land for development [in Utah], designate some land to wilderness and secure passage of yet another pipeline, this one from the Colorado River to booming St. George."[47] In April 2013, when Utah's governor announced he would not sign off on a deal between the two states, this solution collapsed. Another complication was introduced in February 2014, when the Center for Biological Diversity filed a lawsuit in US District Court seeking to overturn a decision by the Bureau of Land Management to allow the pipeline to be routed through public lands.

Ecosystem Resilience and the Adaptive Cycle

Ecosystem resilience is understood as the ability of an ecosystem to adapt to changes without collapsing or undergoing a qualitative "phase shift" to a different type of ecosystem. Ecologists have proposed the concept of the adaptive cycle as a way of understanding ecosystem resilience. According to this cycle, an ecosystem goes through distinct phases in order to reach multiple steady states. There are four stages of the cycle: growth or exploitation, conservation, collapse or release, and reorganization. The phases from exploitation of natural resources to conservation and then to release are slow-moving processes. However, moving from release to reorganization of the ecosystem is rapid and can result in irreversible qualitative changes. The Great Basin is a fragile ecosystem that must be managed to maintain enough resilience to withstand a qualitative change to another type of ecosystem. To succeed, the goal of management must be to ensure that the exploitation of natural resources occurs at a rate that can be replenished. The most important aspect of preserving resilience is maintaining biodiversity in order for the ecosystem to endure disturbances and to replenish itself. Clinging to the habits and perspectives of the Lords of Yesteryear may cause the eventual collapse of the Great Basin's ecological system. Grazing must be regulated, invasive plants such as cheatgrass must be controlled, juniper woodlands must be prevented from displacing sagebrush ecosystems, and the numbers of wild horses and burros must be managed. All of these goals must be accomplished while accommodating ranching, mining, and other economic activities. Obviously, urbanization complicates the equation.

Climate change further complicates the ability to manage ecosystem resilience in the Great Basin. The predicted change in temperatures in the years ahead will depend upon the emission of greenhouse gases, and it will vary in parts of the Basin depending upon topography. The areas of the Great Basin that experience warmer temperatures will experience more wildfires and will undergo an increasing cheatgrass invasion. Wildfire seasons will lengthen. Stream flows will become more variable, and lower stream flows in the summer will negatively impact water use and increase groundwater pumping. While the growing season for crops would be lengthened with warmer temperatures, sufficient water will be a major obstacle to agricultural production.[48]

The Great Basin ecosystem is balanced on a fine line between resilience and an irreversible ecological transformation. More information about climate change and its impacts is needed in order to preserve ecological systems. In the past scientists believed that the goal was to maintain a steady state, but today it is understood that ecosystems are not static. They are always undergoing change. Society must move beyond concern for depletion of resources and begin to focus on ecosystem cycles and how they impact our use of resources if it wishes to achieve ecosystem resilience.[49] The challenge is to know when a qualitative shift or tipping point has been reached. We simply do not know when, or if, that will occur in the Great Basin.

The Problem Is Politics

The Great Basin is a fragile ecosystem, and the current politics that involves the Basin add to that fragility. Urban population growth is increasing pressure on the Basin's ecosystem. It is also driving management priorities and policies at both the local and the regional levels. Population growth in the

rim cities also places much pressure on the rural areas by adding to air pollution and depleting scarce water resources. Added to this tension is the
conflict that occurs between states and local governments and the federal
government. Much of the Basin, 70 percent, is public land.[50] States are under
pressure to follow federal environmental mandates, but environmental policies constantly press up against population expansion and the imperative of
economic growth.

The Great Basin has a long history of conflict between states, localities,
and the federal government. Politically, much of the region leans Republican,
but that does not tell us much about future planning and management decisions and how they will be made. For example, the city of Fallon, Nevada, has
been run by solid Republican majorities for years. At the same time the city
is engaged in long-term comprehensive planning that would be anathema to
Republican politicians in other parts of the Basin. Public leaders in the Salt
Lake City region have also been open to environmental regional planning.
While the city itself tends to lean Democratic, the surrounding area is conservative. Environmental planning can occur regardless of political ideolo-
gies. The key is that the federal government and states must work together to
address conflicting values regarding land use and protection of the ecosystem: environmental protection versus economic growth, the cultural symbol
of wild horses and burros versus the need to manage the rangeland the herds
use, and urban population growth versus rural and agricultural interests.

The federal government and the states must be able to cooperate, but
current policies tend to be top-down and constrain the ability of states to
manage land uses within their boundaries. Interstate cooperation is difficult
because, except for Nevada, states only partially overlap the Great Basin.
Because John Wesley Powell failed to convince Congress more than a century ago to create jurisdictions based on watersheds, ecological boundaries
do not coincide with political jurisdictions. Despite the conflicts this circumstance creates, it is imperative that the federal government and states work
together to address environmental degradation in the Great Basin; in addition, states within the Basin must find a way to cooperate with one another.

Achieving a sufficient level of policy coordination seems impossible at
the moment, and this task would be complex in any case because it must
combine the capacity to make policy that reaches across jurisdictions while
retaining enough flexibility and local autonomy to respond to the varying conditions within the Basin. The federal government might hypotheti-
cally create an overarching framework, but this would require that political

leaders in the Basin to reconsider their long-standing hostility toward federal authority of all kinds. The problem, in the end, is more about the adequacies of politics than about the limitations of science.

NOTES

1. Sarah R. Hurteau et al., "Relationship Between Avifaunal Occupancy and Riparian Vegetation in the Central Great Basin (Nevada, U.S.A.)," *Restoration Ecology* 17, no. 5 (2009): 722–30.

2. Beverly P. Smaby, "The Mormons and the Indians: Conflicting Ecological Systems in the Great Basin," *American Studies* 16, no. 1 (1975): 35–37.

3. Paul F. Starrs and John B. Wright, "Great Basin Growth and the Withering of California's Pacific Idyll," *Geographical Review* 85, no. 4 (1995): 417.

4. Rebecca J. Rowe, Rebecca C. Terry, and Eric A. Rickart, "Environmental Change and Declining Resource Availability for Small-Mammal Communities in the Great Basin," *Ecology* 92, no. 6 (2011): 1366–75.

5. Erica Fleishman, Jeanne C. Chambers, and Michael J. Wisdom, "Introduction to the Special Section on Alternative Futures for Great Basin Ecosystems," *Restoration Ecology* 17, no. 5 (2009): 704–6.

6. See, for example, Mary M. Rowland et al., "Habitats for Vertebrate Species of Concern," in *Habitat Threats in the Sagebrush Ecosystem: Methods of Regional Assessment and Applications in the Great Basin,* edited by Michael J. Wisdom, Mary M. Rowland, and Lowell H. Suring (Lawrence, KS: Alliance Communication Group, 2005), 163–204.

7. Charles Wilkinson, *Crossing the Next Meridian: Land, Water, and the Future of the West* (Washington, DC: Island Press, 1993), 2.

8. Bureau of Land Management, "Fact Sheet on the BLM's Management of Livestock Grazing," http://www.blm.gov/wo/st/en/prog/grazing.html.

9. Alicia Torregrosa and Nora Devoe, "Urbanization and Changing Land Use in the Great Basin," in *Collaborative Management and Research in the Great Basin: Examining the Issues and Developing a Framework for Action* (Fort Collins, CO: US Department of Agriculture–Forest Service, 2008), http://www.fs.fed.us/rm/pubs/rmrs_gtr204.pdf, 10.

10. Vernon Robison, "Bunkerville Rancher Holds Out Against Federal Officials," *Moapa Valley Progress,* April 18, 2012, http://mvprogress.com/2012/04/18/bunkerville-rancher-holds-out-against-federal-officials/.

11. Christi Turner, "The Revolt That Wouldn't Die," *High Country News,* May 12, 2014, 3, 5.

12. US Government Accountability Office, *Livestock Grazing: Federal Expenditures and Receipts Vary, Depending on the Agency and the Purpose of the Fee*

Charged, GAO-05-869, September 2005, http://www.gao.gov/new.items/d05869 .pdf.

13. Bethany A. Bradley and John F. Mustard, "Identifying Land Cover Variability Distinct from Land Cover Change: Cheatgrass in the Great Basin," *Remote Sensing of Environment* 94, no. 2 (2005): 204–13. This represents 7 percent of the land cover.

14. Kris Zouhar, "Bromustectorum," US Forest Service, http://www.fs.fed.us /database/feis/plants/graminoid/brotec/all.html#INTRODUCTORY.

15. "Do Fence Me In: Cattle Enlisted in the Great Basin to Reverse the Cheatgrass/Wildfire Cycle," *Fire Science Brief*, no. 64 (2009): 1.

16. "Cheatgrass and Wildfire," Colorado State University Extension Fact Sheet no. 6.310 (May 17, 2012), http://www.ext.colostate.edu/pubs/natres/06310.html.

17. Marcia Wood, "Western Juniper and Cheatgrass," *Agricultural Research* 57, no. 6 (2009): 20–21.

18. US Forest Service, "Pinion-Juniper Woodlands," http://www.fs.fed.us/rm /reno/research/ecosystems/pinyon-juniper/.

19. David M. Engle, Bryan R. Coppedge, and Samuel D. Fuhlendorf, "From the Dust Bowl to the Green Glacier: Human Activity and Environmental Change in Great Plains Grasslands," in *Western North American Juniperus Communities: A Dynamic Vegetation Type* (New York: Springer, 2008).

20. C. E. Kay, "The Evils of Pinyon and Juniper," first published in *Mule Deer Foundation Magazine* 10, no. 5 (2010), also available at http://westinstenv.org /ffsci/2010/10/22/the-evils-of-pinyon-and-juniper/.

21. US Fish and Wildlife Service, "Greater Sage-Grouse," March 2011, http:// www.fws.gov/mountain-prairie/species/birds/sagegrouse/GreaterSageGrouseFact -Sheet2011.pdf.

22. US Forest Service, "Pinion-Juniper Woodlands."

23. Wild Free-Roaming Horses and Burros Act of 1971 (Public Law 92-195).

24. Sally Spencer, US Bureau of Land Management, interview, July 13, 2012.

25. Jay Paxson, environmental specialist, City of Elko, Nevada, interview with the authors, June 29, 2012.

26. Spencer interview.

27. International Society for the Protection of Mustangs and Burros, http:// www.ispmb.org/index.html; Hidden Valley Wild Horse Protection Fund, http:// hiddenvalleyhorses.com/main.php/main.php; Save Our Wild Horses, http://www .saveourwildhorse.com/index.htm.

28. J. Stephenson, "Air Pollution: Air Quality, Visibility, and the Potential Impacts of Coal-Fired Power Plants on Great Basin National Park, Nevada," GAO *Reports* (serial online), July 27, 2009, 1.

29. G. Xian, "Analysis of Impacts of Urban Land Use and Land Cover on Air Quality in the Las Vegas Region Using Remote Sensing Information and Ground Observations," *International Journal of Remote Sensing* 28, no. 24 (2007): 5427–45.

30. Christopher Smart, "Utah Pollution: Bad Air Quality, Elevated," *Salt Lake Tribune,* January 8, 2011, http://www.sltrib.com/sltrib/home/51006311-76/pollution -utah-county-lake.html.csp.

31. Stephenson, "Air Pollution." See also Jennifer Robinson, "NV Energy Backs Off Coal-Fired Ely Energy Center; Air Force Objects to Solar Plant," *Las Vegas Review Journal,* June 23, 2009, http://www.lvrj.com/news/breaking_news /48923992.html.

32. The information about Owens Lake and air quality was provided to the authors from an interview with Nik Barbieri, Great Basin Air Quality Management District, City of Keeler, California, June 14, 2012.

33. Mark Long, environmental health specialist, Inyo County, California, interview with the authors, June 11, 2012.

34. Nevada Mining Association, FAQs, http://www.nevadamining.org/faq /index.php. Nevada considers mines that abut one another as a single mine. Thus, the word *location* is used.

35. Deidre Page, "Stop Giving Away Nevada's Gold!," *Reno News and Review: Opinions,* September 23, 2010, http://www.newsreview.com/reno/stop-giving -away-nevadas-gold/content?oid=1750703.

36. US Geological Survey, "Western Region Gold Deposits," http://minerals .usgs.gov/west/projects/nngd.htm.

37. Center for Biological Diversity, "Mining," http://www.biologicaldiver sity.org/programs/public_lands/mining/index.html.

38. Associated Press, "Toxic Chemical Pollution Up 2.1% in Nevada from 2006– 07," March 21, 2009, http://www.oregonlive.com/environment/index.ssf/2009/03 /toxic_chemical_pollution_up_21.html.

39. Center for Biological Diversity, "Mining."

40. US Geological Survey, "USGS Programs in Nevada," http://pubs.usgs.gov/fs /FS-028-96/#HDR05.

41. Employee from the Nevada Division of Environmental Protection, Bureau of Water Pollution Control, interview with the authors, July 17, 2012.

42. Jeanne C. Chambers, "Water Resources and the Great Basin," in *Collaborative Management and Research in the Great Basin.*

43. Bob Conrad, "State Engineer Releases Water Right Rulings for SNWA's Pipeline Project," Nevada Department of Conservation and Natural Resources, http://dcnr.nv.gov/2012/03/state-engineer-releases-water-right-rulings-for -snwas-pipeline-project/.

44. Henry Brean, "Water Authority: New Report of $7.3 Billion Pipeline Cost Is Worst-Case Analysis," *Las Vegas Review-Journal,* August 23, 2011, http://www.lvrj .com/news/water-authority-new-report-of-7-3-billion-pipeline-cost-is-worst -case-analysis-128231803.html.

45. John L. Smith, "Pipeline Planners Ignore Input They Need Most," *Las Vegas*

Review-Journal, May 27, 2012, http://www.lvrj.com/news/pipeline-planners-ignore -input-they-need-most-154692655.html.

46. Lynn Davis, Nevada Field Office Manager for the National Parks Conservation Association, "Draining Great Basin: National Parks Conservation Association Expresses Concern over Nevada Groundwater Pipeline," http://www.npca.org /news/media-center/press-releases/2012/draining-great-basin.html.

47. Emily Green, "Not This Water," pt. 4 of "Quenching Las Vegas' Thirst," *Las Vegas Sun,* June 22, 2008, http:/www.lasvegassun.com/news/2008/jun/not-water/.

48. Jeanne C. Chambers and Michael J. Wisdom, "Priority Research and Management Issues for the Imperiled Great Basin of the Western United States," *Restoration Ecology* 17, no. 5 (2009): 707–14.

49. Adapted from Zachary Smith, *The Environmental Policy Paradox,* 6th ed. (Upper Saddle River, NJ: Pearson, 2013).

50. Alicia Torregrosa and Nora Devoe, "Urbanization and Changing Land Use in the Great Basin," in *Collaborative Management and Research in the Great Basin,* 10.

Cheatgrass Empire

Public Lands as a Contested Resource

ERIKA ALLEN WOLTERS AND BRENT S. STEEL

PUBLIC LANDS IN THE GREAT BASIN have become the subject of both a national and a regional debate concerning the proper use and long-term well-being of rangelands, forests, and riparian zones. Historically, grazing and to a lesser extent timber extraction have been the primary economic products derived from public lands in the Basin, with mineral extraction and fossil fuel collection taking a position of secondary importance in most (though not all) areas. However, public concern for wildlife habitat, protection of fish species, wilderness preservation, recreational access, and other nonextractive use values associated with these lands has increased substantially since the 1970s, and the primacy of management for grazing, timber, and mining has become the subject of increasing controversy and litigation, particularly with regard to federal forest- and rangelands.[1] At the heart of this debate are differing values and interests concerning the natural environment and the proper relationship of humans to their ecological surroundings. These views, in turn, are connected to different conceptions about how the management of common-pool natural resources ought to be provided for in the contemporary setting.

The Great Basin is one of the most endangered ecosystems in the United States.[2] The management of fragile ecosystems such as this requires a new way of thinking about the delicate balance of human needs (and wants) while sustaining and improving the integrity of the rangeland as a complete ecosystem. The surveys conducted for this study find that Great Basin residents are dissatisfied with current management of the Great Basin ecosystem, instead favoring the active management of rangeland and other resources. A large proportion of the Basin's residents support biocentric values, increased participation by local (noncommodity) communities in management decisions, and the protection and conversion of wilderness areas from economic uses such as livestock grazing. These values are the product of the rapid urbanization of the Basin and signal a deep and growing cultural divide. It is certain that the policy influence of urban areas will grow over time; indeed, cities may even become the epicenter of political and economic power in the Basin. These are momentous changes in a region primarily known for its empty spaces and conservative cultural attitudes. Our surveys reveal sharply differing value orientations toward the environment and the management of public lands in the Great Basin Desert. Clearly, urbanization is changing this, the driest desert in North America, just as it has previously altered the political, social, and geographic landscape of regions that have experienced urban growth in the past.

Value Change Concerning the Environment and Natural Resources

In the decades following World War II, a number of fundamental changes transpired in the industrial nations, especially those usually identified as the "Western democracies."[3] In contrast to the prewar period, economic growth in the 1950s and 1960s was so rapid that fundamental structures of society were altered, and social commentators began to note a new stage of development. This new stage or phase of socioeconomic development in advanced industrial society has been assigned the label "postindustrial" in the social science literature on modernity and postmodern intellectual thought.[4]

A large number of studies examine in considerable depth the social, economic, and political implications of postindustrialism.[5] Although there is some disagreement among scholars, a few central features of the postindustrial age are, by now, well known. Postindustrial societies are characterized by the economic dominance of the service sector over manufacturing and agriculture; complex nationwide communication networks; a high degree of economic activity based upon an educated workforce employing scientific knowledge and technology in their work; a high level of public mobilization in society (including the rise of new social causes such as the civil rights movement, the antiwar movement, the antinuclear movement, and the environmental movement); increasing population growth and employment in urban areas (and subsequent decline in rural areas); and historically unprecedented societal affluence.[6]

These features of postindustrial society have altered social values, particularly among younger people, with an increasing emphasis on "higher order" needs (self-actualization) have supplanted more fundamental subsistence needs (basic needs, material acquisition) as motivation for much societal behavior.[7] Value changes entailing greater attention to "postmaterialist" needs have brought about changes in many types of personal attitudes—including those related to natural resources and the environment.[8]

What this means for natural resource policy is that structural changes in the economy featuring the growth of urban service economies (or "the core") and the concomitant decline in natural resource rural economies (or "the periphery") have increased the influence of urban service areas. This influence derives from the greater economic and political power of urban elites and workforces, their superior technical expertise, their substantial knowledge and information base (that is, scientific knowledge, policy process knowledge, timely access to information, and so forth), and control of mass communication channels.[9] Further, with the advent of postmaterialist value orientations in these core urban service areas, urban mass publics and elites have formed belief systems concerning natural resource issues and land use policy in the periphery that are quite different from the growth-oriented views that predominated in the past. Increasingly, then, natural resource–based communities at the periphery become subject to the environmental protection rules devised by governmental agencies located in urban cores.[10] This state of affairs eventually leads to sharp conflict because land use practices and policies imposed on the periphery challenge the values and "way of life" of rural citizens.[11]

Factors Associated with Changing Natural Resource Management Paradigms

Most scholars investigating the topic of postindustrial society tend to agree that a relatively small number of key socioeconomic factors have led to the development of conflicting core versus periphery natural resource management paradigms, resulting in frequent policy conflict and occasional policy stalemate in advanced industrial societies.[12] Leading examples in the Great Basin include the three-decade-long Sagebrush Rebellion, the decade(s)-long battle over use of Yucca Mountain as a nuclear waste storage facility, and the ongoing proposal by the Southern Nevada Water Authority to run a three-hundred-mile pipeline from Las Vegas to rural Nevada and Utah (the pipeline would pump fifty-seven million gallons of water and cost $15.5 billion). Among the most salient factors generally thought to be involved in driving these conflicts are those included in the following discussion.

Population Change

Postindustrial societies have experienced a shift in population from periphery to urban areas. For example, during the 1980s through 2010 more than one-half of all rural counties in the United States lost population, while urban counties (which include both urban and suburban communities) grew at a rapid rate.[13] In most cases this encouraged the rural outmigration of highly educated and skilled younger workers. These population dynamics have increased the economic and political power exercised by urban elites at the expense of the periphery.[14] This pattern is especially evident in the Great Basin because it has been experiencing one of the highest (or perhaps the highest) urban growth rates in the United States.[15] Between 1990 and 2004 the population almost doubled from 2.9 million to 4.9 million people.[16] By 2006 more than 60 percent of Great Basin residents lived within or adjacent to the urban core;[17] at the same time rural areas were experiencing depopulation, an aging population, and economic decline.[18]

Economic Change

With the development and growth of the urban tertiary sector (and subsequent decline in the manufacturing, natural resource, and agricultural sectors) in the West, employment grew much more rapidly in urban than rural areas.[19] In addition, unemployment and poverty rates were significantly higher and wages were significantly lower in the periphery when compared to the urban core.[20] Substantial economic decline in the rural periphery often leads to an imperative to increase natural resource extraction in order to sustain community viability, while growth in urban service industries creates a contrary preference for the nonmaterial uses of natural environments.[21] The contradiction between these two imperatives provides fertile ground for contentious and often bitter conflict.

Historically, much of the economic base in the Great Basin derived from extractive industries such as mining, farming, ranching, and, more recently, recreation and gaming. However, recent economic downturns have illustrated how reliance on an economy based on little diversity results in fragile and vulnerable local economies as well as economic problems at the state level. For example, in 2012 Nevada ranked among the top states for unemployment, with 11.6 percent of Nevada residents unemployed.[22] Because the interior of the Great Basin region is one of the least developed areas in the nation, natural resource development and use could provide economic stability and potential profitability to the region.[23] With increasing efforts to secure energy domestically, opportunities exist within the Great Basin for development of natural gas, coal, and oil as well as renewable energy sources such as solar and geothermal power.[24] However, continued development of energy resources will exact an environmental toll on the region that significantly affects rural communities. Since energy development is currently a primary disturbance factor in the Great Basin,[25] additional energy development adds to the challenges already threatening its ecosystems.

Technological Change

The role of technological innovation and change is central to the relationship between core and periphery. Technological innovations have led to increased efficiency and productivity in manufacturing industries, agriculture, and natural resource extraction and processing industries. In the past work on public lands was labor intensive, but it is now primarily technology intensive, which speeds outmigration to urban areas. In addition, technological advances have led to a more central role in the (core) economy for theoretical and mathematical knowledge and for research and development investments as opposed to physical capital. This in turn has led to an enhancement of the importance of universities, think tanks, and the diverse media devoted to the creation and transmission of specialized information. As a result of these changes we now have the capacity to generate far more information about the condition and consequences of land use patterns than in the past (for example, satellite photography, geographic information system maps), and this information has become increasingly available to individuals, interest groups, political elites, and investigative reporters.[26] In the Great Basin there has been a dramatic growth in high-tech industries, particularly in Utah. While other states have struggled in the recent recession, Utah has continued to produce new high-tech jobs. Of an estimated twenty-eight thousand new jobs created in 2012, a majority were in the high-tech sector.[27] In addition, Salt Lake City ranked fifth among fifty-one metropolitan areas in high-tech growth.[28]

The state of Nevada is trying to capture some of Utah's success in high-tech development. For example, the Nevada System of Higher Education has brought together the Universities of Nevada at Reno and Las Vegas, Nevada community colleges, and the Desert Research Institute to form the Nevada Renewable Energy Consortium, facilitates renewable energy research and development within the state. Each institution participating in the consortium focuses on an array of alternative energy technology ranging from wind and solar to biomass and geothermal energy.[29] The ultimate goals in this endeavor are to make Nevada a leader in the research and development of renewable energy, develop a workforce to implement renewable energy projects,[30] and create a niche in renewable energy projects that relies on the urban cores for research and development and the rural periphery for the implementation of the projects.

Value Changes

Some observers have suggested that the rise of the environmental movement was, in great measure, a product of the vast socioeconomic changes evident in postwar advanced industrial societies.[31] The development of environmental consciousness has resulted in the open questioning of many of the traditional political and economic institutions of modern society.[32] These changing value orientations pose serious consequences for land use in the periphery, and they have led to the articulation of two conflicting natural resource management paradigms concerning the use of public lands. These conflicting paradigms have been well articulated by Brown and Harris.[33]

The two competing natural resource management paradigms identified by Brown and Harris—derived from the ideas of Gifford Pinchot and Aldo Leopold, respectively—have been labeled the "Dominant Resource Management Paradigm" and the "New Resource Management Paradigm." The former worldview is founded on the anthropocentric belief that the management of federal forests and rangelands ought to be directed toward the production of goods and services beneficial to humans. The latter paradigm has emerged more recently and grown rapidly in popularity in postindustrial society. It is based on a biocentric view toward management that emphasizes the goal of maintaining intact all the elements of natural ecosystems and is best summarized in the words of Leopold: "A thing is right when it tends to preserve the integrity, stability, and beauty of the biotic community. It is wrong when it tends otherwise."[34]

A passage from William Kittredge's Who Owns the West? captures the essence of these conflicting paradigms and describes how they apply to the situation many western communities now find themselves in: "Again our culture in the West is remixing and reinventing itself. It's a process many locals, descendants of people who came west only a few generations back, have come to hate; some think they own the West because their people suffered for it, and in that way they earned it. They feel that it's being taken away from them, and they're often right; they think they are being crowded out, and they are. They feel that nobody in greater America much cares about their well-being or dreams, and they are right."[35] The following sections analyze data collected in the Great Basin in surveys conducted in 1998 and 2011. The responses to these surveys show that the processes described by Kittredge are taking place in the Great Basin. Clearly, a long-standing cultural divide is widening.

Methods
Sampling

The data came from two surveys, a western US regional random household survey conducted in 1998, from which a subsample of Great Basin respondents can be extracted, and a 2011 Great Basin random household survey that replicated the 1998 study. Sample frames were provided by the same national survey research company for both surveys. Dillman's total design method guided mail survey design and implementation.[36] For the 1998 western regional survey, we surveyed more than 4,000 households and received 2,140 responses, for a 53.5 percent response rate. Out of the 2,140 surveys returned, 1,051 respondents lived in or adjacent to the Basin (including residents of Las Vegas and Reno). For the 2011 study we designed a survey to replicate the size and distribution of the one conducted in 1998. We sent three waves of mail surveys to 2,300 randomly selected households and received 1,070 responses, for a 46.5 percent response rate.

Survey Instrument

Survey questions were designed to reveal attitudes toward management of federal rangelands, knowledge about the environmental condition of federal rangelands, the degree of confidence in organizations and institutions involved in range management, attitudes about the relative influence that different rangeland constituencies should have on policy development and implementation, and the attributes of respondents that might influence their responses, including their overall attitudes toward the relationship between society and the natural environment as well as demographic characteristics. Many questions were adapted from a recent study of public attitudes about federal forest management in Oregon and in the United States,[37] and a survey of public attitudes toward public rangeland management in the West.[38]

The primary attitude and belief measure was constructed from a series of questions asking people for their level of agreement with statements about rangelands and range management. For each question respondents were asked to choose a response of 1 (strongly disagree), 2 (disagree), 3 (neutral), 4 (agree), or 5 (strongly agree). For statements about the environmental condition of rangelands, respondents could also choose a "don't know" response. Interestingly, no more than 4 percent answered "don't know" to any single question; data from the "don't know" responses were excluded from our analysis.

Respondents were asked to give their views about "federal lands such as those managed by the Bureau of Land Management and the U.S. Forest Service," with particular attention to rangelands. To ensure continuity in the responses, we provided a definition of "rangeland" from the several that are available.[39] The definition we chose was: "places that have arid climates, where grassland or desert environments are *more common* than heavily forested ones (although forested areas may be present)."

Results
Changing Natural Resource Values

In both the 1998 and the 2011 surveys, respondents were asked to indicate their level of agreement or disagreement with a variety of statements concerning society-environment relationships. The survey results unequivocally demonstrate strong support for elements of the New Resource Management Paradigm; indeed, 63.1 percent of respondents in 1998 and 74.7 percent of respondents in 2011 agreed and strongly agreed with the statement that "wildlife, plants and humans have equal rights to live and develop on the earth." Higher proportions, 80.5 percent in 1998 and 89.7 percent in 2011, agreed with the biocentric statement, "humans have an ethical obligation to protect plant and animal species." This is in contrast to support for statements pertaining to the Dominant Resource Management Paradigm where only 32.7 percent of respondents in 1998 and 27.8 percent of respondents in 2011 agreed or strongly agreed with the statement, "plants and animals exist primarily for human use." Further, only 36.2 percent in 1998 and 32.9 percent in 2011 agreed with the statement that "humankind was created to rule over the rest of nature." While one may take issue with the leading wording of these statements[40] or question the commitment to supportive behavior on the part of responding individuals,[41] they do indicate strong support for protecting natural environments in the Great Basin. The same high level of support for environmental protection has been documented in a number of studies of the "New Environmental Paradigm" conducted by Riley Dunlap and his associates in recent years.[42]

As noted earlier, a number of scholars have documented a widening generational gap regarding attitudes toward the environment and natural resources.[43] These differing value orientations are closely linked to postmaterialist values among younger people. The surveys provide empirical support for these findings. For most of the indicators of orientations toward the society-environment relationship, younger respondents express greater concern for protecting nature than do older respondents. The most striking finding is for the first indicator, where in 2011 only 2.7 percent of the eighteen-to-twenty-nine age group agreed with the statement, "plants and animals exist primarily for human use," which compares to a 48.3 percent agreement among the sixty-one-plus age group. Similarly, in 2011 only 15.2 percent of the eighteen-to-twenty-nine age group agreed with the statement, "humankind was created to rule over the rest of nature," compared to 46.2 percent of the sixty-one-plus age group. These findings portend increasing intergenerational conflict over the use of public lands in the Great Basin. It seems clear from this survey evidence that Roderick Nash's theme of an emerging "rights of nature" ethic is deeply imbedded in the value systems (the "hearts and minds") of contemporary American youth.[44] Similar studies of intergenerational beliefs and opinions on a variety of public policy issues confirm that a high proportion of younger people support a proenvironmental stance.[45]

Public Rangeland Perceptions, Attitudes, and Policy Preferences

A major purpose of the 1998 survey was to investigate public knowledge, beliefs, and management preferences concerning public rangelands in the western United States. Rangelands cover approximately 80 percent of the Great Basin and provide livestock grazing, wildlife habitat, recreational opportunities, and "water resources for the rapidly urbanizing Western states."[46] The management of these rangelands—most of which are on publicly owned lands managed by the Bureau of Land Management and US Forest Service—has been the subject of political conflict for decades.[47] From the long-simmering feud over grazing fees to the use of prescribed fire and herbicides for land management, public rangelands have become the subject of increasing controversy and litigation.

The US Department of Agriculture has recently reported that more than 50 percent of Great Basin rangelands are degraded, with "many more at risk because of reoccurring drought and wildfires."[48] To what extent are

TABLE 1
Policy Preferences for the Management of Public Rangelands

	1998 Percentage Agree and Strongly Agree	2011 Percentage Agree and Strongly Agree
More wilderness areas should be established on federal rangelands.	62.9	72.7
Livestock grazing should be permitted in rangeland wilderness areas.	29.1	27.6
Greater protection should be given to fish such in federal rangelands.	77.1	77.6
Greater efforts should be made to protect rare plant communities on federal rangelands.	73.7	75.7
Endangered species laws should be set aside to preserve ranching jobs.	16.3	15.8
Federal rangeland management should emphasize livestock grazing.	23.1	22.0
Greater efforts should be given to protect wildlife on federal rangelands.	76.8	77.9
Ranchers should pay more than they do now to graze livestock on federal land.	68.0	69.2
	N > 1,048	N > 1,068

NOTE: The scale used is: 1 = strongly disagree, 2 = disagree, 3 = neutral, 4 = agree, 5 = strongly agree.

TABLE 2
Preferences for Grazing Fee Policy

	1998 (%)	2011 (%)
Ranchers should be able to graze their animals on federal lands free of charge.	7.2	5.8
Ranchers should continue to pay about what they currently pay to graze on federal land.	12.6	13.4
Grazing fees charged to ranchers should be raised to fair market value, but the change should be gradual to let ranchers adjust to new economic conditions.	41.4	43.4
	41.4	43.4
Grazing fees should be immediately raised to their fair market value.	16.0	13.9
Ranchers should not be allowed to graze their animals on federal lands no matter how high the fee.	22.8	23.4
	N > 1,042	N > 1,061

Great Basin residents aware of this situation, and what are their management preferences for mitigating degradation (if any)? In the 1998 and 2011 surveys we asked citizens about their perceptions concerning the condition of public rangelands. The results showed that there is a strong public perception that public rangelands are in trouble and that the situation is getting worse. The statements that were most likely to gain agreement referred to watershed issues: loss of riparian vegetation and declining water quality. There also was growing concern about overgrazing; in the 1998 survey 60.2 percent were worried about overgrazing, but this proportion had risen to 73.5 percent by 2011.

Given that a significant percentage of respondents perceive public rangelands to be in a state of degradation, what policies do they prefer to mitigate and improve conditions? Generally speaking, the data displayed in table 1 indicate that Great Basin residents favor policies consistent with the New Resource Management Paradigm. Residents favor protection for nonmarket rangeland resources and a shift away from commodity-oriented management. Respondents did not support the current policy that allows livestock grazing within wilderness areas in either 1998 or 2011, and the percentage of residents supporting the establishment of new wilderness areas increased from 62.9 percent in 1998 to 72.7 percent in 2011. Large majorities also favored greater protection of fisheries, wildlife, and rare plant communities and disagreed that range management should emphasize livestock grazing. In both 1998 and 2011 large percentages of respondents thought that ranchers should pay more than they do now to graze livestock on federal land. In addition, when asked to choose among five statements about the grazing-fee system, the majority of respondents in 1998 and 2011 favored increasing fees to "fair market value" either "immediately" or gradually, "to let ranchers adjust to new economic conditions" (see table 2). Clearly, respondents were not altogether insensitive to the economic upheavals that may result from a fee increase.

Confidence and Influence

Both the 1998 and the 2011 surveys also asked respondents about how much confidence they have in agencies and interest groups involved in public rangelands management and how much priority these groups should be given in the policy process. We found that in 1998 and 2011 public confidence in conservation groups was higher than commodity groups and most agencies (see table 3). Of the three resource agencies that have the greatest responsibility for range management, respondents expressed less confidence in the Bureau of Land Management. The US Fish and Wildlife Agency enjoyed the highest level of confidence, followed by the US Forest Service, but it is important to note that even higher percentages expressed "hardly any" confidence in either of these agencies. In both 1998 and 2011 public confidence for Congress was much lower, almost on par with the oil, mining, and livestock industries. The oil industry attracted the higher level of distrust.

TABLE 3
Confidence in Agencies and Interest Groups to Responsibly Manage Federal Rangelands

	1998		2011	
Question: How much confidence do you have in the following government agencies and interest groups to responsibly manage federal rangelands?	Hardly Any (%)	A Great Deal (%)	Hardly Any (%)	A Great Deal (%)
Federal agencies:				
Bureau of Land Management	44.6	19.0	40.2	19.5
US Forest Service	36.2	26.3	35.4	25.8
US Fish and Wildlife Service	34.3	30.6	36.5	29.8
Commodity interests:				
Livestock	51.3	14.7	51.9	13.8
Mining	51.7	8.8	54.2	8.1
Oil/gas	30.9	8.7	34.5	6.7
Other:				
Congress	67.9	6.5	68.8	5.5
Conservation groups	22.5	30.9	22.9	30.0
	N > 1,038		N > 1,054	

NOTE: Response categories provided were: "Hardly Any Confidence," "Some Confidence," and "A Great Deal of Confidence." "Some" responses are not reported in this table.

TABLE 4
Preferred Group Priority in Federal Rangeland Policy

Question: How much priority should be given to the needs of the following groups when making federal rangeland policy?	1998 Mean 1 (s.d.)	2011 Mean (s.d.)
Affected local communities	2.63 (1.77)	2.61 (1.78)
Government natural resource agencies	3.68 (1.77)	3.73 (1.78)
Affected local industry	3.91 (1.73)	4.07 (1.77)
Conservation groups	4.30 (1.91)	4.21 (1.92)
State public opinion	4.33 (1.75)	4.28 (1.73)
National public opinion	4.49 (1.70)	4.39 (1.73)
Congress	5.16 (2.18)	5.09 (2.16)
	N > 902	N > 924

NOTE: Response format provided: 1 = highest priority to 7 = lowest priority.

Respondents were also asked to rank seven broad groups according to how much priority their needs should be given when decisions about federal rangelands are made (see table 4). As we previously found, there is a high level of support for giving priority to the needs and desires of local communities. However, respondents made a distinction between local *communities* and local *industry*. In addition, respondents in both 1998 and 2011 ranked natural resource agencies as second highest in priority. Perhaps this signals a recognition that these agencies are ultimately responsible for management of public rangelands in the Great Basin and that public management is needed. Congress ranked dead last.

Implications for Natural Resource Management

If only one message were to be drawn from these surveys, it is that there has been and continues to be widespread public disapproval of current public lands management in the Great Basin, and this reflects a growing disenchantment with commodity-focused management as well as a belief that conditions on the public lands are deteriorating. These results reflect a marked shift from the Dominant Resource Management Paradigm to the New Resource Management Paradigm. Many citizens of the Great Basin believe that public rangelands are overgrazed and seriously eroding, that they are losing riparian vegetation, and that conditions are getting worse instead of better. At the same time, respondents supported the multiresource and biocentric management of these lands to enhance fisheries, wildlife, and rare plant species. Public and private sources of information are generally distrusted. We found little public confidence in the livestock industry. Ranchers, like others who earn their living from public lands, may be seen as foxes in the henhouse, deriving great benefit from grazing on public lands while actively contributing to growing ecological management concerns.

The rapid urbanization of the Great Basin virtually guarantees that urban-rural and the intergenerational battle lines will sharpen in the years ahead. However, if a focus on local community interests becomes an important goal of rangeland management, it is possible that conflict can be reduced. A cooperative plan for rangeland conservation is the key. Ultimately, what is at stake for all residents both in the core and in the periphery areas of the Great Basin is an extremely fragile desert ecosystem that supports both urban lifestyles and rural needs.

It is our hope that this research will contribute to an informed and productive dialogue on difficult value trade-off issues across the urban-rural and younger-older dividing lines of society. If we note that the state of Nevada (the Silver State) just fifty years ago was the most rural state in the nation and that it is now the most highly urbanized, we begin to get a good sense of the scale and scope of change affecting the citizens of the Great Basin. In this circumstance public deliberation and dialogue are essential. As Jane Mansbridge has argued, we need to move "beyond advocacy democracy" to achieve some sort of policy learning.[49]

Although there is no assurance that collaborative processes will lead to consensus, it is also clear that some noteworthy successes at collaborative environmental policy negotiations have occurred.[50] Civic journalism can do much to promote a level of public discussion and deliberation that may lead to a "coming to public judgment."[51] Federal government agencies, which frequently face challenges to their legitimacy and authority, would, in particular, benefit from a collaborative style aimed at bridging the political and cultural divide that has emerged in the Great Basin.

NOTES

1. Brent S. Steel, Richard Clinton, and Nicholas P. Lovrich, *Environmental Politics and Policy: A Comparative Perspective* (Boston: McGraw-Hill, 2003); Julia Wondolleck, *Public Lands Conflict and Resolution: Managing National Forest Disputes* (New York: Plenum Press, 1988).

2. Alicia Torregrosa and Nora Devoe, "Urbanization and Changing Land Use in the Great Basin," *U.S. Geological Survey* (2008), http://www.fs.fed.us/rm/pubs /rmrs_gtr204/rmrs_gtr204_009_013.pdf.

3. Russell Dalton, *Citizen Politics in Western Democracies* (Chatham, NJ: Chatham House, 1988).

4. Paul Rosenau, *Post-modernism and the Social Sciences: Insights, Inroads and Intrusions* (Princeton, NJ: Princeton University Press, 1992).

5. Daniel Bell, *The Coming of Post-industrial Society* (New York: Basic Books, 1973); Martin Heisler, ed., *Politics in Europe: Structures and Processes in Some Postindustrial Democracies* (New York: McKay, 1974); Samuel P. Huntington, "Postindustrial Politics: How Benign Will It Be?," *Comparative Politics* 6 (1974): 147–77.

6. Bell, *Coming of Post-industrial Society;* William A. Galston, "Rural America in the 1990s: Trends and Choices," *Policy Studies Journal* 20 (1992): 202–11; Ronald Inglehart, "Public Support for Environmental Protection: Objective Problems and Subjective Values in 43 Societies," *PS: Political Science and Politics* (March 1995):

57–72; Ronald Inglehart, *Culture Shift in Advanced Industrial Society* (Princeton, NJ: Princeton University Press, 1990).

7. Paul R. Abramson and Ronald Inglehart, *Value Change in Global Perspective* (Ann Arbor: University of Michigan Press, 1995); Inglehart, "Public Support for Environmental Protection"; Inglehart, *Culture Shift in Advanced Industrial Society;* Scott C. Flanagan, "Changing Values in Advanced Industrial Society," *Comparative Political Studies* 14 (1982): 99–128; D. Yankelovich, *Coming to Public Judgment: Making Democracy Work in a Complex World* (Syracuse, NY: Syracuse University Press, 1991).

8. Mary Ann Steger et al., "Political Culture, Postmaterial Values, and the New Environmental Paradigm," *Political Behavior* 11 (1989): 233–54.

9. John C. Pierce et al., *Citizens, Political Communication, and Interest Groups: A Study of Environmental Organizations in Canada and the United States* (New York: Praeger, 1992); Christopher A. Simon, Brent S. Steel, and Nicholas P. Lovrich, *State and Local Government: Sustainability in the 21st Century* (Oxford: Oxford University Press, 2011).

10. William Dietrich, *The Final Forest: The Battle for the Last Great Trees of the Pacific Northwest* (New York: Simon and Schuster, 1992).

11. Matthew Carroll, *Community and the Northwest Logger: Continuities in the Era of the Spotted Owl* (Boulder, CO: Westview Press, 1995).

12. Steel, Clinton, and Lovrich, *Environmental Politics and Policy*, chaps. 3–4.

13. Simon, Steel, and Lovrich, *State and Local Government*, chap. 1.

14. Steel, Clinton, and Lovrich, *Environmental Politics and Policy.*

15. Torregrosa and Devoe, "Urbanization and Changing Land Use."

16. Ibid.

17. Ibid.

18. Ibid.

19. Galston, "Rural America in the 1990s."

20. L. Gorham and B. Harrison, *Working Below the Poverty Line: The Growing Problem of Low Earnings in Rural and Urban Regions Across the United States* (Washington, DC: Aspen Institute, 1990); I. Shapiro and R. Greenstein, *Fulfilling Work's Promises: Policies to Increase Incomes of the Rural Working Poor* (Washington, DC: Center on Budget and Priorities, 1990).

21. Max Nicholson, *The New Environmental Age* (New York: Cambridge University Press, 1987); P. Stern, O. Young, and D. Druckman, eds., *Global Environmental Change: Understanding the Human Dimensions* (Washington, DC: National Academy Press, 1992); Daniel Yankelovich, "How Changes in the Economy Are Reshaping American Values," in *Values and Public Policy,* edited by Henry Aaron, Thomas Mann, and Timothy Taylor (Washington, DC: Brookings Institution, 1994).

22. Bureau of Labor Statistics, "Local Area Unemployment Statistics"

(Washington, DC: US Department of Labor, 2014), http://www.bls.gov/web/laus /laumstrk.htm.

23. Torregrosa and Devoe, "Urbanization and Changing Land Use."

24. Nora Devoe, "Energy Development in the Great Basin," in *Collaborative Management and Research*.

25. Jeanne C. Chambers, Nora Devoe, and Angela Evenden, "Collaborative Management and Research in the Great Basin: Examining the Issues and Developing a Framework for Action," in ibid.

26. Shanto Iyenger and Donald E. Kinder, *News That Matters: Television and American Opinion* (Chicago: University of Chicago Press, 1987); Douglas Kellner, *Television and the Crisis of Democracy* (Boulder, CO: Westview Press, 1990).

27. Jasen Lee, "Tech Execs Tout Utah as Key Growth State," *Desert News*, January 14, 2011, http://www.deseretnews.com/article/705364520/Tech-execs-tout-Utah-as -key-growth-state.html?pg=all.

28. Joel Kotkin, "The Best Cities for Technology Jobs," *Forbes*, November 18, 2011, http://www.forbes.com/sites/joelkotkin/2011/11/18/the-best-cities-for -technology-jobs/.

29. Desert Research Institute, "Nevada Renewable Energy Consortium, 2014," http://www.dri.edu/nvrec.

30. Ibid.

31. Lynton K. Caldwell, "Globalizing Environmentalism: Threshold of a New Phase in International Relations," in *American Environmentalism*, edited by Riley Dunlap and Angela Mertig (Philadelphia: Taylor and Francis, 1992); Steel, Clinton, and Lovrich, *Environmental Politics and Policy*.

32. Claus Offe, "New Social Movements: Challenging the Boundaries of Institutional Politics," *Social Research* 52 (1985): 817–68.

33. George Brown and Charles Harris, "The USDA Forest Service: Toward the New Resource Management Paradigm?," *Society and Natural Resource* 5 (1992): 231–45.

34. Aldo Leopold, *A Sand County Almanac* (Oxford: Oxford University Press, 1949), 262.

35. William Kittredge, *Who Owns the West?* (San Francisco: Mercury House, 1996), 5.

36. Don Dillman, *Mail and Telephone Surveys: The Total Design Method* (New York: John Wiley, 1978).

37. Bruce Shindler, Peter List, and Brent S. Steel, "Managing Federal Forests: Public Attitudes in Oregon and Nationwide," *Journal of Forestry* 91 (July 1993): 36–42.

38. Mark W. Brunson and Brent S. Steel, "National Public Attitudes Toward Federal Rangeland Management," *Rangelands* 16 (1994): 77–81.

39. Jerry L. Holechek, Rex D. Pieper, and Carlton H. Herbel, *Range Management: Principles and Practices* (Englewood Cliffs, NJ: Prentice Hall, 1989).

40. Steven R. Brechin and Willett Kempton, "Global Environmentalism: A Challenge to the Postmaterialism Thesis," *Social Science Quarterly* 75 (1994): 245–69.

41. Riley Dunlap, J. D. Grieneeks, and Milton Rokeach, "Human Values and Pro-environmental Behavior," in *Energy and Material Resources: Attitudes, Values, and Public Policy,* edited by W. A. Cann (Boulder, CO: Westview Press, 1983).

42. R. E. Dunlap et al., "Measuring Endorsement of the New Ecological Paradigm: A Revised NEP Scale," *Journal of Social Issues* 56, no. 3 (2000): 425–42; Steel, Clinton, and Lovrich, *Environmental Politics and Policy.*

43. Russell Dalton, "Citizenship Norms and the Expansion of Political Participation," *Political Studies* 56 (2008): 76–98; Inglehart, "Public Support for Environmental Protection."

44. Roderick Nash, *The Rights of Nature: A History of Environmental Ethics* (Madison: University of Wisconsin Press, 1989).

45. Dalton, "Citizenship Norms."

46. US Department of Agriculture, "Great Basin Rangelands Research Unit" (2012), http://www.ars.usda.gov/main/site_main.htm?modecode=53-70-00-00, 1.

47. Deborah Gordon, "Western U.S. Demonstrates Scale of Climate Challenge," *Huffington Post,* December, 12, 2012, http://www.huffingtonpost.com/deborah-gordon/oil-drilling_b_2288700.html.

48. US Department of Agriculture, "Great Basin Rangelands Research Unit," 1.

49. Jane Mansbridge, *Beyond Advocacy Democracy* (Chicago: University of Chicago Press, 1983); Hank Jenkins-Smith and Paul Sabatier, "The Dynamics of Policy-Oriented Learning," in *Policy Change and Learning: An Advocacy Coalition Approach,* edited by Paul Sabatier and Hank Jenkins-Smith (Boulder, CO: Westview Press, 1993).

50. Edward Weber, *Bringing Society Back In: Grassroots Ecosystem Management, Accountability, and Sustainable Communities* (Cambridge, MA: MIT Press, 2003).

51. Peter Dahlgren and Colin Sparks, *Communication and Citizenship: Journalism and the Public Sphere in the New Media Age* (New York: Routledge, 1991); E. Fouhy, "The Dawn of Public Journalism," *National Civic Review* 83 (1994): 261; Yankelovich, *Coming to Public Judgment.*

The Solace of Empty Spaces

Searching for Tourists in America's Outback

ANAHIT TADEVOSYAN AND DENNIS R. JUDD

SINCE THE POST–CIVIL WAR ERA, popular conceptions of the American West have been informed by themes heavily laden with romanticism and myth. With the end of the Indian wars, Buffalo Bill's Wild West extravaganza played to enthusiastic crowds at every stop, and well into the twentieth century writers found a ready market for a literature recounting (or inventing) a stylized interpretation of the western experience. With the coming of the railroads, the American West became increasingly accessible to affluent tourists who wanted to see it for themselves. Before they stepped onto the first railcar, however, they already knew what they expected to see because artists and writers had already constructed the West as an exotic realm of otherworldly surprise and beauty. What they "saw" left them with a sense of wonder and awe: a seemingly endless panorama of jagged mountain horizons; canyons carved deep into the earth; glaciers, sky-blue lakes, geysers; and an exotic menagerie of wildlife. When the West became scripted in this way, it came into focus in the American imagination as an assemblage of iconic places and dramatic landscapes.[1] Those parts that did not fit the script were rendered virtually invisible, places to be passed through and endured on the way to much-anticipated destinations.

Although it occupies almost a third of the sprawling region between the Rockies and the Sierra Nevada—what people refer to as the Intermountain West—the Great Basin remains largely unknown to most Americans. Well-publicized tourist sites are scattered throughout most of the West, but the Basin has few places that tourists intentionally seek out. The Grand Canyon of Arizona draws approximately 4.3 million visitors a year; by contrast, the Ruby Mountains of northern Nevada, the most accessible and scenic of the mountain ranges of the Great Basin, see only about 40,000 visitors. With an average of about 70,000 visitors in recent years, the Great Basin National Park is one of the least crowded in the park system because, as the Park Service readily admits, it does not seem much like a national park at all: "Called dead, barren, and desolate, visitors are surprised to find it's alive, fruitful, and full of wonders."[2] For tourists, the Great Basin is the hole in the donut, the missing middle, because it is hard to fit it into the standard western script.

The Great Basin was never the backdrop for dramatic tales of nineteenth-century explorations, unless one counts the disastrous experience of the Donner Party. Nor did it hold the promise of the twentieth-century leisured lifestyle associated with California. James Cowden, who passed through in 1853, described the desert he encountered in a dismissive tone emulated by the generations of travelers who followed in his wake: "From Fort Larramie to the Nevada Mountains, a distance of twelve or fourteen hundred miles, wild sage constitutes three fourths of the vegetation to be seen. I would give more for one county in Iowa than for all of it, except perhaps Salt Lake Valley. Can't see any use for so much desert country, for certainly it is good for nothing only to hold the rest of creation together."[3]

The coming of the railroad and the automobile did little to erase the frequently expressed opinion that crossing the Basin was a psychological and physical trial. A train passenger in 1932 complained, "One gets up in the morning and looks out one's window at the landscape. Six hours later one is, seemingly, in exactly the same place, and it has changed little at bedtime or the next morning." Even today such perceptions persist. As noted by Soren Larsen and Timothy Brock, "For most Americans, the Great Basin is nothingness. In the popular imagination the basin is a dry, crater-pocked land of endless scrub populated by tarantulas and jackrabbits. It is seen as a place without use or value, a wasteland that has intimidated the most intrepid of travelers."[4] The Basin has been widely regarded as an unattractive place not because it lacks a script, but because the one written for it by generations of travelers has been mostly unappealing. Finally, in recent decades the urban growth that has come to it offers some hope that there may be, at long last, a reappraisal of its narrative.

Tourism in the American West

In 1785, nine years after the United States declared its independence, Thomas Jefferson was serving as the ranking American diplomat in France when he entered into a bet with Georges de Buffon, the renowned French naturalist of the day. To rebut Buffon's claim that the animals and plants of North America were inferior to those of Europe, Jefferson commissioned a hunter to shoot an American moose and have it shipped to Paris. When this first specimen proved to be less impressive than Jefferson thought necessary for the purpose, he commissioned a second hunting party and put the stuffed carcass on display in the lobby of his Parisian hotel. Though he never managed to convince de Buffon that America's natural endowments were equal to France's, Jefferson became, in effect, the de Buffon of North America, defending the wildlife and natural life of his newly formed country as superior to anything that could be found in Europe.

Jefferson's attempt to elevate America's stature in the eyes of Europeans reflected the new nation's need to define a distinctive American character and identity. Uncharted wilderness provided that opportunity, and the West beckoned like a blank canvas waiting for the brush. A growing fascination with this unknown region fueled the transition from discovery and exploration to settlement and, finally, to tourism. In the eighteenth century members of the aristocratic classes thought they needed go to Europe to experience refined culture; in the next, visiting the American West became an equally compelling goal for European royalty. Finally, almost a century after Jefferson's futile attempts to prove America's grandeur, "Americans were content that their geography equaled Europe's cultural past. Some daringly referred to Switzerland as the Colorado of Europe, inverting a historic American sense of inadequacy in the face of Europe's attractions."[5]

Making the West accessible to tourists was not a straightforward task. Robert Edmund Strahorn, a prominent promotional writer in late century, recognized that a western identity needed to be shaped if it were to draw anyone but the most intrepid of travelers. Settlers were expected to put up with all manner of hardship, but visitors expected something else entirely.[6] To solve the problem, the promotional writing of the time promised that a trip to see the scenic wonders they read about could be undertaken in comfort and security.

The completion of the transcontinental railroad in 1869 forever changed the experience of a westward journey. The Pullman car offered comfort and eliminated the need for a hazardous overland journey. Travelers were able to reach their destination in days rather than weeks. This altered not only the act of travel but its purpose: "Unlike the early overland stagecoach and steamboat companies, transcontinental railroads promoted tourism as an end in itself."[7] To boost ridership, railroad companies aggressively promoted a mythical version of the western landscape and historical experience. One example is the cooperation between the Santa Fe Railroad and the Harvey Company, which sought to market the Southwest by appropriating carefully selected features of Indian culture. Displays of Indian life, artfully constructed by Santa Fe and Harvey, were shown at World's Fairs, at regional expositions, and in Harvey hotels and shops. Such displays included Indian-made objects as well as "live" Indians, all artfully curated to please tourists and potential tourists. In Fred Harvey's Southwest, "the combination of a subjective tourist gaze and the mobility of the train afforded tourists the free-dom to choose the objects of consumption," and thereby reduce a complex region to a few selected sites and artifacts.[8]

The Grand Canyon presented a perfect opportunity for affirming Amer-ica's identity through its landscape: "The more majestic the scene, the more celebrated it became; the more singular, the more valued." When the railroad industry realized the canyon's potential, it transformed it from "a fearsome landscape [to] a precious object." In 1905 the Atchison, Topeka & Santa Fe Railway developed a route with a stop at the canyon's south rim and built the luxurious El Tovar Hotel, which provided breathtaking views down into the canyon. Almost overnight the Grand Canyon was drawn into the realm of mass tourism, and at that point it was transformed from a place for explo-ration to an obligatory stop on an increasingly well-defined tourist circuit: "The visitor replaced the explorer, the Kodak snapshot the grand canvas, the inscribed overlook the monographs, atlases and personal narratives of its bold creators."[9] Likewise, Yellowstone National Park found a tireless pro-moter in the Northern Pacific Railroad. By the mid-nineteenth century pro-moters billed Yellowstone as a wonderland, and the few upper-class travelers who were able to reach it by the 1870s were eager to champion its virtues.[10] In 1883 the Northern Pacific launched a public campaign designed to induce tourists to schedule a train trip to see it, and when President Chester Arthur visited it that same year, Yellowstone began to attract national and interna-tional attention. Promoters realized that exploiting Yellowstone's potential would require pleasant accommodations, restaurants, and reliable transpor-tation.[11] Hotels went up, built from local lumber and leaving stumps that are visible to the present day. The development of Yellowstone as a tourist des-tination was the product of marketing for commercial purposes, and in this way nature was turned into a commercial commodity and a cultural cliché. Within a few years a growing rail network provided access to a scattering of other scenic places sprinkled throughout the West.

While the railroads provided access to a few heavily marketed iconic sites, in the twentieth century the automobile allowed tourists to explore all cor-ners of the American West. After World War I, when cars became available to the members of the middle class, the number of riders taking coach class travel dropped dramatically. "The automobile took them from the locales overwhelmed by tourism, the railroad depots, the plazas, the towns, the seemingly inauthentic and corrupt places, and transported them to areas where the intrusions of the modern world were limited to the drivers and their vehicles."[12] Travelers were no longer bound to the confines of steel rails, and while railroad travelers were often presented with a fixed itinerary, automobile travelers enjoyed a wider range of options. Today, although Amtrak takes people to stunning places in reasonable comfort, it will never again compete with the car or, for that matter, with the airplane.

In the second half of the twentieth century, the travel tourism of an earlier era gave way to an incredibly eclectic mix of leisure, sports, and entertainment activities. Iconic tourist sites will always be on the itinerary, but the climate and topography of the West also lend themselves to an endless variety of recreational opportunities, and these are marketed relentlessly. Sports such as climbing, backpacking, skiing, fly fishing, rafting, hang gliding, BASE jumping, and countless other activities appeal to people looking for something that feels like adventure; dude ranches, resorts, and spas provide luxury and comfort for those who wish to experience their nature less raw. Throughout the West tourism is a leading sector of state and local economies, and despite the changes that have come to the industry, western tourism still offers a unique blend of experiences not available anywhere else.

Tourism in the Great Basin

People have been restlessly moving to the four cities on the Great Basin's rim. Although they live in a sparsely populated desert environment, the daily experience of most people living in the Basin is urban.[13] In the desert outback one is not likely to encounter crowds. By contrast, people come by the planeload to experience the entertainments of Las Vegas and to ski and gamble in and near Reno and Lake Tahoe. Throngs of skiers head for the slopes above Salt Lake City and visit Temple Square and other Mormon sites. And although Boise lacks a clear brand that might be associated with tourism, the local economy would be in trouble without it.

Perhaps because there may be no other choice, the absence of crowds is a selling point for the Great Basin Business and Tourism Council, which boasts, "One of the best things about Great Basin is the low number of visitors. This is truly a place to get away from it all. If you come in the spring or fall you might not see anyone for hours on backcountry trails." The Basin's uncluttered vistas may not be enough of a draw for most tourists, but for those who love the desert it is a luminous and sacred place. Richard Francaviglia, who has elegiac prose about his love affair with the Basin, writes of "the Great Basin's powerful—biblical-like—landscape: deep basins, salt lakes, well-watered oases, forested mountains, and remote archeological sights . . . [suggest] a grand past. In the Great Basin, faith and landscape conspire to resurrect old myths and create new ones."[14] The self-proclaimed desert rats of the Basin regard it as a place of special and unmatched serenity, solitude, and beauty. For them, if people began to show up in large numbers Yogi Berra's favorite aphorism would become a painful reality: "Nobody goes there anymore because it's too crowded."

Those who take the time to explore beyond the urban orbit will find awe-inspiring landscapes and panoramas. They might, for instance, come across the Craters of the Moon in Idaho, where the jagged fields of lava look as if they erupted from the ground just yesterday. The Basin contains rank on rank of mountain ranges, and those with enough elevation are sky islands containing plant and animal communities found nowhere else. Great Basin National Park and the Ruby Mountains rise from the desert floor to summits topping ten thousand feet. The eastern escarpment of Steens Mountain in southeastern Oregon stands more than a mile above a sagebrush plain and salt playa; on its western slope startling U-shaped canyons cut by ancient glaciers slice directly into the rising arc of the mountain from the desert floor.

Sometimes, features that might ordinarily repel people become popular attractions; for example, thousands of curious tourists brave summer heat to gaze on the craters left by nuclear explosions at the Nevada Test Site. For decades the Bonneville Salt Flats near the Great Salt Lake has been a gathering spot for racers pursuing land-speed records, and in recent years some of these events have moved to the desolate and remote Black Rock Desert of northwestern Nevada. What attracts the racers is exactly what doomed the Donner Party: square miles of salt blown absolutely flat by the desert winds.

Black Rock has also become the site for the internationally publicized annual event called Burning Man. Burning Man began in the 1980s on the beaches of California, but the waterless and featureless salt playa of the Black Rock desert turned out to be a better home for the thousands who gather each summer for an uninhibited expression of avant-garde culture. Black Rock City, LLC, the organization that stages the festival, is a "$23 million-per-year concern with 40 full-time employees, hundreds of volunteers, and a non-profit arts foundation that doles out grants." Its current success is a far cry from the festival's beginnings in the late 1980s, when Burning Man consisted of "a small group of friends torching an effigy on San Francisco's Baker Beach." When the spectacle began to draw crowds numbering into the hundreds and then thousands, the organizers began searching for a new venue. In a recent interview the cofounders of Burning Man explain why they chose a Nevada salt pan:

> There were a few philosophical underpinnings to Burning Man, but the one that got us to the desert was the Zone concept Carrie came up with. The idea was that you would cross an imaginary barrier, and after that you'd be in an alien land where anything could happen. . . . When you reach the point where you can see the desert open up, it's amazing. We'd piled into this station wagon and thrown some potatoes on the manifold to cook, and when we got to the edge of the playa there was nobody there. Nobody anywhere. We got there at dusk, which is my favorite time. You look out, it's like the goddamn surface of the moon.[15]

What the faithful hope to find at Black Rock is a place of power and spiritual significance; like so many people who love the desert, the isolation and solitude are the main draws. The flood of tourists who come to the cities of the rim are seeking an entirely different experience. Tourism is the number-one industry in Nevada, generating billions of dollars of revenue each year. In November 2010 Nevada received 3,806,348 visitors; in the same month Las Vegas welcomed more than 2.93 million visitors—three-fourths of the total visitors to the state. Reno accounted for most of the rest. The Nevada Tourism Commission promotes more remote areas but almost as an afterthought; without Las Vegas, it would have little to do. Between the ski slopes of Salt Lake City and the neon lights of the Las Vegas Strip lie empty stretches of land punctuated by clusters of small towns whose only claim to distinction is the occasional dude ranch or hot springs.

Reno's Struggle for Identity

Reno cannot be understood without reference to its setting, that is, as a city situated uncomfortably between the neon lights of Las Vegas and California's beaches. Reno has a history deeply steeped in sin, and for more than a century its boosters have tried to draw a veil around the sordid parts of its past. To some degree this path has been forced upon it because it has been so thoroughly eclipsed by its neighbor to the south. Visitors are encouraged to compare the culture of Las Vegas to the friendlier and more genuine Reno,

"a vision of wholesomeness . . . and a feeling that there is enough room for
. . . everybody."[16] Such claims leave Reno in an awkward position. It is not,
and can never be, Las Vegas; nor is it California. As a result for more than
a century it has struggled to craft a distinctive identity that will set it apart
from both.

In 1868 a reporter for the *San Francisco Times* chronicled his journey west
over the Sierra Nevada on the Central Pacific Railroad. From Sacramento
to the slopes of the Sierra, his account consisted of glowing references to
"green meadows" and "beautiful cascades." Upon entering Nevada, however,
his journey took a decidedly unpleasant turn, with the landscape "drearier
and more depressing at every mile," with "no trace of vegetation other than
the dusty blue sage brush, whose monotonous bunches alone hide the sterile
sands."[17] The reporter thought Nevada had one saving grace—the immense
silver lode that had been discovered in the Comstock region. Reno was the
gateway for people heading for the Comstock, and although Comstock put
Reno on the map, its early prosperity came at a price. Reno acquired a reputation as a rough town riddled by violence and sin, and the tawdry reputation would prove to be hard to shake.

By 1870 Reno's population had barely reached 1,000, though the number
of people passing through to Comstock ensured that the city's streets were
always filled. "The completion of the railroad may have enabled more people
to visit Nevada, but at the same time this also allowed them to compare the
state more easily and directly to its neighbors. And in many minds, the contrast only served to accentuate the state's inferiority to them."[18] At the same
time that Reno was struggling, the state began to encounter difficulties of its
own. In the late 1870s the Comstock mining district went bust, and the mining magnates and miners quickly fled. The Comstock collapse left the state
with a sharply reduced population and an economic depression that endured
until the turn of the century. Sin, in the form of relaxed gaming laws, vice,
and easy divorce, kept it afloat, though barely. To improve their prospects
Reno's business class struggled to distance the city from the sorry reputation
of a state known for its boom-and-bust cycles and the ghost towns sprinkled
throughout the desert. Reno, they thought, was destined for better things; all
they had to do was burnish its image.

Eager to build its economy, Reno's promoters tried to bring the city closer
to the cultural mainstream, but not too close. This strategy required local
boosters to walk a fine line between virtue and vice. While Las Vegas was

cultivating a booming industry of gambling, promiscuity, and leisure, Reno tried to make itself slightly tamer, with a "gayety and friendliness" guided by "tolerance, not license." At a critical juncture Reno forged a partnership with the motion picture industry, which was struggling to balance the restrictive standards imposed by the Motion Picture Production Code of 1930 against demands by film audiences for racy material. Nevada's casinos and six-week divorce law provided the foundation for the production of such films as *Merry Wives of Reno*. In the 1930s the motion picture industry developed a handful of films focused on Reno divorces, and the theme of scandalous fun was incorporated into every inch of the city, from shops and beauty parlors to courthouses.[19]

The melding of permissive laws and western hospitality found a perfect expression in divorce ranches, which began opening in the late 1920s. To attract well-healed divorcées and celebrities, Reno's ranches provided luxurious surroundings, organized shopping trips, and ample numbers of ranch hands (often referred to as "cowboy-gigolos"). Divorce ranches provided both an escape from troubles back home and a taste of western adventure. Shops supplied the clothing needed to help temporary residents blend into the western landscape, and nightclub owners renovated their interiors to project an Old West ambience.

Las Vegas's meteoric postwar rise came at Reno's expense. While the former played on a national and international stage, Reno tended to draw weekenders from San Francisco and other West Coast cities. Once again Reno's promoters undertook a search for a new brand. In the 1960s they hit upon a strategy that tightly linked the city with Lake Tahoe, a sparkling jewel located just forty miles west. Today, Reno's tourism comes as a Reno-Tahoe package deal. A Web search for "tourism in Reno" returns to the Reno-Tahoe official tourism page. In Nevada Lake Tahoe's "South Shore" is divided between Washoe, Douglas, and Carson City counties; California's "North Shore" is divided between Placer and El Dorado Counties. A website that aims to aid travelers in deciding between the two shores describes the Nevada side as an entertainment hot spot:

> South Shore, the Nevada side, brings the carefree, have fun and forget yourself attitude that the state is famous for. With plenty of casinos, liquor stores, restaurants, arcades, shows and entertainment easily found. South Shore invites those who want to have a lot to do and a lot of excitement." The Californian North Shore, in contrast, is promoted for its scenery: ". . . North Shore is all

about keeping calm and enjoying the solitude the lake has to offer. Many Californians and long time vacation homeowners visit North Shore and soak up the lack of the excitement and lights present just down the street. . . ."[20]

The artful attempt to combine nature with the pursuit of pleasure is not working as effectively as Reno's promoters might hope. A 2011 winter survey of the South Shore revealed that the California side was doing better, but that South Shore tourism was more local than national. In a 2010 meeting sponsored by the Tahoe Douglas Visitors Authority, promoters and planners worried that their message was not getting through: "We need to capitalize to let people know how much we love this place and that they can too. Gaming is still important, but it's going through a metamorphosis. We need to broaden our appeal beyond skiing and gaming."[21] Despite an ambitious program to turn the Truckee River into a whitewater park, its downtown still looks tired and tattered. Remaking its image will not be easy because Las Vegas holds an unchallengeable position as America's playground. What goes on in Reno does not necessarily stay in Reno; a lot of it has moved to Las Vegas.

Las Vegas: From Flyblown Crossroads to Fantasy City

Las Vegas has long been promoted as a pleasure paradise. Comedian Lewis Black extols the devilish pleasures of the city: "The reason you should go to Las Vegas is because, for only the second time, the second time, ever, they have rebuilt Sodom and Gomorrah. It's back!! And you have the opportunity to see it before it turns to salt." Writer Chuck Palahniuk has said that Las Vegas "looks the way you might imagine heaven must look at night." Las Vegas is America's leading convention city because it seamlessly combines work with play. An experiment in the 1990s aimed to make the city family friendly, but its failure resulted in an unapologetic reversion to form. The MGM Grand, which began promoting a "Wizard of Oz" theme in 1993, quickly removed any signs of Dorothy and her friends. Families may, and do, bring their children with them on a Las Vegas vacation, and all of them may find wholesome fun, but wholesome is not the city's main draw.

Las Vegas sprang up as a rest stop on the Old Spanish Trail, lending a brief respite to travelers on their way to California. Until well into the twentieth century it remained little more than a flyblown crossroads. After passing through many hands, the rights to the site were sold in 1902 to Montana senator William Clark, who had a long-standing intention of building a railroad that would join the Union Pacific mainline in Utah with Southern

California. When his endeavor proved successful, Las Vegas solidified its status as a stopover for passing travelers.[22] A cluster of clubs sprang up to provide entertainment for the train's passengers, and the two blocks near the station became the city's red-light district. When it became clear that the city could not rely solely on the business generated by the most raucous of the train's passengers, local entrepreneurs began promoting spas and entertainment. In 1924 a dude ranch was built to attract vacationers and divorcées, construction began on a resort near town, lakes were dug for boating and swimming, and the city's first golf course began taking shape. In the late 1920s local boosters managed to persuade the state to finance a highway to make the city more accessible to Californians. And, finally, the legalization of casino gambling in 1931 vastly improved the city's prospects.

Las Vegas's decisive turning points came with the building of the Hoover Dam and the onset of World War II. The origins of the dam can be traced to California's insatiable demand for water and power and the New Deal's interest in building reclamation and hydroelectric projects throughout the West. During its construction the Hoover Dam quickly became a man-made equivalent to a wonder of nature, and tourists flocked by the thousands to see the newest engineering marvel and release their "pent up desires for travel and entertainment to erase the memories of the 'hard years.'" The tourist onslaught necessitated accommodations and recreation, both of which could be found only in Las Vegas. By 1945 air-conditioning had been installed in every casino, hotel, restaurant, and entertainment venue, this at a time when whole-building cooling systems were almost unknown. Through the years a willingness to experiment has been the city's secret to success. Las Vegas's constant renewal and innovation have allowed it to prosper: "Like a chameleon, [Las Vegas] has been able to change colors as the need arose: beginning as a ranch area, it became a railroad town, and then a dam getaway, then a recreation center for troops and defense workers, and now a Mecca for world tourism."[23]

Las Vegas has been hailed as "the first city of the twenty-first century, the place where desire meets capital, where instinct replaces restraint, where the future of a society . . . takes a form that had been inconceivable even a generation before."[24] The city's population in 2010 was still a modest 584,000, but it seemed much larger because it received more than 39 million visitors in the same year. The hotel occupancy rate of 85 percent is more than twenty points above the national average.[25] And the future looks bright: Clark County's gaming revenue increased from $369,286,977 in 1970 to $9,222,906,000 in 2011.[26]

From 2007 to 2011 surveys showed that people visited Las Vegas primarily to vacation, gamble, or attend a convention or corporate meeting. The pleasures of Las Vegas make up a brand of tourism that does not fit the traditional western script. Stunning landscapes may matter elsewhere, but not in Las Vegas. The Las Vegas Official Visitor Guide website leads with "what happens in Vegas stays in Vegas" and follows by promising, "This is your town. This is your stage. Most grown up adventures start with these five words: Welcome to Fabulous Las Vegas. Sleeping is optional, but you will need a hotel room for costume changes." While travelers to the Grand Canyon may seek to *find* themselves in the vast landscape, those traveling to Las Vegas seek to *lose* themselves in a world that promotes the shucking off of inhibitions in favor of an alternate identity. Perhaps it is for this reason that Nevada has one of the highest divorce rates in the country—"quickie" chapel marriages preceded by a night of debauchery and indulgence are conveniently easy to annul in the morning.

Salt Lake City, Skiing, and the Games

Salt Lake City is the anchor city in the four-county Wasatch Front metropolitan area and serves as the government, commercial, and industrial center for Utah and much of the Intermountain West. It is also the regional center of banking and finance and the largest retail and wholesale market in Utah.[27] Salt Lake's tourism industry is based largely on skiing. Eight ski resorts are located within a radius of fifty miles, and the number of skiers has increased nearly 29 percent since the 2002 Winter Olympics.

Numerous studies have examined the impact of the Games on Utah's economy, and most of them have reached the conclusion that the Games did not significantly alter the state's economic landscape. Although the Olympic venues remain in use today, they are losing rather than generating income. Home owners who thought they could make a killing by renting out their homes to tourists did not, and public financial support for maintaining the facilities has fallen in the wake of a weak economy. If the Games did not directly bring significant economic growth, what *did* they do for Utah? In an interview former governor Mike Leavitt asserted the Winter Games gave the state a brand. In his words, "'I traveled a great deal as governor and before the Olympics I would have to explain where Utah was. After the games I would just say: Utah, you remember the 2002 Winter Olympic Games—Oh, Yes. I remember.' We were now identified with this powerful symbol and people had something that set us apart."[28]

Establishing a brand is critical to tourism, and skiing seems to have worked for Utah. Tourism spending in Utah has gone up $2 billion since the 2002 Games. Delta added an international flight from Salt Lake City to Paris. The Games globalized the state by attracting investment from world-renowned hotel chains, federal funds for the construction of rail and high-way transport, and investment from foreign and domestic sports companies (for example, Amer Sports, Hart Ski, and Smith Optics are now located in Ogden). The president of Amer Sports Americas eagerly stated, "Before the Olympics, they thought of Colorado when they thought of North American skiing. The Olympics changed that. When the time came [to pick a North American site], they were familiar and comfortable with Utah."[29] A decade after the Olympics, Utah's ski industry sold 42 percent more lift tickets than it had a ten years before. Since the Olympics, the number of foreign and US visitors to Utah grew from 17.3 million to 20.2 million in 2010.

For all this success, there are far fewer skiers on the slopes of Utah than in Colorado, even when one accounts for the differences in the states' popula-tions. As of the 2010–11 winter season, there were twenty-nine ski areas in Colorado but only fifteen in Utah.[30] In 2011 the state of Utah recorded 4.22 million skier days, which generated direct expenditures of $1.2 billion. By contrast, in the same year Vail resorts in Colorado reported 5.33 million skier days. In an attempt to improve its numbers in January 2012, the Utah Office of Tourism launched a $1.2 million advertising campaign in New York and Los Angeles designed to persuade skiers that Utah's powder is better than the snow in Colorado or anywhere else. Utah, it promised, has the "Greatest Snow on Earth."[31]

One of Utah's disadvantages is that skiing is the main activity, and the off-season is not as well developed as in Colorado. Colorado resorts are not only premier ski destinations; places such as Aspen, Telluride, and Crested Butte also attract a large number of hikers, climbers, mountain bikers, and fly fish-ermen in other seasons, and summer residents choose among any number of haute cuisine restaurants, festivals, and entertainment events. Utah's resorts are also premier ski destinations, but only Park City and nearby Sundance, the site of the annual Sundance Film Festival, have a lot to offer the rest of the year.

Boise's Favorable Press

Anyone aware of Boise's past would have concluded it was an unlikely candidate for tourism. Early in the twentieth century it established itself as a regional center for the prosperous agricultural region that runs along the floodplain of the Snake River, and until late century it remained a modest and attractive small city, charming but hardly exciting. Today, its most promising asset is a downtown containing an eclectic and unusual mix of architectural styles dating back to the city's nineteenth- and early-twentieth-century origins. The terra cotta, sandstone, limestone, and granite-faced buildings displayed a fascination, at different periods, with turrets and mansard roofs, Romanesque and classical Revival, Art Deco, and even, in one case, with what some might call Egyptian Revival.[32] If this assemblage had been left in place, it would undoubtedly constitute one of the most interesting and complete architectural collections of any city in the American West.

Unfortunately, in the 1970s the city's civic leaders fell into a late love affair with urban renewal clearance even after it had been discredited everywhere else. By 1974 Boise's ambitious program of demolition was so successful that *Harper's* pronounced it "the first American city to have deliberately eradicated itself." The plan to construct a huge mall to shore up Boise's place as a regional center came to a sad end that left unsightly buildings and weed-filled lots. Over the years the downtown has been reconstructed, and it is generally inviting, thanks mainly to the stone buildings that survived the wrecking ball and a skillful blend of public spaces and urban amenities. Even so, in 2010 a reporter noted that "downtown Boise gives the impression that it has recently been visited by an exceedingly tidy bombing raid conducted by planes that cleaned up after themselves."[33]

Despite this regrettable legacy, tourism has become a multimillion-dollar industry in Boise, and the city has attracted an outpouring of attention from national and international publications as a city offering an exceptional quality of life. Albertsons, Morrison-Knudsen Construction, Ore-Ida Foods, Micron Technology, and the Hewlett-Packard printing division were all located in the metropolitan area in the 1990s, and the presence of so many corporate headquarters transformed the city into a magnet for young people working in managerial and high-tech services. Despite the fact that all of them except Micron left over the next decade, Boise's population continued to grow, in part because outdoor recreation provides a foundation for a distinctive western lifestyle revolving around a high level of urban amenities and outdoor pursuits.

For at least two decades Boise has benefited from an admiring and even fawning press coverage. It has been put at or near the top of the list as a "best city" for, among many other things, raising kids, pursuing business careers, and retiring; it has also been called a top turnaround city, a most physically active city, a top music city, a most inventive city, a top undiscovered market, a top "super city of the future," an exceptionally healthy city—and the "top city" lists go on and on. The praise has been heaped upon the city from a wide range of publications with national and international reach: *Time*, the *Wall Street Journal, USA Today, Forbes, CNN Money, Sports Illustrated, National Geographic Adventure, Parenting,* and *Kiplinger's Personal Finance.*

The flood of favorable press has served the city well, but Boise's ability to attract visitors is probably due more to the local corporate-employee presence than to the city's attractiveness as a tourist destination. In 1959 civic leaders pushed for the formation of an auditorium district and the construction of several meeting and event centers. Little came of these early efforts; indeed, in 1976 the city's tourism bureau was still financed by a minuscule budget and run by a single employee. By 1982 the bureau, now working under the direction of the Boise Chamber of Commerce, hired several more employees, and plans were put in place to build the Boise State Pavilion arena, the Velma V. Morrison Center for Performing Arts, and a convention center. The newly formed Idaho Travel Council promised a modest amount of funding to the city, and the convention bureau took the official title of the Boise Convention and Visitors Bureau. After printing brochures and using the scraps for business cards, the bureau made a concerted effort to document the city's assets in photos. The combination of marketing and new infrastructure bore fruit. In the 1980s the bureau brought visitors to the city for a rally, resulting in an estimated ten-million-dollar gain for the city's economy. Boise went on to host the National Governors Conference, the US Cycling Championships, the Special Olympics World Winter Games, and the Iron Man 70.3 triathlon, among other events.

Most of the city's efforts have been focused on selling Boise as an event destination, as revealed in the slogan "If you believe you can bring an event to Boise, you can bring that event to Boise." For the most part it appears that tourism, broadly defined, is a by-product of event attendance. It is doubtful that Boise is a destination for many visitors coming from beyond the region, and the bureau seems to recognize this fact. Today, the Boise Convention and Visitors Bureau boasts, "Boise is many things. Urban and outdoorsy.

Wild and relaxing. Friendly and unforgettable. You can explore it all here. Plan a meeting. Prepare your visit." The "Professionals: Meetings + Tour + Sports" tab, for instance, is placed ahead of "Visitors."

Constructing a Regional Identity

Outside its four major cities the Great Basin lacks a tourist script because as a geographic and ecological entity, it has yet to find a comfortable place in the popular imagination. The desert outback does not fulfill the expectations most people have when they go west for relaxation and fun, and the cities on the Basin's rim are so different from one another that they do not fit a consistent tourist profile. For a lot of visitors, the landscape beyond the urban bubble looks like a wasteland. Many of the people who live in the Great Basin learn to love the desert for its stark landscapes, serenity, and solitude. A photographer specializing in Great Basin and Nevada photography captions one of his photographs, taken in Nevada in winter, with this observation: "There's beauty in the fine details of jack frost, clear cold air and the endless horizons of the Great Basin."[34] Those who appreciate desolation find it to be endlessly fascinating.

It is possible that in the years ahead the isolation and emptiness of the desert may come to be regarded as more virtue than vice. In the case of Reno and, to a lesser extent, Salt Lake City, some of the recent growth can be attributed to the influx of Californians seeking "spiritual rehab": "Feeling swamped by the size of California's cities, they feel that they can invest more easily in Salt Lake or Reno and can have a hand in making them their own."[35] But there is a danger that urban growth will reincarnate the very thing that people have been trying to escape. The threat comes from two directions: the metropolitan areas of the Basin are growing, and as they do so they are likely to impact the desert ecosystems that stretch beyond the urban boundaries. Tourism and recreation use resources at a prodigious rate; this, after all, is why Las Vegas continues to grow and why it needs so much water. Consider that a group of four people playing a round of eighteen holes of golf on a Las Vegas course will use the same quantity of water as the average American family uses *in a month*.[36] The costs of using water on this scale are everywhere apparent. In 2009 workers blasted through the limestone surrounding the reservoir next to Lake Mead, which supplies 90 percent of Las Vegas's water. Battling the worst ten-year drought in history, the crew hurried to lay new pipe because another one, which supplies 40 percent of the city's water, was in danger of being left dry by the falling water line. Contractors are currently laying the pipeline to access the bottom of Lake Mead to keep the water flowing even if the lake's surface continues to fall.[37]

Because so much of the Great Basin is in public land, much of it seems remarkably unspoiled, and a growing number of people living in the Basin cities want to keep it that way.[38] Urban residents are demanding a voice in environmental and resource policies that impact the thinly populated reaches of the desert.[39] Preserving this fragile desert will not be easy. In 1889 Rudyard Kipling traveled up the Pacific Coast; in his *American Notes* (1891), he celebrated the splendid scenery and the open vistas, but also complained of westerners' fatal attraction to materialism and the eagerness to sell off natural resources in exchange for profit and progress. The Basin has not been immune to such temptations.

Although the Great Basin is not likely to shed its image as "America's resolutely unblooming wasteland," it may yet manage to burrow into the American imagination.[40] The website for the Great Basin National Heritage Area captures both the drawbacks and the advantages of the desert in this disarming appraisal:

A visit to the Great Basin National Heritage Area is all about the scenery and the other heritage feature [Lehmann Caves]. Expect a beautiful dark night sky full of stars. Expect spectacular sunrises and sunsets. Expect long vistas of more than 60 miles punctuated by jutting mountains and broad valleys. Expect a spiritual experience that helps you define your place, not only in the world, but in the universe. Expect friendly people and clean, reasonable priced accommodations. Do not expect a plethora of upscale hotels, franchise restaurants or gourmet foods. Do not expect frequent gas stations, rest stops or mechanical services. Expect to be enchanted and expect to look forward to your next return.[41]

The interesting question is whether these qualities will survive the urbanization taking place on the Basin's rim. It is a fragile desert, and it is now called upon to sustain both the natural environment that gives it a unique identity and the cities that provide people easy access to it. Writer Tim Sullivan has observed, "Great cities are possible here. They'd better be."[42] Whether great cities can coexist with a desert so easily harmed by the hand of man is another matter entirely.

NOTES

1. Hal K. Rothman, *Devil's Bargains: Tourism in the Twentieth-Century American West* (Lawrence: University Press of Kansas, 1998), 32.

2. Great Basin National Park, "What Is the Great Basin?," http://greatbasin.areaparks.com/parkinfo.html?pid=13111.

3. Elizabeth Raymond, "When the Desert Won't Bloom: Environmental Limitation and the Great Basin," in *Many Wests: Place, Culture, and Regional Identity,* edited by David M. Wrobel and Michael C. Steiner (Lawrence: University Press of Kansas, 1997), 71.

4. Ibid., 75; Soren Larsen and Timothy Brock, "Great Basin Imagery in Newspaper Coverage of Yucca Mountain," *Geographical Review* 95, no. 4 (2006): 517.

5. Rothman, *Devil's Bargains,* 32, 40.

6. David M. Wrobel, *Promised Lands: Promotion, Memory, and the Creation of the American West* (Lawrence: University Press of Kansas, 2001), 29.

7. Carlos A. Schwantes, "No Aid and No Comfort: Early Transportation and the Origins of Tourism in the Northern West," in *Seeing and Being Seen: Tourism in the American West,* edited by David M. Wrobel and Patrick T. Long (Lawrence: published for the Center of the American West, University of Colorado at Boulder, by the University Press of Kansas, 2001), 227–47.

8. Leah Dilworth, "Tourists and Indians in Fred Harvey's Southwest," in ibid., 146, 158.

9. Stephen J. Pyne, *How the Canyon Became Grand* (New York: Penguin, 1998), 23, 115, 116.

10. Paul Schullery, "Privations and Inconveniences: Early Tourism in Yellowstone National Park," in *Seeing and Being Seen,* edited by Wrobel and Long, 227.

11. Ibid., 28.

12. Rothman, *Devil's Bargains,* 143.

13. Tim Sullivan, *No Communication with the Sea: Searching for an Urban Future in the Great Basin* (Tucson: University of Arizona Press, 2010), xiii.

14. Great Basin Business and Tourism Council, "Great Basin National Park," http://www.greatbasinpark.com/gb_national_park.htm; Richard Francaviglia, *Believing in Place: A Spiritual Geography of the Great Basin* (Reno: University of Nevada Press, 2003), 18.

15. Brad Wieners, "Hot Mess," *Outside,* August 24, 2012, http://www.outsideonline.com/outdoor-adventure/events/Hot-Mess.html.

16. Sullivan, *No Communication with the Sea,* 26, 27.

17. Alicia Barber, *Reno's Big Gamble: Image and Reputation in the Biggest Little City* (Lawrence: University Press of Kansas, 2008), 13, 14.

18. Ibid., 21.

19. Ibid., 137, 127, 136.

20. Eric Morgan, "Lake Tahoe—North Shore Versus South Shore," *Articles Base*, February 7, 2008, http://www.articlesbase.com/sports-and-fitness-articles/lake -tahoe-north-shore-versus-south-shore-326880.html.

21. Lake Tahoe Visitors Authority, "South Shore Intercept Survey" (Winter 2011), 5–7, http://tahoesouth.com/ltva/LTVA.org/Winter_Intercept_Survey_2011 .pdf; Kathryn Reed, "Bleak Numbers Force Tourism Officials to Rethink Message," *Lake Tahoe News*, March 9, 2012, http://www.laketahoenews.net/2010/03 /bleak-numbers-force-tourism-officials-to-rethink-message/.

22. Michael S. Green and Eugene P. Moehring, *Las Vegas: A Centennial History* (Reno: University of Nevada Press, 2005), 1.

23. Ibid., 106, 249.

24. Rothman, *Devil's Bargains*, xi.

25. Rossi Ralenkotter, "The State of Las Vegas Tourism," *Las Vegas Review Journal*, December 4, 2011, http://www.lvrj.com/opinion/the-state-of-las-vegas-tour ism-134985353.html.

26. Las Vegas Convention and Visitors Authority, "Historical Las Vegas Visitor Statistics (1971–2011)," http://www.lvcva.com/getfile/80/Historical%201970%20 to%202011.pdf.

27. City Data, "Salt Lake City: Economy," http://www.city-data.com/us-cities /The-West/Salt-Lake-City-Economy.html.

28. Andrea Smardon, "Utah's Olympic Legacy: The Impact of the 2002 Winter Games. Part Two: How the Games Affected Utah's Economy," KUER *Local News*, February 14, 2012, http://www.kuer.org/post/utahs-olympic-legacy-impact -2002-winter-games-part-two-how-games-affected-utahs-economy.

29. Mike Gorrell, "Olympics Gave Utah a Five-Ring Economic Boost," *Salt Lake Tribune*, February 20, 2012, http://www.sltrib.com/sltrib/money/53506266-79 /utah-ski-olympics-salt.html.csp.

30. National Ski Areas Association Press Release, September 1, 2011, http://www. nsaa.org/nsaa/press/sa-per-state.pdf.

31. Visit Utah Official Tourism Website, "Utah Winter Ads Debut in New York and Los Angeles," January 5, 2012, http://www.visitutah.com/articles/view /Utah-Winter-Ads-Debut-in-New-York-and-Los-Angeles/101/.

32. For an enlightening tour of Boise's architecture, see Charles Hummel, Tim Woodward, and Jeanne Huff, *Quintessential Boise: An Architectural Journey* (Boise, ID: Boise State University, College of Social Sciences and Public Affairs, n.d.).

33. John Reuter, "Razed and Confused: Boise's Turbulent History of Urban Renewal," *Boise Weekly*, August 4, 2010, http://www.boiseweekly.com/boise /razed-and-confused-boises-turbulent-history-of-urban-renewalContent?oid =1713334.

34. Taken from Mike Sevon Photos, specializing in "fine images of Nevada and the Great Basin." http://www.mikesevonphotos.com/great-basin-landscapes.

35. Sullivan, *No Communication with the Sea*, 26.

36. Charles Fishman, "The Big Thirst: Nothing's Quite So Thirsty as a Las Vegas Golf Course," Fast Company, April 25, 2011, http://www.fastcompany.com/1749643 /the-big-thirst-nothing-s-quite-so-thirsty-as-a-las-vegas-golf-course.

37. Henry Brean, "Concrete Work at Lake Mead Resumes After Windy Day," *Las Vegas Review-Journal,* March 7, 2012, http://www.lvrj.com/news/concrete-work-at -lake-mead-resumes-after-windy-day-141841383.html.

38. See "The Fragile Desert: Managing the Great Basin's Environmental Crisis," this volume.

39. Paul F. Starrs and John B. Wright, "Great Basin Growth and the Withering of California's Pacific Idyll," *American Geographical Society* 85, no. 4 (1995): 434, http//:wwwjstor.org/stable/215918.

40. Raymond, "When the Desert Won't Bloom," 86.

41. "The Great Basin National Heritage Area: Travel Information," http://www .greatbasinheritage.org/great-basin-travel-information.html.

42. Sullivan, *No Communication with the Sea,* xiii.

The Cities on the Rim

Constructing the "Quality of Life" City

"Boise Is Best"

ERIN DAINA McCLELLAN

BOISE HAS BEEN AWARDED many accolades in city rankings over the past decade. Between 2004 and 2012, Boise has appeared on lists that deem it a top healthy city; a top music city; a top turnaround town; a great place for paddling; a top adventure town; a best place to retire; a most physically active city; a most underrated city; a top college football town; a top city for green building; a top bike-friendly city; a best city for raising kids; a best city for business, careers, and economic growth; a most inventive city; a top undiscovered market; a top "super city of the future"; a "Sportstown USA"; and a best city to live, work, and play. In addition, it has been said to have some of the nation's best urban parks, workplaces for commuters, and carbon footprint. The sources of these rankings range from *Time*, the *Wall Street Journal*, *USA Today*, *Forbes*, *CNN Money*, and *MSN* to *Sports Illustrated*, *National Geographic Adventure*, *Parenting*, and *Kiplinger's Personal Finance*.[1] Each of the rankings may be read as a "text" reflecting a *discourse*[2] that shapes the ways people come to know Boise. Whether people have never seen Boise or whether they have lived in Boise their whole lives, these texts guide everyone to see the city as having some attributes that are deemed more important than others. Quality-of-life discourses, in particular, have become ways of reflecting what desirable cities should entail; such discourses presented Boise in glowing terms.

A closer examination of what Boise "is" according to these top-ten lists reveals a lot not only about the city, but also about how "best" is constructed. Demographic and economic statistics show Boise to be successful, in part, because increased growth is most frequently interpreted as an unalloyed virtue for all cities and urban areas. Other statistics meant to measure various aspects of quality of life (for example, percentage of population over the age of fifty as an indicator of "best place to retire") and specific economic performance (for example, job growth) attempt to reflect success in other terms. Some of these "best" rankings rely upon sets of previously collected data such as the US Census Bureau, while others use complicated indexes that give an impression of scientific sophistication and objectivity. Despite the range of methodologies used to rank "best cities," Boise consistently does well when compared to other cities and metropolitan areas. However, there is more to measuring quality of life than just results.

In this chapter I first examine the discourse constructing Boise as "best" as it is revealed through best-city rankings that feature Boise, Idaho, and appear in four leading publications. In relation to one another, these sources provide a remarkably consistent portrait of Boise as a city offering an exceptional quality of life, though not for the same reasons. I then provide a rhetorical analysis of these texts as a way to explain how particular values and motivations are embedded in these rankings. My reading of these four texts reveals how these "best" city rankings simultaneously shape their readers' conceptions of what is best about Boise, in particular, while simultaneously contributing to larger discourses about what makes cities have a high quality of life more generally. Finally, I discuss the need to move beyond the recognizable discourse of quality of life in Boise in order to question the ways in which such a discourse influences our understandings of cities like Boise in significant ways. As illustrated across the texts included in this discourse about how Boise is "best," the subjective and value-laden measures of evaluating a city have tangible consequences—both positive and negative. The cities included (and excluded) in such rankings and the diverse people they account for will inevitably interpret the significance of these constructions of a "successful" city differently. It is worthy of our time to critically assess how this happens if we are to productively address the diverse needs of any urban population.

"Boise's Best" . . . Retirement and Child-Rearing, Working and Playing?

For many years Boise's mayor has been fond of citing acclamatory comments from city rankings sources in his annual State of the City address. Between 2004 and 2012 the summary from these State of the City addresses has boasted that Boise is (among other things), the best city to retire; the best city for raising a family; the best city to live, work, and play; and the best place for business. A close examination of four specific texts that represent each of these four types of rankings that were included in the mayor's annual State of the City address summaries can provide insight into how Boise is portrayed differently in each as a "successful" city.

Text 1: The Best City to Retire

In 2011 *CNN Money* ranked Boise number three of twenty-five "best" cities to retire, under the caption "Each of these towns offers amenities galore for the post-work crowd—plus a cost of living that's pretty darn sweet." Boise's "City Stats" are compared to the "Best Places Average" and include several statistical indicators: median annual family income, job growth percentage (2000–2010), percentage of test scores above and below state average in reading and math, personal and property crime incidents, restaurants within fifteen miles, high and low temperatures in July, median age, and a variety of other financial, housing, school, and quality-of-life indicators, such as the percentage of population over the age of fifty, median home price, top state income tax (with a notation that Social Security income is exempt in Idaho), and a cost of living index.

This collection of statistical information appears alongside an aerial shot looking northward down tree-lined Capitol Boulevard, with the capitol building as the dominating and central feature. The accompanying text addresses a topic that seems entirely detached from the numbers: "If you're the type who can't survive without your symphony, art, and theater fix, you may have resigned yourself to staying in some pricey coastal burg during retirement. . . . Boise is no Manhattan. But its thriving cultural scene includes an opera company, a philharmonic orchestra, and a ballet. . . . Catch shows at Boise State University's Morrison Center for the Performing Arts. . . . Or hit the annual Shakespeare Festival at the city's 770-seat outdoor amphitheater." The last two sentences of this mini-essay change the subject yet again with a reference to the city's natural setting—"Residents also enjoy all the outdoor activities you might expect of a city that's flanked by mountains and bisected by a river full of fish"—and with an anecdotal reflection: "Another plus: Violent crime in Boise is a little more than half the national average."

Text 2: The Best City for Raising a Family

In 2012, *Forbes* listed the Boise metropolitan area as the second "best city for raising a family." The authors compared the one hundred largest metropolitan areas by "median income, overall cost of living, commuting delays, crime statistics, school quality, and housing affordability," while also referring to "low crime and high school quality" and the "chance to mix urban and outdoor lifestyles" as additional positive attributes. A statistical profile of Boise "at a glance" displays a map along with a dizzying array of metropolitan statistics on major industries (namely, technology, tourism, mining, farming), metro product growth, median annual household income, median home price, unemployment percentage, job growth percentage (2010), cost of living percentage above and below the national average, percentage of population with "college attainment," and net migration (2010). Finally, the reader is given the opportunity to see Boise's ranking on other *Forbes* lists published in the magazine. These reveal that Boise is ranked number eighteen among best places for business and careers, number eight in the cost of doing business, number seventy-one in job growth, and number ninety-eight in education. The plethora of data makes for daunting reading, but a sharp eye might immediately notice that the tangential reference to Boise's education ranking does not seem to align with the in-text reference to Boise's "high school quality."

The eclectic mix of indicators used by *Forbes* indicates that an extraordinary number of things determine whether a city is friendly for families. As one would expect, economic growth and development are important: "The high-tech industry has become increasingly important to Boise over the years, though the economy remains diversified with its government and business sectors continuing to be strong influences." A list of "key companies," statistics on employment, and a roster of college and university campuses seem to support this point. But a host of other factors are also brought into the equation; for example, there are statistics on housing, education, and a quality-of-life index. However, the authors also provide a list of museums, take note of Boise's annual jazz festival, and comment on the "vibrant section known as the 'Basque Block' [which is] representative of the second largest ethnic Basque community in the U.S." No clarity is offered about what "raising a family" entails, and no recognition of the varied ways that people might choose among countless criteria that make a city a good place to raise one is provided.

Text 3: The Best City to Live, Work, and Play

In 2008 *Kiplinger's Personal Finance* published a list of the top-ten "best cities to live, work, and play." Boise landed a number-four spot. The article framed its criteria for selection by explaining the authors' approach as follows: "[We] look for places with strong economies and abundant jobs, then demand reasonable living costs and plenty of fun things to do." The article discloses that their "numbers guru" applied a "formula [that] highlights cities not just for strong past performance, but also with all the ingredients for future success." The key ingredients of the formula were identified as "a healthy shot of people in the creative class . . . scientists, engineers, architects, educators, writers, artists and entertainers, as they are catalysts of vitality and livability in a city."

According to *Kiplinger's*, several statistical measures were used to determine its ranking; among others, these included metropolitan area population, population growth percentage since 2000, percentage of workforce in the creative class, cost of living index in relation to the national average, median annual household income, and percentage of income growth since 2000. However, these "just the facts" statistics appear next to a stylized Boise Convention and Visitors Bureau photograph of the downtown skyline under white puffy clouds and an azure sky and silhouetted against the shadowed foothills in the background. The article's author admits to "an almost irresistible temptation to desert your desk. Glance northward from the city's orderly downtown business and shopping district, and the majestic slopes of the Boise foothills beckon."

One of the qualities that receives a clear focus in this discussion of "best" cities is the ability to "balance" everyday life, work, and play: "When they're not casting a line or taking in a show, a growing number of Boisians work for local high-tech businesses, the fruits of which make up the state's biggest exports. Micron Technology and Hewlett-Packard are the Boise Valley's two largest employers." The city's economic prospects are boosted by a "high proportion of college graduates . . . 37% compared with the national average of 27%," "plenty of affordable housing," and an "average work commute" of eighteen minutes. A retired high-tech executive is quoted as providing this advice: "When you first arrive, you have to downshift and adjust to a more relaxed pace." Intentionally or unintentionally, the message conveyed in this vignette appears to mix three particular elements of an idealized lifestyle: urban life portrayed in ways that may be seen to reflect suburban ideals, a place where work is both profitable and flexible, and a place worthy of eventual retirement.

Text 4: Best City for Business

In 2004 *Forbes.com* produced a special report that revealed Boise to be the seventh "best place for business" in the nation, explaining, "The best metro areas to launch a business or career often revolve around universities that offer a diverse, educated work force and, especially when they are far from big cities, relatively low costs." A link to more information about the methodology used to determine the rankings is provided, and a separate set of links provides alternative ways to sort "best" cities in a variety of ways (by rank, name, cost of doing business, and population). The article explains that the ranking partially relies on an index of "business cost" developed by an economic and financial firm located in West Chester, Pennsylvania. The indicators in the index include a measure of the quality of the work-force (the "concentration of college graduates and PhDs in an area") plus job and income growth and migration data. In addition, an index created by a Portland, Oregon, consultant is utilized to measure "culture and leisure" across cities.

The statistical profile of Boise includes the usual indicators: population of the city and metropolitan area, percentage of job growth (with no indication of source or date), income growth (also with no reference for source or date), and a list of the major employers (Micron Technology, Mountain Home Air Force Base, St. Luke's Regional Medical Center, Albertsons, and Hewlett-Packard). A two-sentence description of Boise's limitations is provided as a testament to its draw in spite of them: "While not exactly a transportation hub, Boise continues to attract people from all over the nation thanks to low costs and job growth that has risen more than three times the national aver-age during the past five years." A link provides access to a more detailed pro-file and key statistics (advanced degrees, cost of doing business, cost of liv-ing, crime rates, culture and leisure, educational attainment, income growth, job growth, and net migration). A photo featuring the downtown skyline is sandwiched between a row of green trees in the foreground and the notable foothills in the background.

A Rhetorical "Read" of Boise: A Best City for Everything?

A rhetorical read of the four texts that rank Boise as a "best" city—*CNN Mon-ey's* "best place to retire," *Forbes's* "best city for raising a family," *Kiplinger's Personal Finance's* "best city to live, work, and play," and *Forbes.com's* "best place for business"—reveals a larger discourse that presents an idealized ver-sion of Boise. Although this discourse is often interpreted as an objective and complete representation of Boise as a successful city, these texts also con-struct a particular vision of what an "ideal" Boise entails.

Throughout American urban history local boosters have promoted growth as evidence that a given city is prosperous, desirable, and destined for great things. All four of the texts analyzed here treat a "successful" city in the same way. *Kiplinger's* refers to "migration patterns" as an indicator of a "best places to live, work, and play," and all four texts offer a variety of direct and indirect measures of growth. As a western metropolitan area that began to undergo rapid development and growth only in the 1980s, the Boise metropolitan area appears favorably when measured using indicators of growth, and unsurprisingly being conclusively ranked as "successful."

Boise's status as a city is often determined using loose-fitting terms. Although many cities serve as the center of an urban region, or the region as a whole, Boise is often measured using statistics that represent a very expansive notion of metropolitan area. A lack of standardization for how to measure what qualifies as a city across these various texts accounts for large variations in reported population and other statistical representations of Boise. The *Forbes.com* article on "best cities for raising families," for example, compares Boise with cities that are not comparable in size, including New York City and Chicago. All four texts also imply or explicitly state that one of Boise's great virtues is that it offers cultural opportunities and urban amenities traditionally associated with life in these historical urban centers. Thus, the existence of a jazz festival or a single opera company discussed as vibrant "culture" may seem far-fetched, but their mere presence affords seekers of culture something to discover. In these ways Boise's relatively new status and small size in comparison to places such as New York City and Chicago enable it to be measured as either large or small, depending upon how one crunches the numbers, interprets convenience, or otherwise assesses how statistical representations are indicative of "successful" urban life.

Because those who craft (and read) these texts are free to reach a variety of conclusions, there is no resulting universally accepted "truth" about which city is "best" for any of these measures. Arrays of statistics serve an important symbolic and legitimating function, but in the form of a larger discourse these texts combine to create how "best" cities are able to be imagined in particular terms of success. Thus, how people *use* these rankings to justify a given city's association with "best" is a more significant testament to the influence of such rankings than the legitimation of their statistical determination. In the examples provided here, statistics often blend seamlessly with various other attempts to promote a city as ideal. Many times such constructions of ideal simultaneously reflect the values and needs associated primarily with upper-middle-class interests. For example, *Kiplinger's* asserts that the "key to a bright future is a healthy shot of people in the creative class . . . scientists, engineers, architects, educators, writers, artists and entertainers [as] catalysts of vitality and livability in a city." *CNN Money* claims, "If you're the type who can't survive without symphony, art, and theater," Boise is your place to retire. *Forbes* considers a city good if it has qualities such as "bike friendliness, club scene, and coffee houses" as well as "school quality . . . [high] median income levels, housing affordability, and [a lack of] commuting hassles." Each of these descriptions—"a diverse, educated workforce," "a healthy shot of people in the creative class," and enough "arts and culture"—are indeed common ways people characterize quality of life; however, they are notoriously also associated with privilege and associated with what some scholars have discussed as an affordance of the "leisure class," or those who have the ability to think about, make use of, and value particular kinds of work and leisure over others. These distinctions align with the target audiences of the publications in which they are discussed as well.

Statistics, vignettes, colorful anecdotes, personal stories, and photographic representations all serve to (re)present Boise in a particular way. The authors of these texts make choices (albeit not entirely independent of the institutions responsible for printing and disseminating their finished product) about how to present each city in their ranking as legitimately deserving of that ranking. Decisions about editing of layout, naming and language choices, and choice of associated methodological approaches that produce such rankings do not appear in a vacuum. Each occurs in relation to larger institutional missions and value systems that drive such decisions. For example, language choices reflect ideological underpinnings and priorities that inevitably support the sources (and intended audiences) of each of the four texts analyzed here. It makes sense that *Forbes* is interested in helping its readers understand and make decisions about "successful" business, but what happens when that same logic is applied, for instance, to decisions about "successful" parenting? It is important that such associations not be overlooked as these "best city" rankings coalesce to create a larger discourse about "successful" cities that inevitably cross-pollinate logics that might not otherwise be seen to be compatible.

The qualities that come to define a city as an ideal place become so widely accepted that they are regarded as self-evident truisms. What people understand to be "true" about any city affects how that city's branding strategies, visitors and tourists, potential business investors, and residents themselves perceive urban life in that particular city. Rhetorical analysis of these four "Boise's best" ratings reveals a focus on the desires of investors along with two primary demographic groups: the creative class and retirees. There can be little doubt that these are important demographic components of a successful city, but other parts of an urban population may paint a city like Boise in an alternate light.

Complicating Boise's Quality-of-Life Discourse

What makes a city more desirable than other cities is subject to debate. Attempts to create an objective standard able to determine the universally ideal city at any moment in time are futile. When a complex object like a "city" is represented through value-laden judgments like "best" that are veiled in objective, factual accounting measures, a larger consequence looms. When a city is continually (re)presented as "best," particular measures of "success" are privileged in the ways that such a judgment is determined. Alternate indicators of success, however, often become invisible when conversations about "best" cities fail to resonate with particular portions of urban populations. Since metropolitan areas carry with them diverse populations, it is not difficult to see how the target audiences of these rankings' sources may not align equally with all members of an urban population.

When it comes to objectively explaining things like the "best" way to raise a family, one would imagine there are many different ways that such a judgment would utilize indicators of "best" despite the claim that *Parenting* makes about the seemingly uncomplicated nature of the ideal place in which to raise one. While Boise is presented as a "best" place to raise a family by *Parenting* in a way that seems to neatly align with the interests of their largely middle- and upper-middle-class readership, statistics about Boise and the state of Idaho may not be interpreted as desirable by that same demographic. For example, the overall welfare of children has been measured in the state of Idaho as twentieth among the fifty states in overall child well-being, forty-fifth in preschool attendance, and forty-third in the percentage of children covered by health insurance.[3] Idaho appears in the bottom tier of states in requirements for physical education in schools and appropriates only 5.2 percent of the Centers for Disease Control's recommended expenditures for tobacco prevention.[4] And in terms of education, the state of Idaho ranks an abysmal forty-fifth in spending per capita. Other statistics for the Boise metropolitan area also show that it may be lagging in areas related to quality of life. For instance, efforts at constructing extensive bike lanes in the downtown core were deemed a failure, and regional transportation options remain car-centric. The Boise metropolitan area reported 7,286,544 annual passenger miles on public transit in 2009 (in comparison, the annual passenger miles in Salt Lake City were reported to be 255,953,778 and 28,565,128 in Reno).[5] These alternate—and no less truthful—depictions of Boise do not neatly align with other quality-of-life measures that elevate Boise in the rankings. Interestingly, in larger metropolitan areas higher incomes and longer commutes are inversely related.

As this discussion has illustrated, measures of "best" cities are at once opportunistic and constraining. Although the interpretive nature of "best" is not often the focus of discussions about Boise's appearance in such rankings, the considerable (re)presentation of cities in objectively veiled rankings that attempt to produce a universal "winner" continues. It is my contention that ranking cities according to various measures of "success" has less to do with the methodologies and indicators used to determine how they are actually "best" cities, and more to do with the influence that such rankings and explanations have in shaping the larger discourses about them. In other words, when discussing "quality of life" in cities, everyone who is interested in business prospects, family life, recreational opportunities, and relocation can now, after putting these collective rankings side by side, use similar statistics to draw similar conclusions. It is thus not surprising that a city like Boise would want to collectively post these rankings together such that a variety of people can easily draw the same conclusion: Boise is indeed "best!"

As critical consumers of (re)presentations of Boise as best, we must carefully consider the possibility for alternative discourses capable of providing a different perspective about how successful urban life is imagined beyond the relatively uniform indicators provided in the texts. Although such alternative perspectives will not necessarily change the larger discourse about how Boise is best, an understanding that what is "best" for some people may be problematic for others can become recognizable to those who may otherwise blindly accept their ideal city as the ideal city for everyone. Opening up such possibility can simultaneously enable inclusion of voices that may otherwise become unrecognizable parts of the larger choir. In other words, if quality of life is, indeed, the indicator of success by which cities like Boise are attempting to aspire, it is our collective responsibility to ensure that all parts of the choir are well prepared to sing together. After all, the quality of the choir is not determined by the performance of its soprano soloist.

SELECTED SOURCES FOR CITY RATINGS

Badenhausen, K. "Special Report: Best Places for Business." *Forbes*, May 7, 2004. http://www.forbes.com/2004/05/05/05/04bestplacesland_print.html.

Bickers, A. "Boise No. 4." *Kiplinger's Personal Finance*, July 2008. http://www.kiplinger.com/features/archives/2008/05/2008-best-city-boise.html.

"Boise vs. Reno: How Are They Different?" November 14, 2010. From "Reno 2020 Series" published in the *Reno Gazette-Journal*, available starting November 16, 2010, as "Boise Is Smarter, Safer, Richer than Reno—So Which Would You Relocate To?" http://rgj.posterous.coboise-is-smarter-safer-richer-than-reno-so-wh.

"The Cities for Families: Best Cities 2010: Boise, ID." *Parenting*, 2010. http://www.parenting.com/article/Mom/Work--Family/Best-Cities-2010-Boise-ID.

Lexington. "In Praise of Boise: Why Space Really Is the Final Frontier in the Internet Age." *Economist*, May 13, 2010. http://www.economist.com/node/16112080.

Moulton, S. "Best Towns 2010: Boise, Idaho." *Outside Magazine*, August 2010. http://outsideonline.com/travel/travel-ta-idaho-boise-travel-sidwcmdev_150669.html.

Park, A. "Boise Named 5th Best City for Low Carbon Footprint by Brookings Institution." May 30, 2008. http://www.cityofboise.org/Departments/Mayor/News Releases/2008/page30376.aspx.

"25 Best Places to Retire." *CNN Money*, 2011. http://money.cnn.com/galleries/2011/real_estate/1109/gallery.best.

Van Riper, T. "The Best Cities for Raising a Family." *Forbes*, April 4, 2012. http://www.forbes.com/sites/tomvanriper/2012/04/04/the-best-cities.

NOTES

1. See selected city rankings sources, above.

2. This discourse is not simply a way of talking about the city; it is, rather, a complex collection of understandings about what we understand and treat as "urban" in any number of ways. Looking at this discourse through the lens of critical theory, particularly utilizing Foucault's notion of "discursive formation," allows a "read" of these city rankings to expose particular consequences for understanding "best of" in particular ways. In this chapter four texts, taken together, can be seen to construct a "discursive formation" of Boise as a city with an exceptional quality of life. A careful discussion of Foucault and the concept of discourse formation as it applies to this "Boise as best" discourse, however, is beyond the scope

of this particular essay. See Michel Foucault, *The Archaeology of Knowledge* (New York: Pantheon Books, 1972).

3. Annie E. Casey Foundation, "The 2012 Kids Count Data Book: State Trends in Child Well-Being," http://www.aecf.org.

4. American Cancer Society, *How Do You Measure Up? A Progress Report on State Legislative Activity to Reduce Cancer Incidence and Mortality,* 10th ed. (Washington, DC: American Cancer Society, 2012).

5. Stephanie L. Witt and James B. Weatherby, *Urban West Revisited: Governing Cities in Uncertain Times* (Boise, ID: Boise State University, 2012), 113.

The Persistent Possibility of Failure

Making Something of Nothing in Las Vegas

ELIZABETH RAYMOND

PERHAPS NO CITY IN THE UNITED STATES requires introduction less than Las Vegas. Grace of its ubiquity in popular culture, it is familiar to most Americans, even those who have never visited it. Among the four Great Basin edge cities, it easily enjoys the most notoriety. Images of its spectacular nighttime neon skyline are as instantly recognizable as Paris or New York. Its once lurid reputation as the country's "Sin City"—a title inherited from Reno as the latter city declined in national prominence—was created in part by books such as *The Green Felt Jungle* (1963) and *Fear and Loathing in Las Vegas* (1974), then lovingly burnished by movies such as *Bugsy* (1991) and *Casino* (1995).[1] Its prominence continues on contemporary broadcast television, with the popular, long-running CBS crime drama *CSI* and *Vegas*, a period drama on the same network. Loosely based on the city's history, the latter show transported viewers back to the 1960s, to witness a titanic struggle over the city's future between a Mob-affiliated casino manager (played by Michael Chiklis) and a Clark County sheriff (Dennis Quaid) appointed to clean up his domain. Both characters were appealing, and both worlds were credibly portrayed as the archetypal romance of a western showdown between good and evil, revived in period dress. Las Vegas, it seems, is virtually inescapable in the twenty-first century United States.

Dutiful cultivation of this image by the city's skilled publicity apparatus has made Las Vegas an icon of modern American culture. Known the world over as a capital of hedonism, its durable allure has helped to sustain an economy founded on tourism. The desert city attracted almost thirty-nine million visitors in 2011, 16 percent of them from outside the United States.[2] They came, it seems, like moths to a flame, drawn to the irresistible combination of gambling, luxurious resort hotels, ambitious restaurants, and big-name entertainment that has been the city's draw for more than a decade. Although Las Vegas has a giant convention center and hosts an impressive number of trade meetings annually, only about 10 percent of its visitors report going there for that purpose. The vast majority, 70 percent according to customer surveys, make the journey for pleasure. Although their total numbers declined somewhat in the years following the financial collapse of 2008, hotel occupancy rates are once again increasing and the Las Vegas Convention and Visitors Authority (LVCVA) reported that 2011 set a new annual record. The resilient tourist city, it seems, is as irrepressible in real life as in popular culture.

Las Vegas thus looms in the public imagination as a gambling and entertainment mecca. Indeed, its most enthusiastic analyst, historian Hal Rothman, gleefully pointed out that in 1999 it surpassed the real Mecca as "the most visited city on earth."[3] In his loving history of his adopted city, *Neon Metropolis*, he extolled it as "the first city of the twenty-first century," a postmodern, postindustrial creation that survived and flourished not because of any natural advantages, but because it was willing to make and remake itself, so as to be attractive to fickle pleasure seekers. Las Vegas is a place that stages itself primarily for the gratification of outsiders, and they have repaid the favor by flocking there in stupendous numbers.

IT WAS NOT ALWAYS SO. Las Vegas was not initially a significant participant in the economy of legalized vices that Nevada created in the early decades of the twentieth century. Led by political and economic forces in Reno, the state in the 1910s and 1920s actively sought an alternative to the mining and ranching that were then its principal industries. The slowly evolving result, based on a willingness to flout social stigma, was a proto-tourist economy founded on easy divorce, prizefighting, parimutuel betting on horse races, and eventually, in 1931, legalized casino gambling.[4] Las Vegas, hampered by its remote location and small size (a population of just over five thousand in 1930), was not instantly conspicuous in this new world. It was Reno that attracted the lurid headlines in the national press. Indeed, as late as 1942, a national journalist explained the modern entertainment mecca to the south as "a minor-league Reno."[5]

The story of Las Vegas's modern rise to prominence began after World War II, when its now familiar spatial organization emerged. After gambling was legalized and could move into public venues, casinos first opened downtown along Fremont Street, where they still remain. The iconic Las Vegas Strip, however, the area of giant resort casino properties that now stretches along Las Vegas Boulevard, is actually located outside the city in an adjoining township. That expansion began with the opening in 1941 of the El Rancho Hotel. With the luxury of more available space, the El Rancho pioneered a new, suburban style of resort property with amenities such as swimming pools and parking. Others soon followed, including, most famously, the Flamingo, opened in 1946 by Benjamin "Bugsy" Siegel on behalf of a syndicate of organized crime investors. The Flamingo was a luxurious property meant to attract high-end gamblers from population centers in Southern California. It solidified the appeal of the emergent Strip as new and larger casino hotels were built over subsequent decades.[6] Ultimately, it was the Las Vegas Strip that physically came to symbolize Las Vegas to the rest of the world.

The Flamingo Hotel was also important symbolically, because it led to Siegel's 1947 murder by his associates over construction cost overruns and disputed loan repayments. A minor episode in the annals of organized crime, his death arguably launched the modern popular cultural fascination with Las Vegas. Most recently, this has been manifested in the Mob Museum, with its enticing hints of lawlessness, violence, and behind-the-scenes corruption. Officially opened in 2012 as the National Museum of Organized Crime and Law Enforcement, the museum caters to a pervasive nostalgia about the city's era of Mob financing, which extended into the 1970s. With the new museum Las Vegas publicly fashioned itself into "the great American crossroads of acceptable sin." Its image-conscious mayor, Oscar Goodman, dutifully played his part by arranging to be accompanied to most official events by showgirls in full regalia.[7] It was an example of the city's brash appeal to humanity's baser instincts, and also of its protean capacity for reinvention.

Not everyone shared the fascination or admired the city's success. A *New York Times* editorial in 2004 memorably described the city as "a defiant invention," a "monument to American hubris and marketing, a crapshoot to tame the desert and make do on an inch of rainfall a year."[8] Boosters were undeterred by the *Times*'s disapproval, however. In a *Las Vegas Sun* column from 2006, Rothman positively gloated about Las Vegas's remarkable achievement: "It is improbable that any city grew so fast and achieved so much without producing more than smiles on people's faces."[9] The explosive growth of Las Vegas during the past two decades amply supports his claims. Although its basic economic engine of gambling and tourism remained unchanged, the place boomed spectacularly in the final decades of the twentieth century. In 2011 the population of Clark County (a huge physical expanse dominated by the population center of Las Vegas and its surrounding communities) was estimated to be nearly 2 million people.[10] In 1990 it had been only about

770,000. Thousands of newcomers flocked to metropolitan Las Vegas each month, seeking to cash in on its apparently endless cycle of growth and prosperity.[11] The boom they created fed on itself, as the demand for subdivisions, schools, and shopping centers to serve all the newcomers fueled more construction and more jobs, which in turn lured still more new residents who needed to be housed. As people and houses proliferated, residents of Clark County made up approximately 73 percent of Nevada's entire population by 2011. Not just in the popular imagination, then, but in actual political and economic fact, Las Vegas dominates its state.

THE SAME CHARACTERISTICS are also evident environmentally. As it expanded into the desert, the nascent metropolis began to place heavy demands on its limited environmental resources. Perhaps no other edge city is so spectacularly divorced from the exigencies of its physical setting as Las Vegas, which multiplies swimming polls and golf courses in an arid desert that provides a historical average of just over four inches of precipitation annually. During some recent drought years, less than one inch has fallen all year. Water is a scarce and precious commodity in a place where summer temperatures not infrequently exceed 110 degrees. A burgeoning population needing air-conditioning and landscaping only makes matters worse. During the late 1990s and early twenty-first century, while the city's exponential growth rate consistently led the nation and attracted national attention, Las Vegas set out to secure the water that it needed to sustain its own growth and continue entertaining all those millions of happy visitors. In keeping with its publicity and its politics, there was nothing halfhearted about the campaign.

By then Las Vegas was already receiving its full share of the Colorado River water stored in nearby Lake Mead (Nevada's tiny population was allotted a meager 300,000 acre-feet of water in the original 1928 Colorado Compact that divided the river's flow among seven participating states). Despite extensive conservation measures, including a program that paid people to replace water-hungry grass with desert landscaping, water levels in the giant reservoir declined alarmingly during the succession of drought years that began in 2000.[12] With a dwindling available supply, the overcommitted waters of the Colorado River were proving unequal to all the demands being placed on them. Most alarmingly for Nevada, many of those competing claims enjoyed a superior priority. In 1989 the area's water authority, the Las Vegas Valley Water District, recognized the vulnerability of a system that relied on the Colorado River for close to 90 percent of its supply. The district filed claims for "unused" water rights in twenty-six rural Nevada valleys, none of them any less arid than the casino city, but all of them lacking the population base or political power to resist effectively.

Outraged environmentalists characterized these claims as the "Las Vegas Water Grab" and compared the Nevada city unfavorably with a thirsty Los Angeles in the 1920s. That California city's quest to secure a dependable water supply for its growing population notoriously diverted water from Owens Lake and crippled the agricultural community that had depended on it, as well as severely diminishing Mono Lake to the north. Opponents of the "water grab" predicted the same fate for the rural valleys targeted by Las Vegas and its new regional water management arm, the Southern Nevada Water Authority. Conveniently overlooking the city's tremendous growth, as well as SNWA's substantial conservation measures, Mike Davis characterized its motives starkly: "Las Vegas haughtily disdains to live within its means. Instead, it is aggressively turning its profligacy into environmental terrorism versus its neighbors."[13]

Those neighbors organized themselves in an uneasy coalition that included ranchers, national environmental groups, and local Indian tribes. They tried to dissuade the Nevada State Engineer's Office from granting the water rights to SNWA, arguing that the hydrology of the rural valleys was unclear and that both wildlife populations and landscapes sacred to tribal groups would be jeopardized if the water was diverted to slake Las Vegas's thirst. If Las Vegas were allowed to claim all "excess" water rights in the remote rural valleys, they pointed out, there would be nothing left for any alternative development. Rulings in 2007 and 2008 granted the metropolis only part of the 126,000 acre-feet of water it initially sought, but were later overturned by the Nevada Supreme Court. A 2012 state engineer's decision granted SNWA the right to pump almost 84,000 acre-feet of water from the distant rural valleys, although not the nearly 105,000 acre-feet in the district's amended request. In December the plan seemed to move another step closer to realization when the Bureau of Land Management approved SNWA's application for a right-of-way across federal lands for a pipeline to carry the water 263 miles from northeastern valleys to the southern cities. Along with associated power lines, pumping stations, and reservoirs, the gargantuan project was estimated to cost fifteen billion dollars.[14]

It soon became clear that the SNWA's pipeline dream would not be so easily granted. For years the states of Nevada and Utah had been engaged in negotiations that would have allowed Nevada to tap into groundwater lying beneath the Dry Cave, Cave, Delamar, and Spring Valleys of eastern Nevada. Las Vegas was fixated on these valleys because no other source in the Great Basin holds enough water to make a big pipeline project viable. Federal legislation required the two states to reach an agreement before Nevada could access this buried treasure, but on April 4, 2013, Utah's governor refused to sign an agreement that had been reached after years of negotiation. The following December still another obstacle was placed in Las Vegas's path. The Seventh Judicial District of Nevada reversed the state engineer's award of water rights to SNWA, ruling that there was not sufficient evidence that the volume of water projected to be withdrawn from eastern Nevada could be sustained while preserving future water supplies. In February 2014, things became even more difficult for Las Vegas water managers when the Center for Biological Diversity filed suit in US District Court, challenging a decision by the Bureau of Land Management to grant a right-of-way across its land for construction of the pipeline.

Though obstacles loom, and financing for the project is not yet in place, no one in Nevada doubts the political and financial muscle of SNWA once the regulatory issues are cleared. As Hal Rothman sagely observes, "The faith in technology that compels American society forward translates into sheer belief in the desert, and barring a revolution in the way American society does business, nowhere is there less chance of running out of water [than in Las Vegas]."[15] The plans to slake Las Vegas's thirst remain controversial and are addressed in greater detail elsewhere in this volume. From the city's perspective, however, the entire controversy is misguided. What seems like environmental hubris to outside observers like Davis makes perfect sense to residents like Rothman, who applaud a water authority planning sensibly to accommodate the unprecedented population explosion that success has produced in the Nevada desert. As was true for metropolitan Los Angeles a century earlier, explosive growth in twenty-first-century Las Vegas has become its own excuse for water imperialism.

From the perspective of the Las Vegas Valley, reallocation of water from lightly populated agricultural valleys to rapidly expanding urban spaces appears both proper and inevitable. Indeed, to do otherwise would be to ignore the lessons of their own history, oblivious to the very real environmental constraints that have always made permanent habitation in this arid desert place a risky proposition. Continued growth and prosperity cannot simply be taken for granted in Las Vegas, for all the city's apparent brash confidence in the appeal of its image and the permanence of its economy.[16] In

Las Vegas's earliest years, even its basic survival was an open question. Well into the twentieth century, city leaders perennially felt imperiled. Their city was subject to sudden, severe economic shocks emanating from forces that they could not control, beginning with the railroad company that established the town in 1905. Growth was inhibited by the paucity of basic resources such as water and fertile soil. At regular intervals over many years successive generations of residents contemplated the genuine possibility that their town would fail to weather the latest jolt and join the list of failed Nevada cities such as Goldfield or Rhyolite, other once vibrant places that subsided into dereliction when delicate economies failed to diversify and thrive.

This chapter will explore the surprisingly long and consistent history of such tensions in Las Vegas, a place that audaciously advertises its own success even as it labors assiduously to avoid the embarrassing possibility that its prosperity might yet prove transient. The environmental lessons of the twentieth century mining ghost towns that surround it are painfully clear. Nevada's arid expanses and sparse resources have always made it a difficult place to establish and sustain permanent settlements. Time and time again, as their towns withered away, would-be residents faced the harsh reality that their best efforts were not enough. The brash, continuous promotional efforts that built modern Las Vegas, I argue, paradoxically grew from a relentless fear of a similar fate. From this historical perspective, the city's water imperialism is just one more example of the kind of bold action deemed necessary for survival in a place that understands its potential environmental jeopardy. For all its apparent success, Las Vegas still construes itself at some level as contingent, vulnerable to the imperatives of its physical environment. As even Hal Rothman admitted, "Las Vegas had a powerful sense of impermanence."[17]

THE ORIGINS OF LAS VEGAS in 1905 certainly gave little promise of future greatness. The town was created as a division point for a proposed rail line linking Salt Lake City to port facilities in Southern California. Coinciding with the fabulous central Nevada silver and gold mining booms of the early twentieth century (at Tonopah and Goldfield, respectively), the San Pedro, Los Angeles & Salt Lake Railroad needed a supply station with enough water to service railroad workers and trains alike. The company's engineers found it in Las Vegas Valley, where they purchased a ranch property belonging to Helen J. Stewart and planned a town site. To run it they created a subsidiary company, the Las Vegas Land & Water Company. That entity auctioned lots in the town site in May 1905 and quickly sold almost half of twelve hundred lots.

With the railroad and its workers as a foundation, the young city was one variant among myriad Nevada "instant cities" that accompanied the mining booms of the early twentieth century. A creature of its corporate masters, its survival and success were by no means certain. Initially, Las Vegas was eclipsed by the growth and prosperity of Goldfield, in particular. Early purchasers of its lots were speculators, like their counterparts in nearby Rhyolite and Bullfrog, hoping—but not necessarily expecting—to find permanence and prosperity in an unlikely desert location.[18]

Initially, it was a bit difficult for them to envision just how that might happen. One 1906 arrival reported piecing together his income from odds and ends. He posted bills, recovered and sold abandoned ponies, and slept in empty buildings as a night watchman, profiting any way that he could from the discouragement of others less sanguine or resourceful than he: "I done anything I could make money on honest. I bought any second-hand thing anyone wanted to sell cheap enough. We bought cars—the roads was so bad, and the people would get stuck; they didn't know how to drive on the desert, and they'd come in and they'd sell them for anything."[19] Ambitious businessmen similarly sought any advantage they could find, successfully campaigning for the 1909 creation of a new county (named Clark, after railroad owner William A. Clark, the Montana copper baron and US senator), with Las Vegas as its county seat. In the same year they organized themselves into a Chamber of Commerce and began actively to seek new business opportunities that would sustain their infant community. Their efforts would lead to a variety of promotional activities designed to draw more people and more varied business to the railroad town.

There was a definite need for such efforts. The panic of 1907 contracted the national economy and severely discouraged investment in Nevada, as early Las Vegas newspaper owner Charles P. Squires recalled: "Nobody wanted to invest money in Nevada. Most people in the Middle West had never heard of Nevada and those who had did not know what or where Nevada was." Discouraged in his efforts to drum up business capital in those years, he returned in May 1908 to find a town on the verge of collapse: "It was a black-looking world and poor, sick Las Vegas was about the lowest in spirit that a town could get and still keep a post office. There were still some people here, most of them unable to get away and having no place to land which was any better."[20] The viability of the isolated desert town remained uncertain.

Its fortunes rose and fell with the railroad, and its businessmen constantly sought additional economic opportunity that would sustain and increase the permanent resident population.

To that end they formed a Chamber of Commerce and began publishing a series of brochures and articles designed to market Las Vegas to the world. These publications were the first in a long series of efforts at reimagining Las Vegas in whatever fashion might be required to appeal most effectively to the wider world, the characteristic that Rothman noted as the foundation of Las Vegas's success.[21] The Chamber's initial effort in 1911 was a pamphlet produced for the Los Angeles Land and Products Show. A similar example a few years later, entitled *Semi-tropical Nevada, a Region of Fertile Soils and Flowing Wells,* gives a sense of its flavor. Inside pink covers, this publication introduced "a region but little known to the world, in which are fertile lands and flowing waters under climatic conditions which are favorable for growing nearly all California products." Seeking to correct the misapprehension that Nevada was only a barren mining state, the pamphlet explained the reasons for the mistaken characterization and waxed lyrical about the agricultural possibilities of southern Nevada:

> The professional promoter who came to Nevada found something more to his purpose in the mines, with their invitation to the investor to "get rich quick," than in the lands, with their opportunity to get rich slowly and surely. . . . A mine in a desert is romantic, alluring, it gets the money. A farm in a desert seems like an anomaly. Yet a desert is merely a country where there are not many farms. All the world was "desert" until the hand of man made it productive. In this sense, and this only, Nevada is a desert.

To reinforce the point, the pamphlet noted the plentiful springs in the region, including the natural artesian wells that were the source of the nearby Muddy River.

In this and subsequent pamphlets issued through the 1920s, Las Vegas and its environs were enthusiastically presented as an agricultural paradise. After Nevada law required that artesian wells be capped when they were not in use, successive publications promised confidently that the water supply would last as long as it was needed. Photographs in the 1924 version—comprehensively titled *Las Vegas, Center and County Seat of Clark County, Nevada, Is a Thriving Railroad Town Located in the Heart of a Country of Wonderful Undeveloped Resources*—depicted winter lettuce growing in Moapa Valley, as well as asparagus and turkeys. Thompson seedless grapes were illustrated in nearby Mesquite. A 1920 variation added peaches and cotton to the list of agricultural products. Although hydrological knowledge about the source of its water was sketchy, the 1920 pamphlet confidently reported the prevailing belief that the presence of numerous springs with year-round flow demonstrated the existence of a "vast underground water resource."[22]

Early Chamber of Commerce pamphlets were also careful to correct possible misapprehensions about the southern Nevada climate. The advantages of its desert surroundings were mild winters and a healthful climate. Occasional frost meant only that citrus fruit could not be grown successfully. Summer was no threat, either. Assuring readers that heatstroke was unknown, the 1920 publication proclaimed that "a temperature of 105 degrees in Las Vegas is endured with comfort and occasions no particular comment, although a temperature of 85 degrees in any of our eastern cities brings great suffering." It was only slightly less exuberant than the 1914 version, which promised readers that "Las Vegas people can spend their summers in SWITZERLAND and their winters in ITALY or EGYPT without going forty miles from home or outside the confines of their own County." Initially seeking to lure settlers and investors from nearby Southern California, the Chamber highlighted correlations between the two areas in terms of growing season, crops, and climate.

The seeds of the area's environmental optimism were thus sown early by its eager promoters, but climatic appeal notwithstanding, the promised agricultural paradise never developed in Las Vegas Valley. Unlike the fertile Virgin and Muddy River valleys nearby, Vegas Valley soil proved alkali and difficult to cultivate. Artesian wells required substantial initial capital from would-be farmers, and the water supply was not so inexhaustible as the Chamber of Commerce believed. As more wells were drilled, the springs began to fail, and wells had to be sunk deeper to reach water. In time pumps were required to lift the water, which required additional capital investment. After 1914 the Chamber pamphlets dropped all references to the hopeful hypothesis that the drainage from the Carson and Humboldt River sinks of northern Nevada actually flowed south to surface again in Las Vegas. Farming proved not to be the basis for Las Vegas's economic future after all.

In 1920 the city had just over twenty-three hundred residents, and the railroad was still the basis of the fragile economy. Control of the Las Vegas Land & Water Company was purchased by the Union Pacific Railroad Company in 1921, but the company struggled to provide a consistent water supply for the infant city. Pipes made of redwood broke down frequently in the alkali soil, and sanitation was a source of continued complaint by residents. In 1922, after a railroad strike broke out in Las Vegas, the company responded by moving its repair shops and attendant workforce to nearby Caliente. Still the town's major employer, the railroad's redeployment emptied out the town and created what longtime newspaper publisher John F. Cahlan later remembered as "one of the very few depressions ever known to this area." In the aftermath, conditions echoed those recalled by Charles Squires in 1908. As Cahlan recalled, "The economic situation was rather bleak for those who remained." There was still genuine doubt as to whether Las Vegas was viable on its own, without its founding industry.[23]

In response, the Chamber of Commerce developed a new strategy that emphasized location and transportation over agricultural potential. Although railroad connections were still important to the economy, it directed its new campaign to the automobile. Las Vegas eagerly sought inclusion on the official maps of the Arrowhead Trail Association, which was organized in 1916 to promote an all-weather automobile route between Los Angeles and Salt Lake City. In 1924 Governor James Scrugham advised the Chamber to advertise the city by pointing out nearby scenic beauties such as Red Rock Canyon and the Valley of Fire to travelers on the Arrowhead Trail, who might be persuaded to spend an extra night or two in order to see them. By 1927 the new Chamber brochure, sedately titled *Las Vegas and Clark County, Nevada*, had enthusiastically shifted gears. Although photographs of peach orchards and walnut groves persisted, the unpaginated pamphlet enthusiastically presented the county as "located in a central position with relation to all of Scenic Western United States," among which it included Lake Tahoe and Yellowstone Park as well as local sights such as Joshua Tree forest and Mount Charleston resort.[24] Accompanying maps helpfully gave distances to more prominent localities such as Salt Lake City or Reno, but also listed all manner of local accommodations available as options for more leisurely travelers. A separate report on Las Vegas by Chamber executive secretary S. R. Whitehead reported that while the city had up until that time been "largely a railroad town," its recent prosperity could be attributed to the fact that "the opening of a transcontinental auto highway has greatly stimulated its growth." Economic doldrums temporarily avoided, the city's future was once again depicted brightly, though for new reasons.

By the late 1920s a new potential economic boon had seized the Chamber's imagination. With the signing of the Colorado River Compact in 1922, the seven states bordering the river had agreed on a system for dividing the river's flow among themselves, thus making it potentially available for generating electricity and providing a stable source for irrigation. The federal government's interest in flood control spurred congressional action in 1928, when the Boulder Canyon Project Act authorized construction of the first dams in what would become a massive campaign of water engineering on the Colorado and its tributaries. Fortuitously for Las Vegas, one of these dams—initially called Boulder but eventually renamed Hoover—was located on its doorstep, approximately thirty miles to the southeast. Giddy with anticipation, Las Vegas developers and the Chamber of Commerce geared up even before construction of the dam was authorized for a bonanza they eagerly anticipated but couldn't quiet specify the nature of. A new pamphlet in 1924 promoted the city as the "gateway of the GREAT BOULDER CANYON DAM PROJECT, where development of new lands will make new fortunes."[25] Confident that cheap electric power would soon be forthcoming, the pamphlet suggested a possible future for the city as an inland manufacturing center where thousands of men would be employed. Or perhaps the country's largest apricot tree, which was growing in the Las Vegas Valley, augured that more plentiful water would finally produce an agricultural paradise in their midst.

In any event, expectations of the dam project ran high. Las Vegas anticipated becoming the construction headquarters for the massive project and hoped as well to house some of the thousands of workers needed to build the massive dam. Visions of inexpensive power and plentiful water renewed hopes for new growth and prosperity. Resident Leon Rockwell remembered that when the Boulder Dam Project bill was signed, "we got the fire truck out, and—my God, everybody that could, hooked onto it! In carts and baby buggies and everything else—just like they was nuts. . . . There was people that got lit that never had taken a drink before."[26] The Chamber of Commerce procured new stationery that billed their city as the "Gateway to Boulder Dam," complete with a depiction of the dam as it would appear when completed. Hopes of a tourist influx revived again, and the Chamber published new maps highlighting the city's location in relation to the proposed new site for the dam, which had to be moved from Boulder to Black Canyon because of problems with the former site.

Still, construction did not begin until 1931, and when it did the city's hopes proved largely unfounded. The federal government built its own company town of Boulder City to serve the administrative and housing needs of the project. Located far enough from Las Vegas to be free of its influence,

Boulder City was specifically designed to be the antithesis of the struggling railroad town, with its well-known red-light district occupying Block 16. In contrast, Boulder City was a dry community with strict regulations designed to ensure a wholesome atmosphere for families. Meanwhile, Las Vegas played a support role. Railroad facilities were expanded in order to carry the massive amounts of materiel required for the dam, and off-duty construction workers made their way into the city of approximately seven thousand for recreation. Nevada's legalization of gambling in 1931 made the state notorious in much of the nation, but rendered Las Vegas all the more alluring to workers flush with payday cash, especially since gambling was prohibited in Boulder City (and remains so to the present).[27] The city did not prosper to the extent that it hoped, but federal spending on the dam and accompanying infrastructure carried it safely through the years of the Depression at a time when many places with stronger economies were desperately foundering.

Visitors came to see the dam being constructed, certainly, but locals never really expected that influx to be permanent. Journalists forthrightly reported that "when the dam was finished, Vegas was expected to collapse." Newspaper owners Charles and Delphine Squires recounted in their history of Las Vegas that everyone knew the infusion of federal cash was a temporary phenomenon. Even before the dam's dedication in 1935, pessimists were predicting that the city would "revert to its former condition of dullness" once the construction workers had departed.[28] Even with the new attraction of legal gambling, the future in Las Vegas did not seem particularly bright.

This time it was the Elks Club that stepped in to rescue the city. As *Las Vegas Review-Journal* editor John Cahlan recalled, club members began looking in 1934 "for some way to soften the blow when the construction crews on the bid project pulled out. Las Vegas was already feeling the effects of the first cuts of the work force and . . . there were those who figured that, when the dam was completed, the city would slide back into the sleepy community it was before construction started—that was really sleepy." So when carnival barker Clyde Zerby arrived in town proposing a "home town celebration in which all the citizenry could join in and have fun," the Elks devised a frontier celebration they called Helldorado. The western theme of the show was somewhat arbitrary. It was chosen, according to Cahlan, because rodeos had proved popular elsewhere. Mostly, Helldorado, complete with saloon, sideshows, a girlie show, chorus girls, and a Mexican singer, was "the vehicle Las Vegas would use to call attention to the fact that there was a Las Vegas in Nevada [as distinct from its then more well-known namesake in New

Mexico] and that it was a great place to have fun." Residents dressed up in western costumes, staged a mock murder trial, and viewed a "rodeo" composed of a trained Brahma bull.[29]

Aided by the publicity efforts of the Union Pacific Railroad, which advertised the event in Los Angeles, Helldorado became an annual multiple-day event. By 1937 it featured dedicated facilities, with a huge dance hall built from logs cut locally on Mount Charleston. The festivities became part of a newly minted Las Vegas image, now "posing," in the words of *Look* in 1940, "as the last of the roaring frontier towns." Although it had never actually been a frontier mining town, and its ranching years predated establishment of the city, Las Vegas good-naturedly adopted all the familiar trappings. Residents "affect cowboy outfits," *Look* opined, because "it creates 'atmosphere.'" In the photographic feature that accompanied the text, *Look* depicted a genuine prospector surrounded by two attractive young women wearing cowboy hats. There were bars, dance halls, sports books, slot machines, a divorcée in slacks, and the prostitutes of Block 16, who "do their modified strip tease before any of eight little houses." Helldorado Days aptly embodied the new spirit that Las Vegas was projecting, as it created for itself an ersatz western heritage designed to render the lurid less so. In "desert-bound, hell-raising Las Vegas," *Look* pronounced, "men are men and sin is a civic virtue."[30] The western veneer was a crucial element in securing public acceptance of the city's naked appeal to humanity's baser instincts.

The strategy was clearly successful. Cahlan reported that Helldorado never shut down even during World War II, when nonessential travel was severely restricted. At the urging of Nevada's powerful US senator Patrick McCarran, the wartime authorities determined that the festival was "a necessity for the entertainment of the troops and the war factory workers in this area." That ruling was critical if the carnival shows and cowboys were to obtain the gas rationing tickets they needed to reach Las Vegas and put on the festival on which the town increasingly depended to lure visitors. By 1946 Block 16 had been closed as a wartime measure, but Helldorado had been expanded to include female jockeys for the burro race and a bathing beauty contest cheerfully acknowledged to be an anachronism.[31] The Chamber of Commerce updated its stationery in response. While it still featured Boulder Dam, it now also bore the ironic slogan "Still a Frontier Town," part of the newly minted image of Las Vegas that had been created to give tourists a respectable guise for self-indulgence. The 1930s faith in technology, represented by the dam, was replaced by 1940s faith in nostalgia, in the form of the loosely reinterpreted frontier. The western theme embodied by the El Rancho Vegas and Last Frontier resorts on the emerging Las Vegas Strip were all part of this new city image, and Las Vegas was once again saved from a predicted collapse by its residents' innovative recasting of the city to suit a new audience with new tastes.

The pattern of reimagining the city in order to save it from a feared collapse certainly did not end in the 1940s, but it became a less ad hoc effort in 1947, when the Chamber of Commerce established a professional news bureau to counter bad publicity and promote the city's attractions to the rest of the world. The Las Vegas News Bureau had a professional staff of photographers and writers, all devoted to spreading word about the city's friendly western atmosphere and its myriad attractions. They collaborated with the publicity departments of local hotels and casinos, photographing publicity stunts such as the famous "floating craps table" staged in the Sahara Hotel swimming pool in 1953. The result of their efforts, the bureau claimed, "literally transformed Las Vegas from a little known name to one of the worlds [sic] most widely recognized and popular resort areas." Whatever direction the city took in marketing itself to tourists, the news bureau made sure that image was widely disseminated. In 1975 it claimed that nearly all "the hundreds of stories in print and on television each year about Las Vegas" developed from contact with its staff. When it was absorbed by the LVCVA in 1992, the promotional apparatus devoted to attracting visitors to southern Nevada was the envy of the world.[32]

Yet even with a professional staff, ensuring success was hard work. As the Chamber nervously noted in 1949, Las Vegas was beginning to have competition. Whereas in 1932 only six states were spending state money to advertise their attractions for visitors, the number in 1940 had risen to forty-two. New attractions were needed, and new slogans emerged. Although Helldorado Days continued, the exclusively western emphasis diminished. The Chamber's new tourist maps now relabeled Las Vegas "the land of sun and fun," as they promoted winter sports at Mount Charleston and the proximity of natural attractions such as Death Valley and the Grand Canyon.[33] A more sophisticated form of recreation replaced the wild-and-wooly-west theme. Time and again this pattern repeated itself, as the Chamber and later the LVCVA changed directions as required to maintain their city's allure.

Over time this tractability became a part of the city's folklore, recounted in 1965 by John Cahlan in a luncheon speech to civic leaders. At the time Las Vegas's economy was once again in retreat, "about as bad as it ever has been,"

according to Cahlan. He urged his audience not to despair, however, recall-
ing the slogan urged by *Las Vegas Age* editor Charles Squires during an earlier recession: "Don't Sell Las Vegas Short." In the intervening years, Cahlan
claimed: "That slogan has been the guideline for many people and whenever
the bottom dropped out of the economy in Las Vegas, it was dusted off and
hung out, all bright and shiny for everyone to see. Perhaps it is this slogan
that has made Las Vegas great. At least, it has always pulled the citizenry out
of the doldrums and caused them to look for the streaks of sunshine." Doing
his part to seek sunshine, Cahlan was a major force promoting the Southern Nevada Industrial Foundation, a group created in 1959 to try to repair
the damage done by a *Wall Street Journal* article of that year. The report had
portrayed Las Vegas as "constructed on a foundation of shifting sand [so
that] any capital invested here would be buried under a floating sand dune."
Its impact, Cahlan reported, was so devastating that investment in the area
"almost dried up." Rallying swiftly to protect their city's interests, local citizens organized a whirlwind publicity campaign that took them across the
country to address local financial leaders and try "to carve a new image to be
presented to the financial world."[34]

With changes in state regulations that permitted corporate investment
beginning in the 1960s, Las Vegas's finances improved and Mob control
gradually diminished. The cultural habits of plasticity that had evolved
through many less successful decades persisted, however. Las Vegas has
never stopped marketing itself to visitors, recasting its image as required, and
promoting nuclear testing, celebrity entertainers, high culture, or gourmet
chefs as prevailing fashions seem to warrant. Meanwhile, federal authoriza-
tion in 1966 of the Southern Nevada Water Project finally brought funding
for the water line and pumping stations necessary to deliver the state's full
share of water from Lake Mead. When construction was completed in 1982,
the supply was projected to be sufficient for a city of almost two million.[35]
Yet, as we have seen, before the end of that decade, planners were already
seeking new sources of water. Success in southern Nevada was never pre-
sumed to be a permanent condition. Constant, concerted action was imperative to protect against the caprices of climate, economy, and reputation.

The persistent possibility of failure continues to haunt Las Vegas. Its success has been achieved only with considerable, conscientious effort. Numerous examples of communities that did not beat the environmental odds, but
withered instead, still linger nearby. Historically, and even into the present
day, regression threatens. After the years of public attention for its stupefying

growth, the nation's 2008 economic collapse brought unwelcome headlines proclaiming Las Vegas the country's leader in dire statistics such as foreclosure and unemployment rates. From miracle boomtown in 2004, Las Vegas became by 2011 the city with the most negative rating of economic conditions in the entire country, according to a Gallup Poll. Its economic confidence and its job creation index were also among the lowest in the country.[36] In 2012 Las Vegas continued to be at or near the top of the list of US cities with the highest rates of mortgage foreclosure. Tens of thousands of houses were estimated to be empty in the communities that make up metropolitan Las Vegas, and a 2012 article in the *Economist* concluded bleakly that the state of Nevada had "the least diversified economy in America," and as a consequence had nothing to fall back on when tourism and gambling declined in the recession.[37] As was true a century ago, there continues today to be a tremendous disparity between the city's glitzy promotional image and its more chastened economic reality. Although its current challenges may differ considerably in scale, historically, for Las Vegas they are nothing new.

NOTES

1. Ed Reid and Ovid Demaris, *The Green Felt Jungle* (Cutchogue, NY: Buccaneer Books, 1963); Hunter S. Thompson, *Fear and Loathing in Las Vegas: A Savage Journey to the Heart of the American Dream* (New York: Random House, 1976).

2. Many useful statistics on Las Vegas tourism, including historical trends, can be found on the website of the Las Vegas Convention and Visitors Authority, http://www.lvcva.com/stats-and-facts. Unless otherwise noted, statistics on Las Vegas throughout this essay are drawn from this source.

3. Hal Rothman, *Neon Metropolis: How Las Vegas Started the Twenty-First Century* (New York: Routledge, 2002), xix, xi.

4. The process is traced in Alicia Barber, *Reno's Big Gamble: Image and Reputation in the Biggest Little City* (Lawrence: University Press of Kansas, 2008); and C. Elizabeth Raymond, *George Wingfield: Owner and Operator of Nevada* (Reno: University of Nevada Press, 1992).

5. Wesley Stout, "Nevada's New Reno," *Saturday Evening Post*, October 31, 1942, 12.

6. For this and subsequent details of Las Vegas history, see Eugene P. Moehring, *Resort City in the Sunbelt: Las Vegas, 1930–1970* (Reno: University of Nevada Press, 1989); and Eugene P. Moehring and Michael S. Green, *Las Vegas: A Centennial History* (Reno: University of Nevada Press, 2005).

7. The "crossroads" phrase belongs to John L. Smith, "Shadow and Light Converge on Mob Museum," *Las Vegas Review-Journal*, February 14, 2012. Goodman's enthusiastic endorsement of the new image was reported by Deborah Solomon, "What Happens in Vegas," *New York Times Sunday Magazine*, January 14, 2011.

8. "Leaving It in Las Vegas," *New York Times*, June 7, 2004, A26.

9. Reprinted in Hal K. Rothman, *Playing the Odds: Las Vegas and the Modern West*, edited by Lincoln Bramwell (Albuquerque: University of New Mexico Press, 2007), 67.

10. Population estimates for 2011 are from the official website of the Nevada state demographer (http://tinyurl.com/bamrgsr). The figure for the state was 2,721,794, while Clark County's total population was estimated at 1,967,722 people.

11. Even the *New York Times* marveled at Las Vegas's phenomenal growth, in a four-part series entitled "American Dreamers: The Lure of Las Vegas," which ran in the paper between May 30 and June 7, 2004.

12. "Water Outlook Grows Dim for Colorado River Watershed," *Las Vegas Review-Journal*, April 13, 2012.

13. Mike Davis, "Las Vegas Versus Nature," in *Dead Cities and Other Tales* (New York: New Press, 2002), 88.

14. For the early history of the project, see James W. Hulse, *Nevada's Environmental Legacy: Progress or Plunder* (Reno: University of Nevada Press, 2009), 55–70. The recent stages including the most recent state engineer's ruling, issued on March 22, 2012, have been well covered by the *Las Vegas Review-Journal*. The BLM decision is explained by Marshall Swearingen, "BLM Okays Controversial Nevada Water Pipeline," *High Country News*, http://www.hcn.org/blogs/goat.

15. Rothman, *Playing the Odds*, 153.

16. For the origins and persistence of this sense of environmental intractability in Nevada, see Elizabeth Raymond, "When the Desert Won't Bloom: Environmental Limitation and the Great Basin," in *Many Wests: Place, Culture, and Regional Identity*, edited by David Wrobel and Michael Steiner (Lawrence: University Press of Kansas, 1997), 71–92.

17. Rothman, *Neon Metropolis*, xxii.

18. The term comes from Gunther Barth, *Instant Cities: Urbanization and the Rise of San Francisco and Denver* (New York: Oxford University Press, 1975). For an evanescent Nevada mining town contemporary with Las Vegas, and the extensive promotional efforts undertaken to sustain it, see Elizabeth Raymond, "Mining Illusions: The Case of Rawhide, Nevada," in *Changing Mines in America*, by Peter Goin and Elizabeth Raymond (Santa Fe: Center for American Places, 2004), 117–38.

19. Leon H. Rockwell, *Recollections of Life in Las Vegas, Nevada, 1906–1968* (Reno: Oral History Project, 1969), 33.

20. Charles P. Squires and Delphine A. Squires, "Las Vegas, Nevada, Its

Romance and History," 2 vols. (typescript, University of Las Vegas Special Collections Department, 1955), 1:211.

21. Early Las Vegas promotional efforts are extensively documented in the Records of the Las Vegas Chamber of Commerce (MS 96-07) in Special Collections, UNLV Libraries. Unless otherwise noted, all information in this chapter about Chamber of Commerce activities and promotional campaigns comes from that source. Individual pamphlets issued by the Chamber of Commerce are also part of that collection and will be cited by page number in the text unless there is not sufficient reference information provided in the text to identify them. "Semi-Tropical Nevada," quoted in this paragraph, is given an attributed publication date of 1914. Other materials from this collection will be cited (by box and folder number) as LVCC Records.

22. The 1920 pamphlet *Las Vegas and Clark County, Nevada: A Brief Review of Climate, Resources, Growth Opportunities* is given an attributed date of 1917 in the UNLV Special Collections catalog, but internal evidence indicates it was published in 1920. The quotation is from page 5.

23. Moehring and Green, *Las Vegas,* 37–45, 60–63; John F. Cahlan, "Las Vegas Elks Make History," *Las Vegas Review-Journal,* February 18, 1968, 51.

24. Scrugham's visit on May 13, 1924, is recorded in the Chamber of Commerce Minute Book that covers the period from January 1924 to July 1929.

25. "Las Vegas Southern Nevada," n.d., but internal evidence suggests 1924; emphasis added. The pamphlet is found in the Union Pacific Railroad Collection (MS 97-19), Box 11, Folder 18, Special Collections, UNLV Libraries.

26. Rockwell, *Recollections,* 116. It is worth noting that Prohibition was in effect in 1928, so consuming alcohol was technically illegal.

27. For Boulder City as the anti–Las Vegas, see Moehring, *Resort City,* 14–21.

28. Stout, "Nevada's New Reno," 12; Squires and Squires, "Las Vegas, Nevada, Its Romance and History," 2:358.

29. Cahlan's account of the founding of Helldorado comes from his article "How Helldorado Gave Las Vegas Needed Life," *Las Vegas Review-Journal,* February 18, 1968. For a broader history of Las Vegas promotional efforts during the 1930s, see Larry Gragg, "Selling 'Sin City': Successfully Promoting Las Vegas During the Great Depression, 1935–1941," *Nevada Historical Society Quarterly* 49 (Summer 2006): 83–106; and Larry Gragg, *Bright Light City: Las Vegas in Popular Culture* (Lawrence: University Press of Kansas, 2013).

30. "Wild, Wooly, and Wide-Open," *Look,* August 14, 1940, 21–25.

31. The 1946 description is by Jules Archer, in "Paris of the Desert." Originally published in 1946 in *In Short,* the article was reprinted in the *Las Vegas Review-Journal,* August 5, 1990.

32. The 1975 history of the Las Vegas News Bureau, from which all quotations

are taken, is a typescript located in the LVCC Records, Box 2. See also Larry Gragg, "Las Vegas New Bureau," *Online Nevada Encyclopedia,* http://www.onlinenevada .org/las_vegas_news_bureau.

33. The new "Fun in the Sun" campaign emerges in the Chamber of Commerce minutes from 1948 and 1948, LVCC Records, Box 9, Folder 11. The figures on state spending on tourism promotion are from vol. 5, no. 37, September 22, 1949.

34. The text of Cahlan's 1965 speech is located in Box 13, Folder 4, Cahlan Collection, MS 15, Nevada State Historical Society, Las Vegas. His account of the motives for founding the Southern Nevada Industrial Foundation is in Box 13, Folder 2.

35. Moehring and Green, *Las Vegas,* 191–94, 207–10.

36. The results of the 2011 poll were reported in 2012, "Washington, D.C., Area Tops in Economic Confidence in 2011," http://www.thefreelibrary.com/.

37. "Diversifying Nevada: Rolling the Dice," *Economist,* January 7, 2012, http:// www/economist.com/node/21542451/print.

Errant into the Wilderness

Reno's Acts Against Nature

ALICIA BARBER

JUST AFTER MIDNIGHT on the morning of Friday, November 18, 2011, residents of the Caughlin Ranch development in Reno, Nevada, were awakened by the pungent smell of smoke, the harsh shriek of sirens, urgent pounding on their doors, and shouted warnings to flee. As what was later dubbed the "Caughlin Fire" blazed through the night, winds of 50 to 60 miles per hour gusted up to 85 mph and higher, intensifying the destruction that had begun when a few bone-dry branches pitched into a power line and ignited. At daybreak the city awoke to the jarring sight of a hillside in flames, the comforting smell of a winter's hearth transformed into a bellwether of disaster.

As the day progressed, the fast-moving fire perpetually changed course, with flames of up to one hundred feet high, prompting waves of evacuations. For four days it burned through houses, fences, and sheds, casting a fiery glow over the ridgetops. Finally, after scorching 1,935 acres, destroying twenty-eight homes and damaging fifteen more, the fire was declared completely controlled, and residents returned to survey the devastation as a light-falling snow soothed the blackened slopes.[1]

Burning Bushes

The Reno area is no stranger to wildfires, but this one was an anomaly, arriving far later than the usual red-flag season of summer's end, when the annual snowmelt has evaporated and high temperatures desiccate the land. On the border of two climatic regimes—the dry high desert climate of the western Great Basin and the alpine Sierra Nevada—Reno is naturally arid, subject to a "rain shadow" effect, as warm air pushed inland from the Pacific releases its moisture in the high Sierra, sending dry clouds eastward over the city.[2] The onset of autumn generally brings some relief, but 2011 had been an especially dry year, resulting in lower-than-average fuel moisture and heightening the risk of combustion.[3]

Contributing further to the destruction was geography. The Caughlin Fire was sparked along one edge of Reno's "wildland urban interface," or wui, a term used to designate an area "where structures and other human development meet or intermingle with undeveloped wildland or vegetative fuels (see Map 2)."[4] As its signature feature, the Caughlin Ranch development ascends from the valley floor into the piñon and juniper foothills of the Carson Range, which stretches fifty miles southward from Reno along the eastern side of Lake Tahoe and peppers its edge with ski resorts. At its highest elevations, the development enters the Toiyabe Humboldt National Forest, a noncontiguous forest whose disconnected sections fan across Nevada and parts of eastern California. Homeowners perch high above the densely populated valley with the city lights spread out below and timbered slopes at their back.

The desire to inhabit such lofty perches is on the rise throughout the American West. According to a 2001 source, nearly 38 percent of the region's new home construction was on property "adjacent to or inter-mixed with wui."[5] Aspiring residents of these so-called natural areas seek amenities including privacy, spectacular views, larger lots, and proximity to outdoor recreation, and at least through the peak of the US housing bubble in 2006, developers rushed to accommodate them. As a result, the frequency of fires along the wui is increasing, as evidenced by recent conflagrations ranging from the Tunnel/Oakland fire of 1991 to California's Grass Valley Fire (Lake Arrowhead) and Angora Fire (Lake Tahoe), both in 2007.[6] Locally, the Waterfall Fire in Carson City was one of Nevada's most destructive wui fires, scorching 8,799 acres and destroying twenty-one homes in 2004.[7]

In Reno the problem is exacerbated by what Reno Fire Department division chief Curtis Johnson described in a 2005 risk assessment as the city's "aggressive annexation policy . . . expanding the City into even more wildland/ urban interface areas."[8] Indeed, over the past few decades, as the valley has filled from one side to the other with housing developments, office centers, and strip malls, waves of affluent residential developments have surged into Reno's western foothills, from the "master-planned golf community" of Somersett in far northwest Reno southward to Caughlin Ranch. But such expansion hardly requires formal annexation. A large percentage of Caughlin Ranch homes, including a projected new division, the Pines, intended to climb even farther up the mountain, are located on unincorporated land; only 74.7 of the nearly 2,000 acres burned by the Caughlin Fire were within Reno city limits.[9] Continuing south along the Carson Range, upscale developments—many, like Caughlin Ranch, boasting golf courses and country

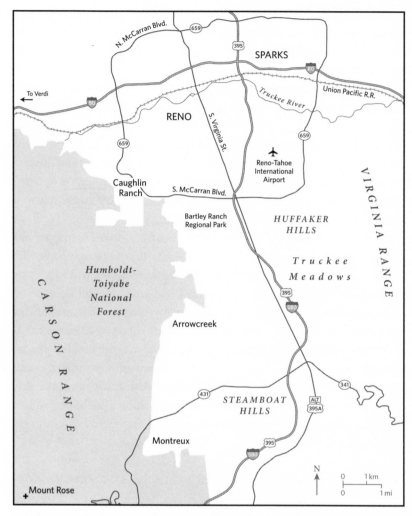

Map 2: Nestled between two mountain ranges, the Reno-Sparks metropolitan area borders the Wildland Urban Interface.

clubs—include Arrowcreek, Saddlehorn, and, finally, a gated assemblage of luxury woodland homes called Montreux, site of the annual Reno-Tahoe Open.

These sites span a wide range of nontraditional, and increasingly vulnerable, locations. As pointed out by the 2005 risk assessment, "Residential developments are designed and built with open space areas of natural vegetation with limited access, on steep slopes, in drainages, with no fuels management program." The problem, then, is not simply one of location, but the failure of many home builders and residents to approach their environment with the requisite caution, to acknowledge that they inhabit what amounts to a latent tinderbox rather than a typical suburb. Avenues for what firefighters deem "fire intrusion" proliferate, in the form of shake and tile roofs, wooden decks, ornamental shrubs, trees, and other vegetation located adjacent to or even on the structures themselves, enabling a "ladder effect" when flames hungrily scale walls draped in trailing foliage. In short, according to the risk assessment, "Although fire codes, defensible space information and fire resistive building materials are available, many of these new structures appear to be built with little or no consideration for maintainable defensible space and protection against wildland fires."[10]

The terms—*defensible space, aggressive annexation policies, fire intrusion* —teem with contention, suggesting the need to defend ourselves, fortress-like, against nature's fury. Writ large, it is a position not confined to residents of these new subdivisions, but common to all who straddle the interface between the urban and the unoccupied, where nature is both treasured commodity and occasional foe. We scale the heights simply because we can. In our ceaseless growth, ever upward and outward, we move boldly into areas once deemed inhospitable or even hostile to human populations, erasing the footprints of lives spent in closer harmony with the natural. We strive to control without compromise. We seek solace without sacrifice. We have, perhaps, forgotten why we are here.

Origin Stories

Five miles south of the Caughlin Ranch development, Bartley Ranch Regional Park tucks into the foot of the Carson Range. The park marked the eastern reach of the Caughlin Fire, which leaped a busy thoroughfare to char its popular trail system, wooden fences, and vegetation, but spared all of the park's structures, which include a row of weathered barns and a picture-perfect, white wood-frame schoolhouse complete with bell tower. This is the Old Huffaker School, built in 1867 and, remarkably, used for its original purpose for eighty-three years.

The fifty-six-acre park both promotes and reflects its western heritage, yet although its historic structures are all authentic, all were refugees from encroaching development elsewhere in the city. The picturesque school arrived here in 1992, restored to its original appearance through the efforts of local history enthusiasts after four decades of use as storage space for a nearby fish hatchery.[11] Originally, it stood two miles east, alongside South Virginia Street, the original highway through town. The constituency it served, however, was not Reno, but Huffaker's, a small community named for its founder, rancher Granville W. Huffaker, a Kentucky native and erstwhile trader who settled the area in 1858, a full decade before Reno's founding.[12]

Unbeknownst to most of its contemporary residents, the area's lineage is one not of urban periphery but community center. Little evidence remains of Huffaker's today, although its echoes resonate in the names of area streets, a modern elementary school, and a cluster of sage-strewn hills that swell up from the surrounding valley floor. A blue Nevada-shaped historical marker languishing in the rear of an insurance office parking lot marks the former site of Huffaker's ranch house next to Thomas Creek, a rivulet now coerced through culverts and conduits to match the rigid lines of south Reno's streets, highways, and commercial strips.

Upon Huffaker's arrival in 1858, Thomas Creek was one of many flowing freely from the heights of the Carson Range into the area long known as the Truckee Meadows, a term familiar to local residents in the name of organizations ranging from the local community college to the regional planning agency. Although often used to denote the entire Reno-Sparks metropolitan area, the term actually describes a far more circumscribed section of the valley, approximately ten miles square, running from the Truckee River, which passes through downtown Reno, southward to where the Steamboat Hills transition into rural Pleasant Valley on the way to Nevada's capital of Carson City.

Open space characterized the Meadows until just a few short decades ago. As the name implies, the Truckee Meadows was a grassy area nurtured by numerous winding waterways culminating in the Boynton Slough, Alexander Lake, and natural wetlands where the eastern edge of the valley approaches the Virginia Range. This was one of the many "Big Meadows" described by mid-nineteenth-century westward emigrants, a welcome expanse of green tules, high wild rye, and bunchgrass that served as a balm to eyes and throats parched by their journey through the "waterless alkali wasteland" of the Forty-Mile Desert in present-day central Nevada. Diaries of Mormon emigrants exploring the western reaches of their newfound land of Zion in the 1850s marveled at the area's "large herds of antelopes" and "grass reaching our horses' girts, thick and luxuriant."[13]

Although far from a lush paradise, the area held promise for agriculture and livestock raising, with swaths of green grasses giving way to broad expanses of native sagebrush, rabbitbrush, bitterbrush, and a broom-like shrub known as Mormon tea. Brigham Young's recall of the Mormon faithful back to Zion amid fears of a federal invasion in 1857 left the area to a handful of traders, farmers, and ranchers like Huffaker who settled on or near the natural waterways of the south Meadows, eventually growing a number of community centers that also included Steamboat, Brown's Station, and Glendale.[14]

Not until a year after Huffaker's arrival did prospectors happen upon the massive Comstock silver lode, triggering the stratospheric rise of Virginia City twenty miles to the southeast and transforming the formerly obscure valley into a dynamic crossroads. Fortuitously located on the direct pathway from the overland trail to the Comstock mining district, as well as a popular route westward to Sacramento, Huffaker's quickly garnered a freight stage station, post office, hotels, saloons, livery stables, the modest wood-frame school, and, by the time Nevada entered the Union in 1864, approximately 300 residents.[15] Increased settlement and the Comstock's demand for beef and butter spurred the creation of a network of irrigation ditches directing water from area creeks and the Truckee River to fields and pastures, making possible the cultivation of twenty thousand additional acres.[16] Leaching alkali, not lack of water, prompted adjustments of crops and techniques to counter the declining fertility of the area's salty soil, in order to populate the valley with alfalfa, onions, potatoes, and, increasingly, cattle, to be sold throughout the region and points beyond.

It was agriculture, ranching, and demand for their products that shaped life in the Meadows, long after the Central Pacific Railroad established a new junction six miles to the north in 1868, christening the new town "Reno," long after Huffaker's became a stop on the new Virginia & Truckee (V&T) Railroad line completed in 1872 to link the transcontinental route to the mines and mills of Virginia City. The 1870 census counted 505 residents of rural areas in Washoe County, 10 percent of whom worked in the town centers of Glendale, Huffaker's, or Steamboat. "The rest," as historian John Townley points out, "were on the land," with all available property in the entire valley snatched up by 1876.[17] This included a few hundred acres purchased by George Andrews, a former gold seeker originally from New Hampshire who carved out the Last Chance Ditch to direct Truckee River water to his thirsty alfalfa fields in 1874. Passing to his wife after their 1892 divorce, the holdings would eventually expand to a ranch of more than three thousand acres, reach high into the Carson foothills, and be managed for decades by George's daughter under her married name, Crissie Caughlin.[18]

The pace, but not the general tenor, of life in the Meadows shifted in the 1880s with the Comstock's decline, and Huffaker's gained a new influx of residents in the form of Italian woodcutters formerly employed by silver barons John Mackay and James Fair.[19] Bolstered by additional immigration in the late nineteenth and early twentieth centuries, the community expanded, while some of the more prosperous ranchers consolidated holdings, creating ranches of several thousand acres each. In subsequent decades community life continued to center around the Huffaker School, the activities of the Brown-Huffakers Farm Center, harvest cycles, and livestock rearing. The ranching tradition was passed along at the University Farm, a site leased since 1915 where students from the University of Nevada's College of Agriculture learned the trade, in keeping with the mission of the land-grant school.

Reno, in contrast, was the favored child of a machine age. Thundering eastward from the Sierra in a shudder of smoke and steel, the Central Pacific Railroad endowed Reno with eternal life, absolved forever of responsibility for its own survival. So long as two slender rails connected it to points beyond, Reno would in some fashion endure, unlike Bullfrog, Rhyolite, Aurora, Ione, and other ill-fated Nevada boomtowns whose urban aspirations died on the vine. Had Reno not been engineered, literally, by the transcontinental railroad, any one of the valley's agricultural centers might have become its primary locus of gradual growth, with perhaps a thousand residents scattered throughout the valley by 1900.[20]

Instead, the machine entered the garden, launching Reno on a new trajectory, one oriented outward, and dizzyingly independent of natural resources vulnerable to sudden depletion or seasonal irregularities. With confident zeal, the town's residents fed their infant city with timber from the Carson Range, denuding its eastern slopes within two decades.[21] Ore discoveries in central Nevada bolstered Reno's status as the state's banking and commercial center, and as the twentieth century dawned, new sources of revenue presented themselves, ventures that did not so much deny nature as transcend it. Not only did prizefighting, migratory divorce, and, by 1931, legalized gambling seem limitless in their appeal, but the resources on which they depended—discontent, greed, and boredom—seemed secure, perennial fixtures of human nature. What need for gold and silver or the proper balance of sunshine and rain when the opportunity for a quick divorce or a quick buck drew waves of consumers who stepped off the Overland Limited like so many shiny new automobiles emerging from a Ford assembly line?

Standardization was the attraction and strength of the migratory divorce industry, exemplified by the term *divorce mill*, applied to any town that offered the expedited service. Simple to explain and to achieve, a Reno divorce was, by 1910, dependable as clockwork, complete with a set timetable, a fixed sequence of steps, and a limited but not overwhelming number of personalized options in the form of lodging, attorneys, and witnesses to testify to one's consistent residence in the state for the designated period. Reducing that period from six months to three months to six weeks by 1931 granted Reno a dominant role in the unusual trade, as guidebooks, articles, novels, and movies further normalized the experience. As Jani Scandura wrote, "While standardized divorce production became increasingly time-efficient in Reno, the product, like the model T, didn't change. Nor did the power dynamics of the Reno factory's patriarchal management structure— the lawyers, judges, politicians, and police—ever substantially alter."[22]

Once a coalition of business and political interests managed to secure the permanent legalization of gambling by the state in 1931, it too became a regular fixture on Reno's burgeoning urban landscape, its prescribed games and behaviors governed by rules and, increasingly, regulatory enforcement. Blackjack, roulette, poker, and keno flourished in their balance of predictability and randomness, nurturing hopes that continued repetition of the same action could in fact produce a different result, a second chance, a new beginning. Each pull of the slot machine arm erased the last, offering the endless promise of changing fortune, unaffected by skill, exertion, or the vagaries of nature, human or otherwise.

Errant into the Wilderness

Other than its physical location on the railroad line, geography played little role in Reno's nascent ventures into entertainment and tourism. And so initially, Reno's success in these arenas had little impact on the physical contours of the south Meadows, still considered well out of town. In 1930 Reno's city limits reached less than two miles south of the Truckee River, with the "Huffaker district" an additional four miles distant. The area's open spaces were, however, increasingly appealing to city dwellers who saw these lands through an urban lens, casting the nearby rural environs as a playground for tourists, diversion-seeking divorcées, and wealthy capitalists like themselves.

The financial means of such players, such as George Wingfield, enabled them to purchase large swaths of open land. A former rancher who had made a fortune in the central Nevada mining boom of the early twentieth century, Wingfield had moved to Reno, where he launched a chain of twelve banks and operated numerous hotels. He also became ensconced as Nevada's chief political kingmaker, playing a key role in the state's legalization of gambling and loosening of divorce laws. In 1914 Wingfield bought one hundred acres of a ranch two miles south of Reno formerly belonging to Nevada governor John Sparks, establishing a stable for breeding thoroughbred horses. Wingfield then helped to orchestrate legalization of parimutuel betting on horses in the 1915 state legislative session, and by 1917 his property, named the Nevada Stock Farm, housed more than six hundred horses, both purebred and mixed breed. He also held a seat on the Nevada State Racing Commission, racing his horses internationally, a form of leisure specifically catering to sophisticated tastes.[23]

Nearby, other entrepreneurs, shrewdly noting visitors' intrigue with the region's frontier heritage, transformed working ranch operations of various sizes into vacation resorts, offering standardized western experiences where tourists of all types could learn to ride horses, witness cowboys of varying authenticity, and generally enjoy the rustic surroundings in an atmosphere of comfort and even luxury. Guest ranches soon peppered the region, with the highest density found in the rural spaces south of Reno, where visitors— primarily female divorcées—could immerse themselves in some semblance of ranch life while remaining conveniently close to the city's more cosmopolitan amenities. The advent of the automobile brought the southern reaches of the valley closer than ever, liberating travelers from the constraints of the V&T railway or the new streetcar lines that provided limited routes into the surrounding countryside.

Basking in the reflected glow of the Hollywood western's golden age, this was ranching as not vocation but packaged entertainment, countryside as commodity. Huffaker-area outposts such as the Flying N, the Sierra Gables Dude Ranch, and the Silver Circle Guest Ranch touted their prime locations, "far enough out in the peaceful countryside for quiet beauty and picturesque saddle trails, yet near to Reno's metropolitan conveniences, smart shops, and fascinating recreation," a gentle euphemism for neon casinos and clubs.[24] For years after his own Reno divorce in 1927, heir and society fixture Cornelius Vanderbilt Jr. ran a glamorous ranch south of town, the Lazy Me, where he entertained Hollywood celebrities including Will Rogers, Charlie Chaplin, and Clark Gable, a heady mix lightly fictionalized in his 1929 novel, *Reno*.

After 1931 Vanderbilt's "package ranch divorce" included "six weeks' room and board, a horse to ride, a trip to Reno twice a week . . . a free package of cigarettes per diem, and a free bottle of any liquor they asked for once a week."[25]

Entertaining these upscale visitors was just one way in which outside wealth began to permeate the Meadows, endowing the fields, pastures, and rangelands with a new form of currency manufactured by legislation. The region came into the sights of extremely wealthy outsiders for a myriad of related reasons as the Great Depression descended upon the country. The failure in 1932 of George Wingfield's banking empire was particularly devastating to the 150 Nevada ranches to which his banks had extended loans, ranches already suffering from years of drought and the collapse of the livestock market.[26] The bank failure sent many of these ranches into the hands of receivers who began to sell the land for very low prices. Seizing opportunity, an enterprising real estate broker and developer named Norman Biltz, originally from New England and active in multiple projects around Lake Tahoe, began buying up these properties, particularly along the Carson and Humboldt Rivers, and offering them for sale to out-of-state millionaires attracted by Reno's low taxes on cash and securities. Biltz and his associates purchased lists of Americans worth twenty million dollars or more, sending them personalized leather binders containing a prospectus and a magazine called *Nevada, the Last Frontier*, listing all the state's tax advantages.[27] Once California increased its own state income tax in 1935, the exodus accelerated, and as Reno assumed the mantle of Biggest Little City in the World, local newspapers brimmed with the names of rich and powerful former denizens of Southern California who had joined the ranks of property owners in western Nevada—many of whom left a legacy of philanthropic foundations that have since donated millions of dollars to the region.

Among the Meadows' new proprietors, some more "resident" than others, was Wilbur D. May. A son of David May, founder of the May Company Department Stores, Wilbur was persuaded to move the base of his world travels from California to Nevada. After renting a house in neighboring Washoe Valley for a few years, he purchased the former Lower Holcomb Ranch near Huffaker's in 1940 from rancher Louis Damonte. May, described locally as an "internationally known sportsman, aviator, and big game hunter," bred quarter horses, Black Angus cattle, and Boston bull terriers on the property, which he named the Double Diamond Ranch, after the shapes formed from stacking his last initial, *M*, on top of his first, *W*. He continued to expand his holdings through the 1950s by purchasing contiguous properties such as the large Humphrey Feed Ranch, which fronted the highway.[28] Biltz himself, named the "Duke of Nevada" by *Fortune* in 1954 and "Mr. Big" by *Time* in 1953, personally bought a portion of the Old Lake Ranch, three miles south of Reno, in 1935. Advertised for sale as a "perfect suburban estate" for the past several years, the large ranch was subdivided and sold in tracts. Biltz purchased several hundred acres of it for his personal estate, building three "Williamsburg style" manor homes on what he dubbed his "Gentleman's Ranch."[29]

Other new arrivals were less interested in residing on the Meadow properties their wealth had secured. Known familiarly as "the Major," Max C. Fleischmann of the Fleischmann Yeast fortune, formerly of Santa Barbara, moved to a new twenty-one-room mansion at Lake Tahoe in 1936, but maintained offices in Reno, where he very quickly became known for his generous donations to the educational and cultural activities of his adopted state.[30] Interested more in profit than philanthropy, eccentric millionaire LaVere Redfield moved to Reno in 1935 and started buying immense amounts of property throughout the region—in Reno, along the western foothills, and well into the heights of the Carson Range—according to Norman Biltz, purchasing tens of thousands of acres for a dollar an acre.[31] When the university's South Virginia farm came up for auction in 1955, Redfield was the sole bidder, snapping it up for seven hundred thousand dollars.[32]

Few urban areas, in the Great Basin or elsewhere, experienced expansion in quite this way, as a somewhat idle entertainment for individuals who happened to find themselves in the area for tax purposes and were able to easily acquire holdings of substantial size. But the trend was not confined to new arrivals. By now the Reno machine was churning out its own millionaires, and increasingly they too cast their gaze to the southern portion of the valley, where large amounts of land could still be had as area ranchers called it quits. With their background in the gaming industry, these men's purchases naturally launched speculation of a new casino strip along Virginia Street. In 1953 Harolds Club gambling magnate Raymond I. "Pappy" Smith purchased the Meadows' Peckham and Fife ranches, a total of 350 acres.[33] After real estate broker Norman Biltz decided to sell his Gentleman's Ranch in 1955, a portion of his land was bought by William F. Harrah, who over the past two decades had parlayed a downtown bingo parlor into one of Reno's most successful gambling properties, Harrah's Club. Harrah knocked down Biltz's mansion, constructed his own in its place, named the estate Rancharrah, and entertained legions of performers, politicians, and assorted luminaries over the next two decades.

With the expansion of both the city and its tourist industry, the ranches and farms of the valley center became the target of airport expansion. Level and free of large trees, wires, and mountains, land farmed and ranched for decades provided ample room for future expansion as well as emergency landings. When ranching families refused to sell, the city resorted to condemnation.[34] In 1956 a reporter sat with eighty-year-old matriarch Martha Matley in the century-old ranch house she had lived in for fifty-eight years, a house that would soon be relocated from the airport's path, noting her tendency to flinch whenever jets took off nearby. Later that year the airport and an adjoining Nevada Air National Guard jet field covered land once cultivated for potatoes, onions, vegetables, and apples where the high water table once had provided all the water required.[35]

Although country estates, farms, and ranches still dominated the Meadows at midcentury, several transformations to the landscape signified an era's end, including the closing of the Virginia & Truckee Railroad. Spectators at Huffaker station witnessed the railroad's final run in November 1950, after which the tracks were removed and the right-of-way sold to the state in order to construct a modern four-lane highway from Huffaker Lane south to Steamboat.[36] Modernization also spearheaded construction on a new brick multiroom Huffaker School along Dry Creek, adjacent to the aging building it would soon replace, a site still complete with hitching posts for students to tie their horses and a spring where generations of children once drew buckets full of water to quench their midday thirst. As the old schoolhouse was put up for auction, property values of the surrounding farmland were said to be increasing rapidly with the harvest of a new and relatively untested crop: the residential subdivision.[37]

Still, nothing showed the escalating literal and symbolic value of the Meadows so much as the decision of the Washoe County Fair and Convention Board in 1962 to purchase a triangle of land four miles south of the city center to construct a new convention center and civic auditorium. Located in a determinedly rural setting, across South Virginia Street from the large property LaVere Redfield had snatched up several years earlier, the site choice flew in the face of a Stanford Research Institute recommendation of a central downtown location for the structure. Also surprising to many was the price paid for the land, a cool $1.2 million, said to be approximately seventeen times the amount paid just ten years earlier.[38] Charges of influence

peddling proliferated, particularly as the property's buyer a decade earlier
had been none other than Harolds Club's own Pappy Smith, sure, many
believed, to be angling for his own financial gain.[39]

The board's decision became clearer, although no less controversial, with
revelations of rumored plans for seven hotels to be constructed near the triangle site, including Holiday Inns and at least two luxury properties, one
said to be a $20 million project with a staggering twenty-four stories and
850 rooms, larger by far than any existing structure in Reno.[40] South Virginia Street had clearly become a new field of dreams for casino and hotel
entities emboldened by the recent easing of restrictions that had long confined gambling to a small portion of the city center. In 1961 the Reno City
Council had voted to permit casino properties to operate outside the former
"red line," so long as they included 100 or more hotel rooms, thereby bringing additional tax revenue to the city. With available real estate increasingly
scarce in the dense downtown area, South Virginia Street beckoned, offering
hopes of imitating the extraordinary success of the Las Vegas Strip, which
had emerged out of nowhere on an unassuming highway out of town in the
early 1940s to become a national sensation.

With the decision to construct a second civic auditorium downtown—a
move that pacified some, but enraged others livid at the doubled expense—
Centennial Coliseum (named for the state's 1964 centennial) was completed
on the triangle site, opening in 1965. Two years later the passage of the state's
Corporate Gaming Act opened the door for corporations to invest in gaming operations, leading to the entrance into the industry of companies such
as Hilton, MGM, Holiday Inns, Ramada, and Hyatt.[41] Hilton Hotels secured
80 acres just to the southwest of the Coliseum in 1971 and was said to be
conducting a feasibility study for a "total resort complex" with at least 500
rooms.[42] Speculation about a new south Reno strip intensified after the death
of LaVere Redfield in 1974 made his land, directly across from the Coliseum,
newly available for purchase. Approximately 210 acres of it were said to be
under consideration by Las Vegas gaming magnate Kirk Kerkorian in 1975
for an immense new MGM property, complete with a golf course, shopping
center, and hotel-casinos.[43]

Added to the frenzy surrounding the prospective new casino strip were
proposals to extend the north-south freeway into the Meadows on one of
five suggested routes, construct a modern enclosed shopping center on 86
acres of former farmland, and replace a small country road, Hash Lane, with
the extension of McCarran Boulevard, a wide beltway planned eventually

to encircle the city. Opponents of rezoning the land for the proposed shopping center from residential to commercial feared the impact of a projected eighteen thousand additional cars in the area per day and a lack of sewage capacity for the city, already taxed by surging population growth. After twice rejecting the application for rezoning, the "giant shopping center" plan was finally approved in July 1975, contingent on securing prominent shopping center developer Taubman Corporation, financing an array of road improvements, and constructing a hockey rink to serve city residents. With all the other proposed development in the area, city council members determined that traffic congestion would increase markedly whether or not the shopping center was built.[44]

Everything seemed primed for a transformation of the Meadows into a gaming and commercial paradise, rivaling or perhaps even exceeding the offerings of downtown. But the Reno machine could not control MGM. In November 1975, company executives announced their purchase of lease options on a 110-acre gravel pit site far to the north, conveniently close to both the airport and the north-south freeway and miles from the Centennial Coliseum. The location came as a shock to onlookers expecting the company to choose either the Redfield site or prime land west of town near a projected 237-acre resort complex to be constructed by Harrah's called Auto World, a resort intended to comprise a 500,000-square-foot building to display Harrah's auto collection, a high-rise hotel-casino, and ice-skating rink, trout pond, and Pony Express museum. With plans for the MGM Grand and Auto World proceeding miles away, any hopes for a casino strip south of Reno seemed dashed. Clearly disappointed, a representative for Hilton Hotels diplomatically said, "Like prudent businessmen, we'll just take it in stride," but plans for a nearby Hilton resort also faded into the dust.[45]

With the collapse of major casino plans for the corridor, the trajectory of South Meadows development assumed a more traditional suburban pattern. The proposed shopping center opened in 1979, surrounded by an asphalt field of forty-one hundred parking spaces, with 650,000 feet of climate-controlled retail space, and the pastoral name of Meadowood. A handful of developers maintained lofty visions for the Redfield property into the early 1980s, with one particularly ambitious plan featuring a monorail that linked three hotel casinos to each other and the convention center. A national economic downturn and the competition-driven closures of many downtown gaming properties dashed those hopes, and today the site that once courted MGM houses a Walmart Supercenter, Babies-R-Us, Sam's Club, discount clothing stores, and a handful of chain restaurants. Facing the convention center, the last undeveloped portion of the Redfield property sits barren but for a few billboards and, for the duration of each election season, a crop of campaign signs. The century-old Cochran Ditch slices through one corner of the wind-swept lot, winding its way through dirt and promises, irrigating nothing.

Unnatural Acts

In recent years those seeking evidence of Reno's changing attitudes toward nature need look no further than the Truckee River Whitewater Park, a peaceful oasis in the heart of the city. Its two branches rush past either side of Wingfield Park, a small grassy island named for George Wingfield, the land's donor, whose grand in-town mansion once overlooked it from the north bank. Popular for freestyle and slalom kayaking, tubing, and rafting, the 2,600-foot stretch beckons with standing waves, drop pools, and a series of Class 2–3 rapids. Large boulders on its banks provide ample seating, and in the warmer months hundreds of people gather to try the course, swim, float, and otherwise entertain themselves.

What seems upon first glance to be a natural gem was in fact constructed in 2003–4 as the first leg of a proposed $6 million, twenty-four-mile recre-ation plan for the Truckee River. Designed by Gary Lacy, the park's features were created by heaving seven thousand tons of smooth flat-top rocks and boulders into place alongside the river's banks and contouring concrete to direct its current and ease access to the water. The $1.5 million project also removed unsafe and unsightly iron rebar, concrete flood walls, and a danger-ous dam.[46]

Refurbishing the river was widely considered a critical component of Reno's attempted reinvention in the new millennium. By 2000 the city's local economy had declined precipitously, as the industries it had created sput-tered and failed. A city accustomed to constant growth learned to expect and then demand it, while the human resources on which its prime attrac-tions had come to depend had proved as capricious as deposits of gold or silver, vulnerable not so much to depletion as to changing cultural norms and, most alarmingly, competition from elsewhere. In shaping its economy around industries disconnected from its unique geography, from any natural advantage, Nevada had made itself vulnerable to the ascension of other des-tinations offering the same amenities in settings that were more impressive, more varied, or simply more convenient.

As Nevada's divorce trade dissipated by the 1960s with the loosening of legal constraints nationwide, gaming became the state's chief source of revenue. And in that arena, beginning in the mid-1970s, Reno's reach exceeded its grasp. Over the next few decades, from the overbuilding of its downtown spurred by the construction of the MGM Grand to the rise of Atlantic City and the legalization of tribal and riverboat casinos throughout the country and the explosive success of Las Vegas megaresorts, Reno found itself increasingly outmatched and outnumbered. The interstate, not the railroad, was now the main conduit for the visiting masses, but the assembly line had come unhinged, its output erratic.

With its landscape of shuttered casinos, souvenir shops, and a general sense of decay, downtown Reno in the 1990s displayed the consequences of privileging isolated interior spaces over interconnected indoor and outdoor environments. Jealous of all competitors, its casinos had created all-inclusive resorts geared to keeping patrons within their walls. Tourists were deposited by airport shuttles at the hotel doors, or piloted their own cars into enormous parking garages, and were then conveyed by skywalks and monorails to registration desks, escalated and elevated from casino floor to buffet to hotel room and back again. The industry that once transcended nature now denied it outright, defying circadian rhythms with windowless rooms and twenty-four-hour cafés. The streets outside became collateral damage, creating a self-perpetuating cycle as visitors and residents alike neither walked downtown nor wanted to.

Faced with such economic and aesthetic decline, Reno's leading voices cried out for a strategy to breathe new life into the tourism industry and attract new residents to what many considered a faded gambling town. Thoughts turned to what made Reno distinctive, including the long-neglected river shooting through the heart of the city. But *control* was the watchword. With downtown business owners still reeling from destructive "flood events" in 2005 and 1997, any aesthetic embellishments must retain the high flood walls and bridges required to provide clearance for and protection from the periodic torrents of melting snowpack exacerbated by a century's narrowing of the natural river channel. Memories still stung of the 1997 flood, which not only deluged downtown Reno, but overwhelmed Steamboat Creek and its entire drainage area in the valley's center, coursing three feet of water over the airport and causing more than thirty million dollars in damage to its runways, passenger terminal, baggage handling equipment, and telephone systems.[47] Such was the peril of locating an airport in a traditional floodplain.

To a city desperately seeking stability, seeking it in something as volatile as nature was perhaps the biggest gamble of all. Carefully crafted marketing strategies attempted to secure nature's new role in 2003 with the slogan "Reno-Tahoe: America's Adventure Place" and an accompanying campaign highlighting the nearby mountains, the temperate climate, and the broad array of outdoor activities they enabled. Topping the list were skiing and golf, with seven ski resorts within an hour's drive and fifty golf courses within ninety minutes—attractions that, like the kayak park, engineer the natural landscape into a manicured playground, turning expanses of sage into brilliant green fairways and carving perfectly angled slopes into the mountainside. What nature did not provide, millions of dollars in snowmaking equipment and irrigation could accomplish with ease.[48]

With the mountains still a short drive away, the much-heralded (and heavily subsidized) arrival of major outdoor superstores Cabela's and Scheels, in 2007 and 2008, bridged the gap with grand indoor mountainsides, enormous aquariums, and hundreds of taxidermied animals dutifully posing for customers in climate-controlled, skylit comfort. And in the heart of downtown, the closed Fitzgerald's Hotel-Casino reopened in 2011 as CommRow, later renamed Whitney Peak, a nongaming recreation and dining destination complete with a 7,000-square-foot indoor bouldering park and a 164-foot climbing wall affixed to its outer facade. Its indoor climbing structures made of Baltic birchwood and outside mosaic of seventeen separate belay stations offered visitors urbanized nature at its finest—a rock-climbing wall with no rocks, bouldering with no boulders.[49]

This is a constructed and convenient simulacrum of nature, well suited to the needs of a consumer society, which values what it has destroyed by replicating its form, if not its function. On the far south end of the Meadows, a herd of twenty mule deer stand sentry along the entry gates and walking paths of the Montreux Golf and Country Club, fixed forever in life-size bronze, seemingly unperturbed by the surrounding enclave of luxury homes that pushed out their living counterparts. Bronzed mountain goats grace a nearby ridgetop, placidly surveying the tide of development that eventually caught up to projects such as the Meadowood shopping center and Centennial Coliseum (since renamed the Convention Center), which had initially leapfrogged over existing subdivisions to occupy the countryside.

In the decades to follow, residential development in the Meadows stratified socioeconomically by geographical location and, especially, by elevation. Developments toward the valley's center, like many throughout postwar

America, were more democratic in nature, offering middle-class families spacious living with all the modern conveniences. The 200-acre Smithridge Park, named for Pappy Smith, from whom developers had purchased the land, lay off South Virginia, just south of the convention center. Touted upon its opening in 1962 as "the largest land development and planned community in Washoe County," it targeted the middle class with parks, a shopping center, playgrounds, an office building, and eight hundred individual residential units and garden-type apartments, all "surrounded by the majestic beauty of the countryside."[50]

Deploying similar nature-infused rhetoric for a very different audience were developments such as Lakeside Meadows, offering "country living at its finest in Reno's most exclusive area," alongside the unincorporated Carson foothills to the west. Named for bordering Lakeside Drive (after a man-made lake constructed by the Works Progress Administration several miles north), the 2.5-acre home sites were carved from the former Ladino Dairy Farm, put up for auction by the university in 1960 as the College of Agriculture acquired a larger site in neighboring Sparks. Beginning the following year, the area parlayed existing irrigation systems and "deep rich soil" into enticements for buyers to establish their own stabled country estates "where the mountains meet the meadows," replacing dairy cows with "hobby livestock" and pets such as llamas, alpacas, and donkeys, all just a ten-minute drive from downtown.[51]

The earliest pioneers into this suburban utopia now exuded great defensiveness over their right to maintain it, along with the high property values it engendered. Throughout the 1960s residents of the southwest Meadows protested applications to the Regional Planning Commission to rezone the area for smaller lots, claiming a swim and tennis club at Lakeside Drive and Manzanita would be a nuisance and create a noise problem.[52] One group of two hundred area residents banded together to oppose a plan to rezone 180 acres west of the Huffaker School in order to construct 184 houses and a golf course. Dr. Gilbert Lenz, one of the committee leaders, cited concerns for overcrowding of the Huffaker School and warned that "the granting of land-use changes to permit high density subdivisions in this area would be the beginning of the end for this area of beautiful ranch-type homes."[53] Similarly, a group called "Preserve Our Washoe" formed in the mid-1970s to fight a proposal to extend the north-south freeway on a direct route through the increasingly desirable foothills of the Carson Range toward the Steamboat Hills.[54] By 1990 they had successfully deflected the freeway (now I-580) eastward toward the valley center and also persuaded Washoe County to pass a Southwest Rural Area Plan, to retain the area's existing character of "rolling countryside, dotted with homes, pastures, ponds, wildlife areas and winding country roads."[55]

Soon, the foothills became the only land available for further residential expansion. Because so much of the Meadows already had been consolidated into the hands of a few ranchers and corporate millionaires, a few key trans-fers of ownership from the 1980s onward transformed the area seemingly overnight, filling the fields, pastures, and rocky outcroppings of the val-ley with dense development. On the western side, Crissie Caughlin's heirs optioned all twenty-three hundred acres of the family holdings, and soon after the master plan for the expansive Caughlin Ranch development was approved by the Washoe County Commission in November 1983, spacious homes began to scale the hillside. After Wilbur May's death in 1982, his ranch of more than twenty-four hundred acres in the valley's center was sold to the Southmark Corporation and eventually transformed into a sea of stucco, where early advertisements proclaimed, "Just as the pioneers once braved the untamed high desert, you have forged new territory into Double Diamond Ranch—Pioneer Village is your discovery!" and streets named Comstock, Eureka, and Gold Rush evoke a romanticized yet misplaced mining past.[56]

By 2002 longtime rancher Louis Damonte Sr. had sold all but one hun-dred of his family's painstakingly assembled twenty-three hundred acres in the south Meadows, and the development bearing his name was the target of a surprise land grab by the city.[57] Staff estimated that annexing the Damonte Ranch subdivision, zoned suburban to allow up to three homes per acre, would generate thirty-eight million dollars in tax revenues over twenty years above and beyond the cost of providing direct services to the area. That amount, as a staff analyst indicated, could go a long way toward rebuild-ing and revitalizing Reno's troubled downtown. Despite vocal protests from some county residents, annexation proceeded, as it had already for Double Diamond Ranch and other nearby properties.[58]

Controversy erupted periodically over attempts to develop or annex the last remaining working ranches in the Truckee Meadows, including the Bal-lardini, Bella Vista, and Balsi holdings. Interviewed in 2000 about the impli-cations of developing the Ballardini property, located in the foothills west of Bartley Ranch Regional Park, area rancher Steve Mestre said, "I remember a little lane called Hash Lane. Now it's McCarran. You go to Windy Hill and all you see is rooftops. This is a decision that could result in destroying the last of our ranching heritage. We're down to the last. They have literally developed the whole valley."[59] There was nowhere to go, it seemed, but up.

Coda

Environmental historian Roderick Nash once wrote, "In the morality play of westward expansion, wilderness was the villain, and the pioneer, as hero, relished its destruction. The transformation of a wilderness into civilization was the reward for his sacrifices, the definition of his achievement, and the source of his pride."[60] To the early residents of the Truckee Meadows, the natural world served alternately as adversary and wellspring, a provider alternately bounteous and miserly, to be endlessly coaxed and courted. To those who succeeded them, transforming fields and pastures into suburbia, the land existed to be commodified and developed, to feed an urban machine born of steel rails and one-armed bandits. And once denied ongoing demand for its manufactured games and diversions, the city continued to expand into its outer reaches, this time solely to support the infrastructure it had created, pursuing growth for its own sake alone, the alternative seemingly inconceivable.

It is a process powered by its own momentum. Before the burst of the housing bubble in 2008, a small army of earthmovers etched the outlines of future streets, lots, and cul-de-sacs into acres of compressed dirt and brush on the Meadows' eastern side, just south of the Huffaker Hills. Since abandoned, the ghostly pathways of developments never constructed resonate with both expectation and nostalgia, an inherently American ambiguity. The Truckee Meadows ceased to be a wilderness long ago, and today the urge to urbanize the lingering traces of the wild, to perch precariously along its edges and plow through its remaining sagebrush, seems more compulsive than purposeful, unbound from the pioneer's moral dictates to civilize, or the farmer's struggle to wrest survival from alkali-ridden soil and mountain streams. It is the ambivalence characteristic of a later generation, far removed from its predecessors' focused determination. To the second generation of Puritans, unmoored and alone, distanced from the persecution that had sent their mothers and fathers clinging to the coast of an infant America, the result was a crisis of faith, a questioning of their ongoing errand into the wilderness.[61] Without an unwavering belief in a purpose born of geography and necessity, whose errand were they truly on, and to what end? Why were they here? Lacking the passion of purpose, any motivation for movement, the errand becomes errant, the blind stumblings of a lost generation, endlessly tracing ghostly circles in the dust.

Early one August morning in 2012, a mountain lion was spotted outside Harrah's Casino, in the heart of downtown Reno. Driven downstream by drought or perhaps a jealous rival, the hundred-pound male had grown disoriented in the unfamiliar urban surroundings, eventually finding refuge under an outdoor stage. Once discovered, the animal was quickly subdued with tranquilizer darts, fitted with a GPS collar, and released into the wilds of the nearby Carson Range. The story made headlines across the country not as a warning, but a punch line, a humorous sidebar about a mountain lion rebuffed from entering a casino and quickly returned to its native habitat. But perhaps there is a more sobering message here. Perhaps it is we who are the invasive species, as we machine the meadows into a metropolis, coercing creeks into concrete, and haplessly building higher and higher into the foothills with nothing but winter's flames to beat us back. We have no natural reason to be in this place, yet here we remain, tranquilized by complacency, little questioning the urgent call to grow, build, annex, climb. Perhaps it is we, not the mountain lion, who have lost our bearings and wander confused in a strange land, perpetually dislocated from time and reason, like billboards sprouting in empty pastures, like ashes tarnishing the new-fallen snow.

NOTES

1. Reno Fire Department, "Caughlin Fire After Action Analysis," November 2011, 4–9, http://www.reno.gov/home/showdocument?id=33332.

2. Brian F. O'Hara, "Climate of Reno, Nevada," National Weather Service, updated August 1, 2011, http://www.wrh.noaa.gov/rev/climate/renoclimateupdate .pdf; John M. Townley, *Tough Little Town on the Truckee* (Reno: Jamison Station Press, 1983), 9.

3. Reno Fire Department, "Caughlin Fire After Action Analysis," 5. Figures cited are from the Western Region Headquarters of the National Weather Service.

4. US Department of Agriculture Forest Service, *Federal Wildland Fire Policy,* chartered 1994, revised 2001, quoted in "Fires in the Wildland/Urban Interface," *U.S. Fire Administration Topical Fire Research Series* 2, no. 16 (2002): 1, http://www .usfa.fema.gov/downloads/pdf/statistics/v2i16-508.pdf.

5. Firewise Colorado, *Wildland Fire Preparedness/Education Partnership,* February 2001, cited in ibid.

6. Ready, Set, Go!, "What Is the Wildland Urban Interface?," December 9, 2012,

http://www.wildlandfirersg.org/Learn/content.cfm?ItemNumber=646&navItem Number=505; Jack Cohen, "The Wildland-Urban Interface Problem: A Conse- quence of the Fire Exclusion Paradigm." *Forest History Today* (Fall 2008): 23.

7. Reno Fire Department, "Caughlin Fire After Action Analysis," 4.

8. Curtis P. Johnson, "Recommendation for a Wildland/Urban Interface Risk Assessment for the Jurisdictional Area of the Reno Fire Department," submitted to US Fire Administration National Fire Academy, April 2005, http://www.usfa.fema .gov/pdf/efop/efo38029.pdf.

9. City of Reno website, "Caughlin Fire Fact Sheet," https://www.reno.gov /modules/showdocument.aspx?documentid=32080.

10. Johnson, "Recommendation for a Wildland/Urban Interface Risk Assess- ment," 5.

11. Washoe County Parks, "Valentine's Day Family Open House," press release, n.d., http://www.co.washoe.nv.us/index/display_outreach.html~details=8231; "Old Huffaker School Now Fish Hatchery," *Reno Evening Gazette*, January 27, 1951, 12.

12. Townley, *Tough Little Town on the Truckee*, 44.

13. Nevada State Historical Marker no. 26, produced by the Nevada State His- toric Preservation Office and located at the junction of Interstate 80 and US High- way 95, calls the Forty Mile Desert "a barren stretch of waterless alkali wasteland." Mormon diaries quoted in ibid., 14, 41.

14. Ibid., 44.

15. Ibid., 55.

16. Washoe County website, "History of Washoe County," n.d., http://www .washoecounty.us/clerks/files/pdfs/county_code/history.pdf; Townley, *Tough Little Town on the Truckee*, 137.

17. Townley, *Tough Little Town on the Truckee*, 124–25.

18. Shiela Lonie, *Crissie Caughlin, Pioneer* (Reno: Shiela Lonie, 2004), 72, 123, 162.

19. Townley, *Tough Little Town on the Truckee*, 129.

20. According to John Townley, "Without a transcontinental railroad, Reno, by 1900, would have been another Genoa and its only product, alfalfa, a glut on the market. Maybe a thousand residents would have shared the valley as it found eco- nomic equilibrium at doldrum level after the Comstock went belly up." Ibid., 267.

21. Ibid., 16.

22. Jani Scandura, *Down in the Dumps: Place, Modernity, and American Depres- sion* (Durham, NC: Duke University Press, 2008), 44.

23. C. Elizabeth Raymond, *George Wingfield: Owner and Operator of Nevada* (Reno: University of Nevada Press, 1992), 112–13.

24. Nevada Dude Ranch Association brochure (Reno: Nevada Dude Ranch Association, 1936), "Dude Ranches" file, Nevada Historical Society; Silver Circle

Guest Ranch brochure, University of Nevada, Reno, Special Collections, Donner Trail promotional file, 91-49/2/12, n.d.

25. Cornelius Vanderbilt Jr., *Ranches and Ranch Life in America* (New York: Crown, 1968), 251–53.

26. Raymond, *George Wingfield*, 203.

27. Norman H. Biltz, *Memoirs of "Duke of Nevada": Developments of Lake Tahoe, California and Nevada: Reminiscences of Nevada Political and Financial Life* (Reno: University of Nevada Oral History Program, 1969), 30–36.

28. "Lower Holcomb Ranch Sold to Louie Damonte," *Nevada State Journal*, January 20, 1938, 2; "Holcomb Ranch Sale Announced," *Reno Evening Gazette*, June 13, 1940, 3; "Raymond I. Smith and Wilbur May Buy 3 Ranches," *Nevada State Journal*, December 11, 1953, 2.

29. "Sale of Land Is Ordered by Judge," *Nevada State Journal*, July 26, 1935, 8; ad, *Nevada State Journal*, May 11, 1930, 11; "Nevada: Mr. Big," *Time*, June 15, 1953.

30. "$200,000 Home Nears Completion at Lake," *Nevada State Journal*, December 15, 1935, 1.

31. Biltz, *Memoirs of "Duke of Nevada*," 36.

32. "Redfield Sole Farm Bidder," *Reno Evening Gazette*, December 3, 1955, 1.

33. "Raymond I. Smith and Wilbur May Buy 3 Ranches," 2; "Raymond I. Smith Adds to Holdings on S. Virginia," *Nevada State Journal*, June 12, 1954, 12.

34. "U.A.L. Buys Land to Make Port Larger," *Nevada State Journal*, November 14, 1936, 9; "Airport Project Must Start Soon Engineers Rule," *Reno Evening Gazette*, May 4, 1954, 13; "Airport Site Action Slated," *Reno Evening Gazette*, January 10, 1956, 18.

35. "The Matley Family: A Story of Progress," *Reno Evening Gazette*, November 17, 1956, 16.

36. "State Desirous of Acquiring Right of Way," *Reno Evening Gazette*, July 14, 1950, 13.

37. "Old Huffaker School Is Ending 83 Years of Service; New Structure Is Going Up," *Nevada State Journal*, June 18, 1950, 3.

38. "Fair Board Orders Site Appraisal After Long Debate," *Reno Evening Gazette*, June 27, 1962, 15.

39. "Grand Jury Reports on Hall Site," *Reno Evening Gazette*, December 20, 1962, 1, 15.

40. "Planners Approve Auditorium Site," *Nevada State Journal*, July 11, 1962, 12; "'Strip' for Reno Ready to Start?," *Reno Evening Gazette*, March 28, 1963, 23.

41. Robert D. Faiss and Gregory R. Gemignani, "Nevada Gaming Statutes: Their Evolution and History," Occasional Paper Series, Center for Gaming Research, University of Nevada, Las Vegas, September 2011, no. 10, http://gaming.unlv.edu/papers/cgr_op10_faiss_gemignani.pdf, 5.

42. "Hilton Gives Hotel Plans at Virginia, Hash," *Reno Evening Gazette*, May 4, 1971, 7; "Plan Developing for Hilton Hotel South of Reno," *Reno Evening Gazette*, June 12, 1971, 11.

43. "MGM, Redfield Estate Negotiate over Reno Land," *Reno Evening Gazette*, April 23, 1975, 1, 2.

44. "Giant Shopping Center OKd by Reno Council," *Nevada State Journal*, July 22, 1975, 2. For whatever reasons, the hockey rink and movie theaters never materialized.

45. "MGM Shifts Sites for Casino Bid," *Nevada State Journal*, November 18, 1975, 1; "MGM Plans Hotel," *Nevada State Journal*, October 17, 1975, 2.

46. City of Reno, "Whitewater Park," http://www.reno.gov/index.aspx?page=311; Ryan Brandt, "Reno Enlists Paddles, Not Poker, for a Rebirth," *New York Times*, June 12, 2005, Travel section, 3.

47. State of Nevada Division of Water Resources, "Truckee River Chronology, Part III: Twentieth Century," http://water.nv.gov/mapping/chronologies/truckee/part3.cfm.

48. Reno-Sparks Convention and Visitors Authority, "Reno Tahoe USA," http://www.visitrenotahoe.com/reno-tahoe/what-to-do/golf.

49. CommRow website, "Base Camp," http://www.commrow.com/BaseCamp.asp.

50. "Work Underway on Housing Development South of City," *Reno Evening Gazette*, August 28, 1961, 13; ad, *Nevada State Journal*, April 22, 1962, 40.

51. "Ladino Dairy Farm Is Sold by University," *Reno Evening Gazette*, April 21, 1960, 19; ad, *Nevada State Journal*, February 22, 1961, 17; "Lakeside Meadows Subdivision First Unit Work Is Completed," *Reno Evening Gazette*, April 26, 1961, 3; ad, *Reno Evening Gazette*, May 10, 1961, 22.

52. "Petition Aimed at Balking Plan for Private Club," *Reno Evening Gazette*, November 10, 1961, 20.

53. "Huffaker Area Tracts Opposed," *Reno Evening Gazette*, February 14, 1966, 2.

54. "Opposing Forces Abound in Shopping Center Issue," *Nevada State Journal*, July 19, 1975, 12.

55. Susan Voyles, "Ballardini Property Could House 995 Homes," *Reno Gazette-Journal*, February 9, 2000, A1, A4.

56. Ad, *Reno Gazette-Journal*, September 17, 2000, C14.

57. Don Cox, "Clinging to the Ranch," *Reno Gazette-Journal*, April 22, 2002, A1.

58. Susan Voyles, "City's Bid to Annex Ranch Could Spark Other Claims," *Reno Gazette-Journal*, March 6, 2000, A1, A6; Peg O'Malley, "Your Turn: City Trying to Sidestep Plan Process," *Reno Gazette-Journal*, March 9, 2000, A9; Steve Timke, "Washoe's Growth Outpaces Nation," *Reno Gazette-Journal*, April 17, 2003, C1.

59. Voyles, "Ballardini Property Could House 995 Homes," A1, A4.

60. Roderick Frazier Nash, *Wilderness and the American Mind,* 4th ed. (New Haven, CT: Yale University Press, 2001), 24–25.

61. See Perry Miller, *Errand into the Wilderness* (Cambridge, MA: Belknap Press of Harvard University Press, 1956).

Cowboys and Clerics

Political Culture and Planning Regimes in Salt Lake City and Boise

CHRIS BLANCHARD

AS MORMON LORE TELLS IT, it was July 1847 and Brigham Young had fallen ill. Victim of the Rocky Mountain spotted fever, the leader of the Mormon Saints found himself confined to the back of a wagon for most of the long trek from Nauvoo, Illinois, to the harsh desert valley of the Great Basin. Except for Young's illness, all went according to plan. After investigating several options, by 1844 or 1845 it became a foregone conclusion that the Mormons would strike out along the Platte River and make their way to the Great Basin. It would be a Herculean task to move some sixteen thousand people across the interior of a partially explored continent, but the Mormons were nothing if not good planners. As historian Leonard Arrington noted, "Central planning, organized cooperation, and the partial socialization of investment implicit in Mormon theory" were crucial elements in translating the Saints' vision into reality.[1] Utahans commemorated the settling of the Wasatch Front by building "This Is the Place Heritage Park" in Salt Lake City, attributing the proclamation of "This is the place" to Brigham Young. Others have appropriated the phrase for purposes all their own.

A little more than a century and a half later, the leader of a state north of the Mormon capital was making a pronouncement of a similar sort, albeit to a band of followers who turned out not to be followers at all. In March 2010 the Boise Young Professionals (BYP), a Generation Y adjunct group of the Boise Metro Chamber of Commerce, sat in a packed room of the newly remodeled Idaho capitol building. They were there to hear Governor Butch Otter talk about why, amid declining economic opportunities in the Gem State, Idaho continued to be a promised land for this group of young professionals. *Boise Weekly* reporter Josh Gross gave an account of the governor's address: "He appeared at the podium in cowboy boots, with a traditional old west long-tail coat, looking just a mustache and a 10-gallon hat short of Wyatt Earp, speaking about animal husbandry and high school football, then name-dropping Albertsons, Simplot and Micron as some of Idaho's greatest hits, closing with the slightly puzzling summation that BYP members should stay in Idaho because 'this is where it's happening, and this is where it's going to happen.'"

The group was not amused, nor as hopeful as Young's road-weary Saints more than a century before. "I wanted to see what his vision for the future was. He didn't have any vision, and that's scary," said one attendee.[2] These two anecdotes arise from and represent the two contrasting political cultures of two Intermountain West states: a laissez-faire style fundamental to Idaho's character and the prophetic faith of Utahans in planning and cooperation.

In both states these contrasting cultures have powerfully shaped efforts to address the problems of rapidly growing urban areas. The "Utah Model" of planning, which has drawn national acclaim, is based on a planning regime that has attracted admiration even outside the state. By contrast, the Boise Valley's troubled Blueprint for Good Growth (BGG) was unable to rise above an indifferent state government and squabbling and bickering among local governments. A comparison of these two cases highlights differences between two western states that are typically obscured and little understood by scholars outside the West—and even within it. Scholars have generally assumed that Idaho and Utah are almost the same politically because both of them contain large numbers of conservative and Republican voters. When it comes to state and local governance, however, they are very different, as the two case studies in this chapter clearly demonstrate.

Historical Context

Utah and Idaho both undertook state-level land use planning activities in the mid-1970s, well before urban growth became a driving force in the Intermountain West. In 1974, the year the state legislature passed the Utah Land Use Act, Utah's population among the four counties that make up the Wasatch Front numbered about 1 million. The legislature's action foretold rising concerns about uncontrolled urban growth, but voters defeated the measure when it was put to a popular referendum, largely because of a drumbeat by conservative talk radio hosts who played on familiar western themes of individualism and "big government."[3]

In the 1970s and early 1980s the population along the Wasatch Front boomed even as the national economy languished in recession. The sleepy town of Sandy leaped from 6,438 residents in 1970 to a city of 52,210 by 1980. West Valley City did not even exist as an incorporated placed in 1970, but by the end of the decade it had become a city of 72,299, and today it is the second largest city in Utah. Dozens of incorporations such as these limited the size and population growth of the region's anchor, Salt Lake City, but not the growth of the county overall. In the thirty years from 1980 to 2010, Salt Lake County's population increased from 619,066 to 1,029,655. A similar story emerged in Utah County, just to the south. There, the small town of Spanish Fork more than doubled in size between 1980 and 2000, from 9,825 to 20,246, and then tripled in population between 1990 and 2010. Utah County as a whole followed a similar path, growing from 263,590 in 1990 to 516,564 in 2010. Estimates showed the Wasatch Front region growing from 1.6 million to 2.7 million people by 2018, and to 5 million by 2050. Land use plans in place in 1998 would mean consuming 590 square miles by 2050; in 1998 the front's urbanized area was only 320 square miles.[4] The incredible pace of urban growth drove Utah's leadership to embrace the idea that the time for land use planning had come.

Decades earlier, in the mid-1970s, Idaho seemed to be ahead of the curve. In 1975 the Idaho Legislature passed the Local Land Use Planning Act, an act that still guides land use policy in the state today. This measure came on the heels of state legislation that consolidated all of the transportation departments of cities within Ada County, an increasingly urban region anchored by Boise. These two pieces of legislation seemed to lie outside the norm in a state where the state government rarely wades into what it sees as "local" issues.

While the Wasatch Front had been urbanizing for some time, 1970 marked the first year that more of Idaho's residents lived in urban than rural areas.[5] In 1960 Boise was Idaho's largest city, though not by much. Idaho Falls, located in the heavily agricultural eastern part of the state, was very nearly the same size, with both cities approaching 35,000 residents. But where Mormon settlement, railroad connections, and the Idaho National Laboratory supported eastern Idaho's economy, Boise's future was tied to its emerging status as a corporate headquarters. The Boise Valley was then home to agribusiness giants Ore-Ida and Simplot—the inventor of the freeze-dried french fry. It was also the home of the world's largest heavy contractor, Morrison-Knudsen, most famous as the builder of the Hoover Dam, the San Francisco Bay Bridge, and the Kennedy Space Center. Also located there were Albertsons, the large grocery chain, and Boise Cascade, the forest products giant.

The concentration of corporate headquarters catalyzed a burst of growth in the city of Boise between 1960 and 1970, a period when the population more than doubled from 34,481 to 74,990. At that point the city and the region began to attract firms that had no connection to Idaho's past. Hewlett-Packard's Data Systems Division moved to the west side of town in 1973, where production commenced on tape drives and systems printers, and later HP's industry-leading laser jet printers. In 1978 Micron, a semiconductor manufacturing firm, set up its headquarters on Boise's eastern border. At the west end of Ada County, the city of Meridian's population grew ten times over between 1980 and 2010, from 6,658 residents to 68,516. Sprawling sub-divisions gobbled up farmland and spilled over into sage-covered desert.

Despite growing concerns about the pace of urban growth, state-level interest in regional planning was not forthcoming at the state level. In a state distrustful of all things urban and governmental, Idaho's head start on a plan to facilitate regional planning could not be sustained. Instead, urban growth deepened urban and rural divisions, and state officials turned their back on urban problems. By contrast, Utah's unchecked growth became a concern for people living within and beyond the areas of urban settlement. In Idaho attempts to plan and direct urban growth brought conflict and failure, but in Utah consensus developed around the idea that planning for the future was essential. The two states took different paths because their political cultures pointed the way.

Utah's Planning Efforts Get Under Way

Regional planning efforts in Utah got under way in 1995 when the state legislature agreed to host a well-publicized October 30 summit billed as an effort to protect open spaces, farmlands, and wildlife habitat from rapid urban sprawl. Their efforts preceded a three-day conference hosted by Governor Mike Leavitt on how urban growth was transforming the state. The local press followed the issue intently. Prior to the legislative summit, a *Salt Lake Tribune* headline read "Public Meet Will Focus on Saving Open Spaces." Mirroring the politics surrounding Oregon's Urban Growth Boundary, in Utah rural legislators with farming backgrounds provided most of the leadership for the summit. Senator Leonard Blackham (R-Moroni), a turkey farmer, who had previously cochaired a state task force on urban growth, expressed deep concern that the urban environment was encroaching upon rural land: "Look at Los Angeles—we can see what will become of our valleys if we don't act before long. . . . [W]e need to be smart enough to control our destiny rather than just react to what comes."[6] As it turned out the governor's conference and the legislative summit both fell flat; in the following legislative session, legislators passed not a single bill in support of the summit's goals.

Urban growth, though, was a festering issue that could not be laid to rest so easily.[7]

By August of the following year, county governments along the front decided to revive the issue of uncontrolled growth. Mayor Tom Dolan of Sandy proposed a "Salt Lake County 2020" effort by proclaiming, "We should be planning for the next 25 years. . . . [I]t's just so logical." In the fall planners from several governments working as the Wasatch Front Planning Group produced a twenty-two-page report on how to deal with urbanization along the Wasatch Front. No one read it. To fill in the silence some University of Utah planning students tried their hand, but critics dismissed their massive report as "naïve."[8] The regional councils of government agreed to a rather abstract plan, but it failed to generate any legislative interest. In the following session the legislature made matters even worse by authorizing the creation of townships within the state, which fractured local governance even more than before. Commenting on this pattern of inaction, University of Utah planning professor Gene Carr was moved to note, "Today we've had it drilled into us this cultural obsession with private property rights and in doing so we've lost our sense of community and public interest." In a singular bit of good news, Senator Leonard Blackham noted the legislature's willingness to provide some money and technical assistance to continue the planning process. Despite the low level of interest, enough angst floated in the air to keep the pot simmering, but barely.

Public-sector leaders who remained committed to some sort of regional planning turned to other sources for support. In early October 1996, David P. Gardner, the former president of the University of Utah (1973–83), chancellor of the University of California System, and former head of the Eccles Foundation, delivered a public address in Salt Lake urging Utahans to "take hold of our future . . . rather than drifting into it, [with] our options unclear and unexamined, and as a result, forfeited irrevocably." Two days later the editors of the *Salt Lake Tribune* took a stand in the editorial pages, concurring with Gardner: "If Utahans expect to avoid the extreme urban sprawl, pollution, traffic snarls and gang crime of Southern California, they must become bolder, more creative growth managers. . . . Utahans cannot hear this message often enough."[9] They castigated the legislature for dragging its feet and accused it of bowing to parochial interests.

The disappointments of 1996 gave way to a degree of hope in January 1997 when a start-up group called the Coalition for Utah's Future grabbed the regional planning reins with its newly minted Envision Utah (EU) initiative.[10]

The formidable drivers of this new coalition could not be ignored. Robert Grow, president of Geneva Steel, Governor Mike Leavitt, and Larry Miller, owner of the Utah Jazz and a string of successful car dealerships throughout the Intermountain West, formed a tripartite leadership to back a regional planning effort.

The architects of Envision Utah instinctively understood the importance of controlling the language around the growth issue. For example, Larry Miller told the *Tribune,* "The growth of the last five or six years has been so rapid and had such an effect on quality of life and that has me very concerned. . . . [T]he food workers, the janitors and housekeeping workers can't afford to live here anymore. There's a lack of open space where our kids can play."[11] The focus on the disenfranchised and on "open spaces" rather than "growth management" and "the environment" proved to be invaluable in selling regional planning to a skeptical public. At this critical juncture Envision Utah got a boost from the George S. and Dolores Dore Eccles Foundation—formerly headed by David P. Gardner—in the form of a $500,000 challenge grant. The local media again provided cover, with the *Tribune* quoting then Utah County commissioner Gary Herbert: "Thirty years ago if we had some leader stand up and say 'I foresee the growth. Let's put the roads over here, let's save this land for parks, let's put things in place,' today we would probably erect a statue of that guy. What a leader."[12] A few years later Herbert became chair of Envision Utah and then was elected governor of Utah. The legislature committed $250,000 to the EU coalition for the purchase of sophisticated modeling software. Envision Utah was making progress.

At a November transportation and land use forum artfully crafted language was once again on display. EU chair Robert Grow spoke not of "density" but of "close-knit communities." Architect and planner Peter Calthorpe eschewed these terms altogether, preferring instead a conversation about "urban design and community fabric." Finally, in a rhetorical move probably more effective than any other, a speaker at the forum invoked the name of Brigham Young. Friends of Oregon director Robert Liberty challenged attendees: "I simply cannot believe that a people who were inspired and bold enough to leave their churches, their homes, and their countries to follow a new faith, to build new communities in the wilderness and to design new social institutions, are now trapped by inertia, unable to shape their own future because someone might object. You cannot wait for another Brigham Young to provide the leadership. In order to change direction, the people must provide direction."[13]

Later, in public meetings sponsored by Envision Utah, an actor dressed as Brigham Young appeared alongside Governor Mike Leavitt. From that time forward, references to the Mormon past became a regular feature of a process that sometimes resembled a theatrical production. As noted by one of the planners, "When you do regional visioning, you need to have one foot in history and one foot in prophecy."[14]

In January 1998, now two and a half years into the planning process, Envision Utah gained genuine traction when it announced it had hired renowned architect Peter Calthorpe and noted planner John Fregonese to develop the regional plan for the Wasatch Front. The *Tribune* promptly labeled Calthorpe a "visionary." The Calthorpe-Fregonese team enthusiastically launched a series of public forums in May. Within a few months' time, Calthorpe and Fregonese had conducted fifteen workshops involving more than seven hundred residents in communities all along the front. In these meetings "citizen planners"—the new lingo for "residents"—overwhelmingly endorsed small-scale town or village development that "encouraged community interaction." After analyzing the residents' feedback, the planners developed three alternative planning scenarios: continued development at low density, which would consume an additional 420 square miles of land; a "walkable neighborhoods" plan that would require only 167 square miles of new land; or a "high infill" plan that would discourage single-family subdivisions and would consume the least amount of new land at 111 square miles.[15]

By May 1998 the message was beginning to sink in. Even a Libertarian candidate for the Salt Lake County Commission, Cabot Nelson, wrote an op-ed editorial in the *Tribune* in support of planning: "Cities are the greatest invention of mankind. Unfortunately, misguided philosophies with good intentions have shaped the city in a dehumanizing sprawl. . . . Ultimately the idea is to reshape settlement patterns in Salt Lake County based upon market-driven principles. This would mean more choices in the way we live, travel, work, and socialize."[16]

Despite a growing momentum for the idea of planned growth, when idea met reality opposition was quick to emerge. Perhaps predictably, it erupted first in an affluent suburb that did not want to see urban-style development come its way. The city of Farmington, which is probably best known for its Lagoon theme park, sits equidistant from Salt Lake to its south and Ogden to the north. Like many cities along the front, it is sandwiched between the Great Salt Lake and steeply rising mountains and is pierced longitudinally by Interstate 15. Though the city sits within a highly urbanized corridor, its

residents are convinced that they live in rural America, an impression supported by large-lot development and the presence of numerous equestrian
properties. Residents strongly opposed Palladian Homes' proposed Farmington Green development of 179 homes set in a new-urbanist style.[17]

The next wave of attacks came from the opposite flank. Environmentalists announced their opposition to an element of the plan that would build
a new highway to reduce congestion on I-15. Transportation planners had
initially proposed the controversial "Legacy Highway" project in 1996 to
link Brigham City in the north to Nephi in the south. Environmentalists
believed that the new route would only lead to more automobile use, and
they accused the governor and his staff of manipulating the planning process
to favor state over local policy objectives. The accusation earned them A1
coverage in the *Salt Lake Tribune*. In response, John Fregonese deftly downplayed the importance of the freeway by noting that it was "a few miles of
road in a 10,000 square mile region."[18]

Calthorpe and Fregonese continued on undeterred. By September they
had refined the three scenarios that had emerged from public meetings and
added a fourth—a scenario that preserved a large amount of land for open
space and agricultural uses. Envision Utah announced a plan to begin a
media blitz to educate the public, to commence after the first of the year.[19]

Anticipating the press release, in November the *Tribune* published a pair
of profiles: one of a large family living in Farmington and enduring long
commutes in exchange for its "rural" lifestyle, another of a family with four
kids that left the suburbs for the city. The story line played on predictable and
clichéd themes. For the family in Farmington, cul-de-sacs with little traffic,
abundant wildlife, terrific views, and a rural lifestyle offered unparalleled
advantages. The family that had moved to the city talked about walkabil-
ity, urban amenities, and urban culture. In December the *Tribune* reprinted
the powerful call to action delivered the previous year by 1000 Friends of
Oregon executive director Robert Liberty. Like Calthorpe, Liberty was convinced that Utah's unique political culture would make the planning process
successful. He wrote, "People in this region, perhaps more than any other
region in the nation, understand that a sense of community is created by a
recognition of interdependence, of the need for restraint, mutual respect and
cooperation, not just a respect for property rights." Perhaps even more con-
vincingly, Liberty appealed to conservatives' concerns about fiscal responsibility by pointing out that planning would save money over time and lower
tax burdens.

The Envision Utah process was soon celebrated as a rousing success. Envision Utah kicked off the release of the report in January 1999 with a massive public awareness campaign that included a press tour to the four largest newspapers and four largest television stations in the region. Governor Leavitt appeared in television and radio ads, as did other political leaders and celebrities. The ads directed residents to be on the lookout for a four-page newspaper insert describing the four growth scenarios sketched out by the planners. Envision Utah staff held fifty public meetings, eventually amassing comments from 17,500 area residents. Residents approved what became known as the "quality growth strategy," and local governments began adopting ordinances to accommodate it. A few months later the Utah state legislature adopted the Quality Growth Act.

Today, the Envision Utah model has been copied all over the United States. A recent example includes the "Superstition Vistas" regional plan in Arizona, put together by the Envision Utah team of Robert Grow and John Fregonese. Envision Utah is managing the nation's only five-million-dollar grant award from the sustainability partnership between the Department of Housing and Urban Development, Environmental Protection Agency, and Department of Transportation. The Wasatch Front is in the midst of yet another iteration of the regional plan, Wasatch Choices 2040. In contradiction to any impression that Utah's political culture is antigovernment, residents of the state have developed one of the most envied and emulated regional planning processes in the nation.

Regional Planning in the Boise Valley

In the first decade of the twenty-first century the Boise-Nampa Metropolitan Statistical Area (MSA) was one of the fastest-growing urban areas in the United States. However, despite concerns expressed by political and civic leaders about sprawl and uncontrolled growth, the attempt to craft a land use and growth planning process has been frustrated by indifference by state officials, deep divisions within the region, and the absence of a viable institutional mechanism for bringing all the players to the table. The agency that set in motion the much-publicized Blueprint for Good Growth—the Ada County Highway District (ACHD)—was an unlikely candidate for leading a regional or even a county-wide planning effort. When the district was founded in 1972, local governments in Ada County, unlike anywhere else in the United States, no longer exercised control over the construction or repair of their own streets. The fact that all transportation projects in the county were henceforth administered by the district became a constant source of irritation to municipal officials.

Another problem was that the Blueprint for Good Growth was not created by a coalition to support it or by a philosophical readiness to adopt it; instead, it represented a pragmatic strategy by the Highway District to secure its future. A citizens' ballot initiative launched in 2002 had attempted to eliminate the agency altogether and return the county's transportation responsibilities back to the cities. That initiative failed at the polls, but it prompted the agency's administrators to undertake an effort to repair its public image and shore up its political standing.

Following the 2002 referendum the Ada County Highway District embarked upon the Blueprint for Good Growth. In conception, or at least rhetorically, the plan represented an attempt to connect land use planning in the county, which resided with individual cities, with transportation planning, which had been assigned solely to the Highway District in 1972. Municipal officials were skeptical of the district's proposal, but they agreed to participate in the planning process because it might give them some semblance of influence over the runaway urban development that seemed to be enveloping the Treasure Valley. Officially launched in the spring of 2004 by the ACHD and all the cities of Ada County (Boise, Eagle, Meridian, Star, Kuna, and Garden City), the "Blueprint for Good Growth" was supposed to take eighteen months and be completed in the fall of 2005. As 2006 approached, however, barely an outline of a plan existed, and it would take years for one to emerge. By then, interjurisdictional squabbles dashed any hope that regional land use planning might be forthcoming.

The abstract principle that urban growth should be reined in seemed attractive to many people because of a widely shared nostalgia for a small-town and rural past. On January 2, the *Idaho Statesman* proclaimed that the "Blueprint" would be a powerful tool for shaping the development of the Boise Valley, and the next day it lamented that "small-town Boise lives only in memory." In the three years between 2006 and 2009 the *Statesman* published a total of one hundred articles mentioning the Blueprint, and several of them lamented the loss of rural lifestyles. Cynthia Sewell's September 18, 2006, article on the Blueprint ran alongside a photograph of horseback riders on an outing in the Boise foothills. Rancher Jennifer Ellis waxed lyrical on the virtues of rural life: "the intrinsic values that come along with what we do—working side by side with our kids and our parents, viewing life from horseback: I mean, you just can't beat these things."[20]

As soon as the ideal of planning came up against local political realities, however, the participants in the Blueprint forgot all about their nostalgia to preserve a long-lost past. In February 2006 Skyline Development submitted an application to build 707 homes in one of the most sensitive environmental areas in Ada County, Hammer Flats. The winter home of Idaho's largest population of migrating deer and elk, this area lay just outside Boise's eastern boundary. Officials of the City of Boise expressed their dismay, and an opposition group formed instantaneously.[21] Threats of a lawsuit to prevent Ada County from approving the development floated in the air, and less than three weeks later developers of the Avimor planned community, located just north of Eagle, launched a legal challenge contesting Boise's right to sue the county to stop the project.[22] Officials of three cities condemned Mayor Dave Bieter and the City of Boise for unilaterally claiming the right to influence land use decisions made outside its jurisdiction. The City of Star went further and quit the Blueprint partnership altogether, and the city's mayor wrote an op-ed in the *Statesman* bitterly assailing Boise's alleged imperialism.[23] The mayor of the city of Eagle reported that her city was considering doing the same because it feared the Blueprint for Good Growth might ultimately limit its right to determine its own destiny.[24]

Public feuding became the order of the day despite attempts to quiet things down. Robert Freilich, the lead consultant for the Blueprint process, issued a letter scolding the participants for taking their conflicts to the press, although a few years later he joined the fray when the Blueprint fizzled to an unclimactic collapse.[25] In an April 2006 op-ed published by the *Statesman,* real estate developer Ralph Perez encouraged local officials to focus on urban sprawl, not "urban brawl."[26] When the Los Angeles–based Blueprint consultants came back into town during the summer to urge the coalition members to "think collectively," they faced a daunting task. Only Garden City, a mostly industrial and commercial city surrounded on three sides by Boise, made any moves to align the city's comprehensive plan with the principles enunciated in the Blueprint, but this small town was the only municipality to take such an action in 2006, doing so because of its landlocked status and the fact that it did not control its local streets.[27]

One of the persistent issues in the Blueprint process involved attempts by cities to unilaterally annex land slated for new development with their "area of impact." Robert Freilich, who by trade is a land use attorney, published a legal opinion in late July opposing the City of Star's right to annex new development; only a few weeks later an attorney hired by the City of Eagle wrote an opinion pointedly contradicting him. Freilich quickly fired off a letter to the BGG consortium that the "concept of the regional county plan is in danger of falling to pieces." On September 6 the *Idaho Statesman* agreed, declaring that "the plan is in imminent danger of collapsing completely."

Despite this long train of troubles, by the end of 2006 Freilich had produced a skeleton of a draft plan, but if anything it stirred up things even more than before. Meridian's mayor, Tammy DeWeerd, accused Freilich of being "fractional" and "divisive," and Eagle mayor Nancy Merrill proposed canceling the remaining $280,000 on Freilich's contract to author the implementation phase, adding that she "could count on one hand how many meetings he's showed up for." The mayor of the City of Star, though long absent from the Blueprint process, reaffirmed that his city would "not fund any further BGG activities and will not enter into any further inter-governmental agreements related to the BGG." The Ada County commissioners, however, saw no issue with the consultant, and all three expressed agreement with Commissioner Judy Peavey-Derr: "We can change the contractors, but the questions are still going to be the same."[28] And so they were.

The spring thaw was still a long way off in 2007 when the Ada County Highway District astonished everyone by announcing it was launching an independent review *of itself*.[29] Attempting to put an end to the feuding that had bogged down the Blueprint, in March the agency asked the Urban Land Institute (ULI) to conduct an independent review of the agency. Mayor Merrill of Eagle immediately expressed skepticism: "As I started going through the proposal, it became blatantly clear to me that with the folks they [ULI] are going to interview and the manner it is conducted it is skewed toward ACHD."[30] She announced that her city was considering opting out of the Blueprint process. She was not alone. Boise mayor Dave Bieter groused that Boise residents annually poured millions of dollars into the highway department's coffers, but the city still exercised no control over its own streets. He did of course control the amount his city contributed to the ULI study—nothing.

The county highway department and the City of Boise had long been embroiled in an acrimonious relationship, and it grew worse in 2006. In July of that year the Ada County Highway Department took the city to court over the city's attempt to block expansion of a small west-east collector, Ustick Road, into five lanes. Residents overwhelmingly opposed the agency's plans, but the city's fight was for naught; the highway department widened the road despite noisy opposition. One consolation to the residents was that the leader of the opposition, Sarah Baker, deposed one of the department's commissioners in the next election.

Another sore spot for municipalities was that Ada County did not appear to have any clear standards for approving new development; indeed, the hope that they could exert some influence over land use decisions is what brought them into the Blueprint process to begin with. In the spring of 2007 the Blueprint partners proposed an "adequate public facilities ordinance" that governments in Ada County would presumably adopt.[31] The aim was to ensure that the existence of adequate public facilities, such as roads, water, and sewer, be considered when assessing developers' proposals.

Reading the tea leaves that some sort of planned growth or growth management might be on the horizon, developers rushed to fill the development pipeline with massive subdivisions, most of them outside of municipal boundaries. The county approved most projects with little delay. In Boise developers rubbed salt in the wounds by shoehorning "shotgun houses"—sixteen-foot-wide, two-story, low-budget homes—into any twenty-five-foot lot they could find. Residents were not amused, and toward the end of April, the City of Boise convened an Infill Task Force to determine how best to balance quality design, the preservation of neighborhood fabric, and private property rights.[32]

Summer fireworks commenced when the eight-member Urban Land Institute task force arrived in Boise in June to conduct interviews with area residents and public- and private-sector leaders. The task force combined sentiments expressed in the interviews into a report card on how well the Highway District was performing for its client organizations—the cities. By July the ULI panel made its pronouncement: the Department was performing just fine. This verdict made ACHD administrators feel vindicated, but it left city officials bewildered.[33] Still, municipal officials came out of it with something they wanted: a recommendation that a "local government alliance" should set road priorities. The alliance would be made up of representatives from each city, the county, the highway district, and a citizen selected at large to chair the panel.[34] Though the composition of the panel mirrored what city leaders hoped would replace the elected Highway District commissioners, that proposal found no support in the legislature. Everyone ended up back at square one.

Despite, or perhaps because of, the months of sturm und drang, some officials in Ada County were listening. In July 2007 an Ada County planning

and zoning commissioner recommended a 180-day moratorium on development in the county, and the public expressed strong support.[35] There seemed
to be gathering wave of enthusiasm for the idea of reining in runaway development. Since 1994 researchers at Boise State University had included in
their annual public policy survey an open-ended question, "What is the most
important issue facing Idaho?" By 2007 concern about growth hit an all-
time high, ranking third on the list behind education and the economy. With
municipal elections approaching, candidates finally caught up to the public
at large. In Eagle growth dominated several candidates' platforms. Mayoral
candidate Saundra McDavid led a "Preserve Eagle" slate of candidates, and
council candidate Scott Nordstrom urged that growth pay its own way. In
November slow-growth candidates won two seats on the Eagle City Council,
and it was clear that valley residents in other cities also wanted elected leaders to come to some sort of agreement on growth management.[36]

The enthusiastic embrace of growth curbs turned out to be remarkably
short-lived, and by the end of the summer of 2008 it was clear that Idaho's
troubled foray into regional planning had come to an end. By August the
Blueprint for Good Growth had $612 in available funding in its account,
enough to buy a planner a modest suit, and no implementation plan.
Responsibility for the shell of a planning process was taken over by COMPASS,
the regional metropolitan planning organization established decades before
to comply with the Federal Aid Highway Act of 1962. Like MPOs elsewhere,
COMPASS cannot compel governments to cooperate.[37] With the weak economic climate following the housing bust of 2008, the remaining members
of the Blueprint coalition considered whether it even made sense to continue
contributing to the project. COMPASS estimated the annual costs to administer the Blueprint process at $73,000, but additional funds were not forthcom-
ing. The remaining members of the coalition met seven times in 2010 and
three times in 2011, but to little effect. COMPASS's website makes little reference to the Blueprint, only listing it as "ongoing" as of 2010. After forty-three
news stories or mentions in the *Idaho Statesman* in 2006 and fifty-one in
2007, coverage dropped to five mentions in 2008 and one in 2009. The Blueprint drew not a single piece of coverage in the region's daily paper of record
in 2010 or 2011. With economic growth slowed to a trickle and the housing market still reeling, Idaho's Annual Public Policy Survey showed concern
over growth retreating, replaced by concerns over jobs and the economy. The
regional planning effort, such as it ever was, sank quietly beneath the surface.

Accounting for Different Outcomes

Many scholars still consider the Intermountain West "fly-over country" and thus have devoted little serious attention to the politics of the region. Utah and Idaho have generally been lumped together as conservative, Republican, and Mormon, with little to distinguish them. The contrasting planning processes in the Salt Lake and Boise metropolitan areas show that, in fact, there are deep differences, and that these differences influence public opinion, political leadership, and the ability to build broad-based alliances.

The Envision Utah process relied heavily on state-level influencers—legislators and the governor. By contrast, Idaho's Blueprint process ignored those players or those players ignored the process. Alan Matheson, the former director of Envision Utah and now chief environmental advisor to Utah governor Gary Hebert, explained, "We've tried to involve people of influence in the state in our [Envision Utah's] leadership."[38] As a result, the current and previous three governors of Utah were either board chairs or on the board of Envision Utah. Governor Leavitt's support of the Envision Utah process was a key factor in the success of the initiative, and previous governors and legislators had also expressed concerns about urban growth. Envision Utah also gained legitimacy when former University of Utah president and University of California chancellor David P. Gardner took to the bully pulpit in support of regional planning.

In Idaho, by contrast, state leaders were missing in action. Local advocates for planning never tried to rally influential supporters to their cause, perhaps because the potential pool of leadership is thin. Few Idahoans who make a name and reputation for themselves in other parts of the world—especially in the political arena—ever return to the state. Those who continued to make their home in Washington, DC, after being elected (and unelected) include former US senator Frank Church; his successor, Senator Steve Symms; former US senator and US interior secretary Dirk Kempthorne; and former congressmen Walt Minnick and Larry LaRocco. Strangely enough, former Second District congressman Richard Stallings returned to Idaho after his defeat and won a seat on the Pocatello City Council—a town that only recently passed the fifty thousand population mark. Needless to say, that effectively removed him from having any sort of influence at the state level.

By contrast, Utah has produced what AnnaLee Saxenian has called the "New Argonauts," a class of individuals that have left the state and increased their wealth, experience, and influence in other places and then returned.[39] Former University of Utah president David Gardner is one example, as are former Envision Utah chair, governor, US ambassador to China, and 2012 presidential candidate Jon Huntsman. Having access to individuals with this level of gravitas represents a significant strength for Utah.

Initial calls for regional planning in Utah came from farmers and ranchers who feared what unchecked urban expansion meant for their own livelihoods. This mirrored the regional planning process in Oregon, where rural legislators responded with the region's signature policy, the Urban Growth Boundary. Idaho's effort was driven by an unpopular and often reviled single-purpose urban road agency. Rural constituencies in Idaho still dominate state politics, but they were not involved at all in the Blueprint for Good Growth.

A glaring difference between the two processes was the total lack of involvement of the private sector in Idaho's Blueprint for Good Growth; by contrast, business leaders and foundations actively participated in Envision Utah. Geneva Steel chief executive officer Robert Grow built Envision Utah into the powerful planning organization it is, largely through his tireless "shoe leather" approach that Alan Matheson remembered.[40] Governor Mike Leavitt-and the ghost of Brigham Young were not the only leaders present at the Envision Utah kickoff—also cochairing the planning process was Utah Jazz owner and car dealership magnate Larry Miller. The governor's office and the legislature in Utah each contributed funding to the planning efforts (Idaho's did not), but much of Envision Utah's funding came from private-sector businesses and foundations such as the Eccles Foundation.

Utah framed its planning efforts in a language that leaders of the private sector could embrace. As Alan Matheson explained, Utah's planning process "provides a distinct advantage. We've got a plan in place to insure that this quality of life continues for the next several generations. Your investment will be protected for your employees and those that will come." It should be noted that this was not just spin for the sake of buy-in. The leaders of Envision Utah were also deeply interested in an inclusionary process of implementation: "We're working closely with the development and financial community to make sure that what comes out at the end of the day is a viable response to the market," noted Matheson.[41]

It may seem uncharacteristic that a conservative "run government like a business" state such as Idaho would eschew participation by the private sector. To understand this anomaly, it may be helpful to more carefully examine the mores and philosophies of the two states to better explain their different approaches to urban land use planning.

Two Political Cultures

Utah provides the setting for one of the great dramas in American history. Before the Mormons arrived in 1847, only a few explorers and some scattered bands of Paiute and Shoshone were brave or stout enough to transverse and sometimes inhabit this hostile desert. It required a highly disciplined religious community capable of an unusual degree of collective effort to build a city there. Individualism is a trait deeply rooted in the western psyche, but in Utah it is moderated by an understanding that much can be accomplished through cooperation and collective effort.

Idaho was largely born as a place where people extracted wealth from its natural resources, and it has experienced an almost divine bounty throughout its history, almost without interruption. It has ridden a buoyant wave created by agriculture and natural resource endowments. The state is rich in natural resources—timber, minerals, and even rare earth. At the dawning of the twentieth century, giant reclamation projects funded by the federal government irrigated more acres of land in Idaho than any state in the West, providing it with a rich agricultural base. In the next step, the corporate world found a way to mesh its agricultural endowments with science and created the first freeze-dried potato, and in the process Idaho's first and only billionaire, J. R. Simplot.

The 1960s and 1970s created a boom in these homegrown industries. Ore-Ida became a processed food conglomerate, and Albertsons grew to become one of the nation's premier grocery chains. Having built the Hoover Dam and other infrastructure projects throughout the world, Morrison-Knudsen became, for a time, the world's largest heavy contractor. The vast stands of timber in Idaho produced Boise-Cascade, the forestry products giant, and Trus Joist, a leading wood products manufacturer. Simplot, which created the French fry, grew by leaps and bounds by first selling potatoes and onions to the US Army during World War II and in the 1950s signed contracts to sell fries to the McDonald brothers and their small chain of burger restaurants.

The 1970s brought an HP branch plant—what is today the laser printer division, as well as Micron, which today is one of the world's largest dynamic random-access memory (DRAM) and NAND flash manufacturers. If you have an iPad, iPhone, or iPod, you are probably powered by Micron. Those two tech giants, combined with the Fortune 500 giants already there—in a Boise city with fewer than seventy-five thousand residents in 1980—propped up the state through the recession of the early 1980s. Then the boom started.

In the 1990s and 2000s Idaho, led by its primary urban center, the Boise-Nampa MSA, grew at a remarkable pace. Like everywhere else around the globe, that growth came to a screeching halt in the third quarter of 2008. Idahoans saw real estate prices crash, along with an economy based on construction and retail. Through it all, though, there seems to be an abiding faith that growth will return of its own accord, as it has in the past.

By contrast, leaders in Utah grew concerned in the mid-1990s when in-state career opportunities for homegrown kids dried up. Utahans responded by creating the Coalition for Utah's Future, a public-private partnership that has morphed into Envision Utah. Then came planning for the 2002 Winter Olympic Games and the need to tidy up the Mormon Mecca, Salt Lake City. The story line is clear: catalyst, big event, point of no return, crisis, showdown, and realization of the importance of civic engagement. That cycle has played out in Utah time and time again.

Idaho has never faced the fear of failure, but there are signs that it may not be so lucky in the future. The processes of globalization have consumed local corporations one by one. By the end of the century the corporate giants that had led the boom existed only in memory. Albertsons board of directors turned the venerable homegrown grocer over to a former General Electric executive who sold the company off to Minneapolis-based SuperValu. A similar story repeated itself repeatedly, until only one local firm was left standing. Ore-Ida became a Heinz-owned property, and its operations moved to Pittsburgh. Boise Cascade was broken up and parceled out by a Michigan-based venture capital firm. Little of that capital remains in the valley. Weyerhaeuser acquired Trus-Joist and moved it to the Puget Sound. In perhaps the most painful corporate raid in Idaho history, Morrison-Knudsen, the heavy contractor that morphed from a company built from a few shovels and wheelbarrows in 1912 to the world's largest contractor by 1950, suffered a torturous fate and was finally sold for pennies on the dollar to a Montana-based contractor, Washington Group International, and then URS Corporation in San Francisco. All these events have played out with little comment or notice from public leaders.

Although Idaho's development as an agricultural powerhouse was originally underwritten by federal reclamation projects, that crucial governmental role has never been acknowledged. There is little mystery in Idaho's political culture. English Liberalism is the most logical parent of the political typology in the United States that celebrates limited government, rugged individualism, and self-reliance. John Stuart Mill's *On Liberty* provides a concise discussion of this philosophy, and Idaho's current governor is wont to recite from it, even while referring to the author as "J. W."[42] The communitarian impulse that resides in Utah's culture and politics is matched, in Idaho, by a deep attachment to individualism and self-reliance. Cultures are durable, and the culture of the two states is unlikely to disappear anytime soon.

NOTES

1. Leonard Arrington, *Great Basin Kingdom: An Economic History of the Latter-day Saints, 1830–1900* (Cambridge, MA: Harvard University Press, 1958).

2. Josh Gross, "Butch Otter Explains It All—Sort Of," *Boise Weekly,* City Desk, March 25, 2010, http://www.boiseweekly.com/CityDesk/archives/2010/03/25/butch-otter-explains-it-allsort-of.

3. *The History of Envision Utah* (Salt Lake City: Envision Utah, n.d.), http://envisionutah.org/historyenvisonutahv5p1.pdf.

4. "What's Your Vision of Utah's Future? Salt Lake City Plans Public Workshops in Attempt to Reach Consensus on Growth," *Salt Lake Tribune,* April 10, 1998.

5. Chris Blanchard, "This Urban Idaho," *Idaho Issues Online,* 2005, http://www.boisestate.edu/research/history/issuesonline/spring2006_issues/5f_numbers_06spr.html.

6. "Public Meet Will Focus on Saving Open Spaces," *Salt Lake Tribune,* October 11, 1995, sec. B.

7. "S.L. County Has No Plan for the Future: Planning Efforts Fail to Bear Fruit," *Salt Lake Tribune,* August 26, 1996.

8. Ibid.

9. "Warning: Utah Needs Planning," *Salt Lake Tribune,* October 9, 1996; "Utah's Future Is Here," *Salt Lake Tribune,* October 11, 1996.

10. "Feeling Crowded? Coalition Tackles Wasatch Front Sprawl; Coalition to Get Handle on Utah Growth," *Salt Lake Tribune,* January 14, 1997.

11. Ibid.

12. "Develop the Will to Change Development; Utahns Must Be Ready to Take on Major Challenges; Alternative Futures Require Changing Direction," *Salt Lake Tribune,* November 26, 1998, sec. Utah.

13. "The Up Side of Density: It Can Be Force for Change; Congestion Can Be Force for Change," *Salt Lake Tribune,* November 15, 1997.

14. Alan Matheson, "Chris Blanchard Interview with Alan Matheson," digital audio recording, July 11, 2011.

15. "Enthusiastic 'Visionary' Chosen to Help Plot Wasatch Growth," *Salt Lake Tribune,* January 15, 1998; "Utah Planners Not Big on Big Cities; Workshops Endorse Growth on Village Scale Instead of Salt Lake City–Type Downtowns; Planners Say One SLC Is Enough for Utah," *Salt Lake Tribune,* August 12, 1998, sec. Nation-World.

16. Cabot Wm. Nelson, "Candidate's Urban Counsel," *Salt Lake Tribune,* May 28, 1998, sec. Opinion.

17. "Small Lots in Farmington? Neighbors Fight Cluster Plan," *Salt Lake Tribune,* September 1, 1998, sec. Nation-World.

18. "Critics: Guv Taints Panel on Growth; Highway Politics Closes Minds, They Say; Growth Scenarios All May Envision Legacy Highway," *Salt Lake Tribune,* November 10, 1998, sec. Nation-World.

19. "Envision Utah Will Debut 4 Scenarios for Growth; Coalition Employs Polls, Workshops in Strategy," *Salt Lake Tribune,* September 20, 1998, sec. Nation-World.

20. Cynthia Sewell, "Treasure Valley Growth: Small-Town Boise Lives Only in Memory," *Idaho Statesman* (Boise), January 2, 2006; Cynthia Sewell, "Rural Idahoans Hoping to Save a Bit of Old West," *Idaho Statesman* (Boise), September 18, 2006.

21. Cynthia Sewell, "Ada Gets Plan for Hammer Flat Community," *Idaho Statesman* (Boise), February 22, 2006.

22. Cynthia Sewell, "Avimor to Fight in Court to Build North of Eagle," *Idaho Statesman* (Boise), March 10, 2006.

23. Nate View Mitchell, "Star Seeks Action That's Consistent with Words," *Idaho Statesman* (Boise), March 13, 2006.

24. Cynthia Sewell, "Eagle May Leave Growth Group, but Not Because of Legal Fight," *Idaho Statesman* (Boise), March 11, 2006.

25. Cynthia Sewell, "Planning Consultant Scolds Blueprint Participants," *Idaho Statesman* (Boise), April 7, 2006.

26. Ralph Perez, "Turf Wars Wreck City Planning," *Idaho Statesman* (Boise), April 11, 2006.

27. Kate Brusse, "Garden City Maps Out Its Future," *Idaho Statesman* (Boise), July 24, 2006.

28. Cynthia Sewell, "County and City Growth Plan Meets with Mixed Reviews," *Idaho Statesman* (Boise), December 15, 2006.

29. Cynthia Sewell, "ACHD Orders Independent Study on Whether District Is Needed—Highway District Says It's Willing to Accept That Urban Land Institute Could Recommend Doing Away with ACHD," *Idaho Statesman* (Boise), March 9, 2007.

30. Our View, "Is the Ada County Highway District Still a Viable Entity to Fulfill Transportation Needs?," *Idaho Statesman* (Boise), April 29, 2007.

31. Cynthia Sewell, "Blueprint for Growth Proposes Roads First, Then Development—Ordinance Now Goes to Ada Councils, Commissions," *Idaho Statesman* (Boise), March 18, 2007.

32. Kate Brusse, "Task Force Seeks Better City Infill Policy—Group Wants City Hall to Exercise Its Authority to Regulate Development," *Idaho Statesman* (Boise), April 28, 2007.

33. Cynthia Sewell, "Ada Residents to Have Say on ACHD—National Panel of Experts to Prepare Report Card on District," *Idaho Statesman* (Boise), June 17, 2007.

34. "Local Governments Need to Form Alliance for Roads—OUR VIEW ACHD," *Idaho Statesman* (Boise), July 1, 2007.

35. Cynthia Sewell, "Ada Official Gets People Talking with Call for Valley-Wide Growth Moratorium—Steve Edgar Said He Suggested the Move as a Private Citizen, but Wants Agencies to Take a Breather," *Idaho Statesman* (Boise), July 12, 2007.

36. "What They Say—We Asked the Candidates About Their Views on Eagle's Future," *Idaho Statesman* (Boise), October 21, 2007; "Eagle Mayor, Council Hopefuls See Growth as No. 1 Issue: The Candidates Want to Manage Development So the City Retains Its Roots," *Idaho Statesman* (Boise), October 10, 2007; Cynthia Sewell, "Ada Leaders Inch Toward Joint Planning: Proposed Alliance Will Draft a Plan for How the County and Cities Will Share Powers," *Idaho Statesman* (Boise), November 10, 2007.

37. Statesman staff, "COMPASS Will Take over Blueprint for Good Growth," *Idaho Statesman* (Boise), August 22, 2008.

38. Matheson, "Chris Blanchard Interview with Alan Matheson."

39. AnnaLee Saxenian, *The New Argonauts: Regional Advantage in a Global Economy* (Cambridge, MA: Harvard University Press, 2007).

40. Matheson, "Chris Blanchard Interview with Alan Matheson."

41. Ibid.

42. Dan Popkey, "Hear Otter's Odd Endorsement Speech of Romney, Which Some Knocked for Barely Mentioning the Candidate," *Idaho Statesman Blogs,* March 9, 2012, http://voices.idahostatesman.com/2012/03/09/idahopolitics/hear_otters_odd_endorsement_speech_romney_which_some_knocked_bar.

The Coming Convergence

DENNIS R. JUDD

THE VAST LITERATURE on the American West reflects a national pre-occupation that goes back to the presidency of Thomas Jefferson and the Lewis and Clark Corps of Discovery Expedition of 1804–6. Despite a nineteenth-century fascination with western exploration, the Great Basin remained generally unknown and little noted. It would have remained virtu-ally invisible if not for the Mormons, who threatened to create a breakaway kingdom, and the experience of the Donner Party, which left an enduring image of a fatal desert to be avoided at all costs. As they skirted its northern reaches, immigrants on the California and Oregon Trails filled their jour-nals with accounts of a desolate and unforgiving landscape. A century later the Basin's history was recorded in the remains of hundreds of ghost towns, and its future trajectory seemed foretold by the conversion of desert land-scapes into bombing ranges and nuclear test sites. Although the growth of major cities has brought it somewhat out of the shadows, as Tadevosyan and Judd note in their chapter in this volume, even today the Basin is opaque because it does not conform to most people's imagined West. Considered in this light, the recent rise of four metropolitan areas on the Basin's rim may appear to be curious and even alarming. It is a development that deserves careful attention.

The urbanization of the Great Basin marks a historic turn because, at long last, it brings this peculiar region into a familiar frame of reference. In the years following World War II, the western Sunbelt was transformed into the nation's urban frontier. Federal military spending disproportionately bene-fited cities in the West, and demographics and lifestyle lured young people and retirees to the newer, energetic cities located there. The story line of the New West featured a narrative of cities and urbanization, and its themes may be useful for understanding the social and cultural transformation taking place in what is likely to be America's last urban frontier. Beginning in mid-century Las Vegas mushroomed into a neon metropolis, and by the 1980s

Reno, Salt Lake City, and Boise crested a wave of urban growth that has yet to break. The rise of these four metropolitan areas on the edges of the inland sagebrush empire of the Intermountain West is a remarkable development, and this process will have consequences and present lessons that will reverberate beyond the region where these changes are taking place.

The Great Basin has become the site of a fascinating experiment that seems perfectly designed to determine if great cities can prosper over the long run in a fragile and withholding natural environment. Up to now the ecological systems that surround the Basin have supplied the water resources necessary to sustain the recent surge of urban growth on the desert's rim. The problem that presents itself is that those ecosystems are undergoing the same changes that have come to the Basin. Throughout the American West, climate change and drought are disrupting ecological systems, watersheds are drying—and cities continue to grow. The urban future in the Great Basin is, therefore, likely to become the urban experience elsewhere in the West. For a long time the Great Basin has been thought of as a region set apart, but the characteristics that have made it distinctive may soon be coming to a neighborhood near you.

How It Became a Region Set Apart

The Great Basin Desert occupies about a third of the arid region between the Rockies and the Sierra Nevada, but for most of the nation's history it has resisted all attempts to place it within a narrative of manifest destiny, conquest, and national progress. In his chapter of this volume Todd Shallat argues that photographers and artists of the Great Basin labored to find signs of the machine in the garden, but in the end the desert resisted every effort to subdue it to the hand of man. Even to its keenest and closest observers, the Basin remained terra incognita because it did not fit within the nineteenth-century imperative of technological triumph over nature. This stubborn refusal to conform became even more obvious in the twentieth century, when massive reclamation projects reached into virtually every corner of the West except the interior of the Great Basin. From 1902 to 2007 more than seventy-nine thousand dams of twenty-five feet or higher were constructed in the United States, most of them by the Corps of Engineers or the Bureau of Reclamation; in the West the Yellowstone River is the longest of three that have escaped the engineers' schemes.[1] Notably, after Congress passed the Reclamation Act of 1902, the two reclamation projects undertaken by the Reclamation Service (later renamed the Bureau of Reclamation) were located on the extreme edges of the Great Basin Desert: the Newlands Project near Reno, Nevada (1904), and the Boise Project, which funded the construction of Arrowrock Dam, at the time the highest concrete dam in the world, near Boise, Idaho (1906). The absence of major rivers in the Basin's interior guaranteed that these projects would be the last to be undertaken within the confines of the Basin. In the next few decades, while vast areas of the West were opened up to agriculture and urban development, the Great Basin remained fixed in the past. Only in the atomic age were the agents of technology able to find a way to bend the Basin to their purposes, and this was only when they found a way to make desolation into a useful asset.

Rather than opening opportunities for agriculture and settlement, as in the remainder of the West, the federal government became the owner of vast tracts of public land that were placed off-limits to development. Perhaps for this reason, the Basin's residents have displayed a chronic and often extreme animosity to federal authority. Christopher A. Simon argues in his chapter that nowhere else in the West has the culture of resistance been expressed as often or as intensely as in the Great Basin. The several Sagebrush Rebellions have found their first home there, though to little practical effect: even after decades of fuss and controversy, the federal government's control over its domain remains intact. Despite (or perhaps because of) their practical failures, these movements have made a profound impact on the Basin's political culture. Resentment to government in all its guises is evident everywhere. All through the Basin, governments tend to be weak and underdeveloped. In her chapter Stephanie L. Witt presents fascinating evidence showing just how few resources counties within the Basin counties command. A deep cultural divide has emerged between frontier counties ("rural" does not work well as a descriptor in the Basin) and urban counties. Witt and her coauthor, Brian Laurent, argue that the collision of culture and governance will help determine the future of this region because county governments simply do not possess the resources or personnel to address pressing environmental issues.

Limited governmental capacity acts as a barrier to policy making in a region undergoing rapid ecological change. In their chapter Jessica L. DeShazo and Zachary A. Smith provide a comprehensive summary of the Basin's status as an endangered ecological system. Grazing, invasive species, water withdrawals, mining, and energy development pose significant risks, but is there a political will to address these issues? Their answer to this question is forthright and disturbing: "The Great Basin is a fragile ecosystem, and the current politics that surround the Basin add to that fragility." They argue that it will take intergovernmental cooperation and capacity to address threats to the ecological integrity of the Basin, but it is far from clear how those would be mobilized. In their chapter Erika Allen Wolters and Brent Steel propose a remedy for the gridlock. Their surveys provide empirical evidence that there is a deep and widening cultural divide within the Basin; while ranchers and rural residents resist governmental effort, the residents of urban counties support rangeland management and environmental protection. Urban populations are growing, and one consequence is that in the years ahead an urban constituency may emerge that will mobilize support for policies designed to preserve the Basin's fragile ecosystems. Of course, such change will not come without conflict.

Although they could hardly be more different from one another, the metropolitan regions that sprawl along the desert's rim share two qualities in common: they are growing fast, and a generous dollop of hubris has energized their extraordinary growth. Salt Lake's founders were motivated not by mere boosterism, but by the idea it was the center of a new Zion (from the Hebrew term *Tzion*, "which designated the area of Jerusalem where the fortress stood, and later became a metonym for Solomon's Temple in Jerusalem, the city of Jerusalem and generally, the World to Come").[2] Erin daina mcclellan's examination of the discourse about Boise shows that the city keeps appearing on just about everyone's "best city" list, and local officials amplify the message at every opportunity. As Chris Blanchard describes in his chapter, an unalloyed confidence that the region will continue to grow helps to explain why Boise's metropolitan residents are willing to bet the future on uncontrolled, unplanned sprawl. In her chapter Alicia Barber writes that in Reno's case, hubris is expressed by a defiance of all natural constraints or boundaries: "In our ceaseless growth, ever upward and outward, we move boldly into areas once deemed inhospitable or even hostile to human populations, erasing the footprints of lives spent in closer harmony with the natural." Las Vegas, though, is in a category all its own; it has, in effect, turned hubris into its theme song. There is no other city in America like it. Elizabeth Raymond finds that successive generations of the city's boosters have made a virtue of the fact that Las Vegas has no obvious attributes or natural advantages that might explain its success.

Are there limits to growth? It is not easy to answer this question because, to turn a familiar cliché on its head, the past does not necessarily predict the future. The urbanization of the West took off in the second half of the twentieth century. Studies of the climate record reveal that it was a period of unusually abundant moisture; in particular, the 1970s and the 1990s, when all four metropolitan areas of the Basin were rapidly adding population, precipitation levels were above normal.[3] By sharp contrast, the twenty-first century appears to be heading into an extended "megadrought."[4] The new climate regime will pose severe challenges for cities all over the West. The cities of the rim rely upon watersheds outside the Basin itself, and if these do not continue to supply enough water to the cities that depend upon them, the desert will be forced to yield up whatever it can, at whatever the cost to its ecological health and integrity.

The Coming Convergence: Climate Change, Cities, and Water

Although there has been significant fluctuations in the climate record, the Great Basin has been drying out for the past twenty-six hundred years.[5] Over the past century and a half, "increasing aridity and reduction in grass abundance" has been the norm.[6] As one scientist has observed, this long-term trend is likely to continue, or even become more pronounced: "If the present patterns continue, the Great Basin may experience approximately three hundred years of potentially drier climates. What this implies, is that it could be several centuries before . . . higher levels of moisture return." It is also likely that global warming may trigger "threshold shifts" involving rapid and unanticipated changes in temperature regimes and ecological change.[7] Currently, climate models point to a 10 percent to 20 percent decline in precipitation by midcentury,[8] but rising carbon dioxide levels and the worldwide spread of species into new ecosystems make it likely that ecological change may occur at a faster rate than previously thought.[9] In the Great Basin, streams and riparian oases are rapidly disappearing; according to a recent study, half of all the streams and the systems dependent upon them "are currently in poor ecological condition."[10] These oasis environments are essential to the diversity of plant and animal life of the desert, and without them the Basin's ecology would be reduced to a uniform regime of sagebrush and small shrubs capable of surviving increasingly harsh conditions.

Apart from the effects of climate change, the Great Basin's ecology has been fundamentally altered by human activity—what scientists call "anthropogenic disturbances." Mining, recreational activities, and highway and road building have disrupted ecological systems, and overgrazing and colonization by invasive species have reached into every corner of the desert. From time to time pitched battles have pitted ranchers, mining interests, and rural residents against a national political alliance attuned to the goals of environmental protection. Even if these conflicts are somehow resolved in the years ahead, "the dynamics and complexity of [natural] communities will likely never return to those of the past."[11]

Urban water withdrawals within the Great Basin are likely to accelerate because drought has come to the watersheds surrounding it. Only a few years ago a concern about climate change and diminishing water supplies in the western states was shared mainly by a few climate researchers and (circumspectly) by some water managers. In recent years, however, public awareness has reached a tipping point. A drumbeat of bad news about drought and diminishing water flows has been pouring forth from scientific publications, environmental organizations, and media outlets.[12] A scientific article published in 2008 that estimated a 50 percent chance that Lake Mead might reach "dead pool" by 2021 was covered widely in the press, but was also greeted with some skepticism;[13] only four years later even more startling conclusions in an article published in *Nature Geoscience* received little push back. According to the authors, the worst drought in eight hundred years had already begun to grip the West, and a cascade of ecological effects had already begun to unfold. In an interview one of the *Nature Geoscience* authors summarized the finds: "Areas that are already dry in the West are expected to get drier. We expect more extremes. And it's these extreme periods that can really cause ecosystem damage, lead to climate-induced mortality of forest, and may cause some areas to convert from forest to shrublands or grassland." The evidence, she said, pointed toward a century-long drying that would make the present period appear as "an outlier of extreme wetness." At about the same time, the authors of a study published by the Congressional Research Service stated, somewhat more diffidently, that "a more arid average climate in the American West . . . may be underway," although the data in their report supported a much more confident prediction, as indicated by their use of the term *megadrought*.[14]

Although the severity of the drought regime varies regionally and from year to year, it is already widespread enough to have affected all the major watersheds in the West. Tree-ring studies tracing the volume of snowpack over several centuries reveal that "late-20th century snowpack reductions are almost unprecedented in magnitude across the northern Rocky Mountains, and in their north-south synchrony across the cordillera."[15] Over the next half century, the water available for agriculture and urban use in the West is projected to fall by as much as 20 percent, with the most intense

drying focused on Nevada, Utah, northern New Mexico, and western Colorado.[16] The rising temperatures associated with global warming will bring
"higher evapotranspiration, reduced precipitation, and decreased spring
runoff" in the Colorado and Columbia River basins and in the American
Southwest.[17]

Because the Colorado River is the lifeline for much of the West, its flow is
subject to constant and intense scrutiny. Researchers expect the river's flow
to fall, perhaps sharply, in the coming decades.[18] Popular sources regularly
publish articles under alarmist headings such as "The Colorado River Runs
Dry." Such language may seem hyperbolic, but not enough for comfort. The
baseline for allocating the river's water was established in the first half of
the twentieth century, which "was the wettest or second-wettest century in
the Colorado River basin in at least 500 years."[19] Even without drought, the
increasing demand by urban users would pose serious problems. Obviously,
urbanization and the river's diminishing flows are on a collision course.

Although widespread drought will adversely impact all the cities of the
Great Basin, Las Vegas's problems are especially acute because the Colorado
River watershed is its main source of water. Although 2011 was a relatively
wet year, high temperatures led to earlier than normal runoff,[20] and drought
conditions returned to the Colorado Basin in 2012.[21] A federal study confirms that climate change and population growth will lead to water shortages
in the decades ahead—3.2 million acre-feet by 2060, or five times the amount
currently used by the Los Angeles metropolitan area.[22] Projections like these
explain why the Southern Nevada Water Authority has laid claim to water
resources throughout Nevada and why it is willing to invest $15 billion, or
more, to tap into and transport the Basin's groundwater.

The Great Experiment

It may be useful to imagine the rise of cities in the driest desert of North
America as an audacious (though unintended) natural experiment. A positive result is certainly possible, though even in that case success will be modest, with expanding cities managing to stay one step ahead of diminishing
water supplies. Without doubt water is available that has not yet been utilized. Despite its surface appearances, the Basin hides a treasure trove in the
system of aquifers stretching from Death Valley northward into Idaho, and
Las Vegas is in the process of trying to tap into it. Withdrawing water from
below the surface will profoundly alter the desert's ecological systems.[23] Surface water is not exempt, either. Las Vegas possesses water rights to the rank

on rank of mountains arrayed across the state of Nevada and to the Virgin River, which runs through Zion National Park. Even in the midst of a long-term drought, more water will be found.

A modestly positive result from the great experiment is also possible because water managers have found creative ways to extend available water supplies. Since the mid-1980s water withdrawals in the United States have not increased markedly even with an increasing population.[24] Cities almost everywhere are employing some combination of conservation measures, including (among others) improvements in infrastructure to reduce losses; restrictions on use, such as designated-day sprinkling; gray-water use and recovery; landscaping regulations; and conservation pricing. Because 80 percent or more of water in the West is allocated to agricultural users, there will be opportunities for reallocating scarce water supplies to cities (with, of course, substantial trade-offs in agricultural productivity, food prices, and economic effects). Cities close enough to the sea can invest in desalination plants, although these use huge amounts of energy. Over time, it is certain that water scarcity will bring new technologies and conservation practices on line.

Optimism is needed because a failure to achieve a positive result from the experiment being conducted in the Great Basin would be catastrophic. A legion of skeptics do not think that cities can ultimately prosper anywhere in the desert West. William deBuys believes that the West is facing a train wreck and that "the train must be stopped. But who is willing to stand on the tracks and flag it down?" His answer is that no one will: "The track won't end until the water does." Writer Timothy Egan believes all the measures to put off the day of reckoning will come up short and that even if cities man-age to buy some time, the ultimate outcome is likely to be ugly. "To make Eden in Los Angeles," he says, "should have lasted more than a century. But water brought subdivisions in place of orange groves, and brought rivers of backed-up cars over plains of asphalt, which brought wretched air that killed people who came to Southern California for their health. So, [Las Vegas is] repeating the entire cycle all over again, only the arc from birth to boom to urban suffocation is much quicker this time."[25]

Patricia Mulroy, the general manager of the Southern Nevada Water Authority, seems to be of two minds about the water problem. On the one hand, she has stated her opinion that Las Vegas's expansion is virtually unstoppable: "If you tried to slow growth around here, you'd have chaos, says Mulroy. You can't expect that this community, all these new people and all these *babies* and all these *families*, are going to just go away." On the other hand, she fully appreciates the peril of diminishing water: "People need a fundamental, cultural attitude change about water supply in the Southwest. It's not abundant, it's not reliable, it's not going to always be there."[26]

An accumulating body of evidence supports Mulroy's assessment. If, as expected, a long-term drought unfolds in the West, it will coincide with an event that has never before been witnessed in the historical record: the rise of the sprawling urban conurbations that dot the western landscape from Denver to Los Angeles. In the next few decades the most pressing issue facing the West involves the question of whether cities in that arid landscape are sustainable. However much they may complain about doomsday scenarios, it is clear that even the most optimistic observers do not know the answer to that immensely important question. It is imperative that we discover the answer because it is of great importance not only to cities such as Las Vegas, Los Angeles, or other familiar places in the western United States. More than a billion people on the planet live in regions that face serious water shortages, and this number will rise sharply even before 2050, when the world's population approaches nine billion. Patricia Mulroy, who spends most of her time thinking about such things, is on record as saying, "There's not enough fresh water to handle nine billion people at current consumption levels." Climate models show that by 2040 persistent and extreme drought is likely to spread through parts of Eurasia, Africa, Australia, and the United States.[27] It turns out that the Great Basin is not such a peculiar region after all. Suddenly, it finds itself not a place apart; instead, it is being inexorably drawn into a sweeping twenty-first-century global narrative.

NOTES

1. Daniel McCool, *River Republic: The Fall and Rise of America's Rivers* (New York: Columbia University Press, 2012), 8. McCool states that the Yellowstone is the only western river without a dam, but the Salmon River and the Selway, both in northern Idaho, are designated as "wild and scenic" rivers that have not been dammed.

2. See *Wikipedia.*

3. William deBuys, *A Great Aridness: Climate Change and the Future of the American Southwest* (New York: Oxford University Press, 2011), 9.

4. Christopher Schwalm, Kevin Schaefer, and Christopher Williams, "Reduction in Carbon Uptake During Turn of the Century Drought in Western North

America," *Nature-Geoscience, July 29, 2012,* study reported in "Chronic 2000–2004 Drought, Worst in 800 Years, May Be the 'New Normal,'" *Science Daily,* July 29, 2012, http://www.sciencedaily.com/releases/2012/07/120729142137.html.

5. Robin J. Tausch, Cheryl L. Nowak, and Scott A. Mensing, "Climate Change and Associated Vegetation Dynamics During the Holocene: The Paleoecological Record," in *Great Basin Riparian Ecosystems: Ecology, Management, and Restoration,* edited by Jeanne C. Chambers and Jerry R. Miller (Washington, DC: Island Press, 2004), 34–35, as well as the several studies cited therein. See also Jerry R. Miller et al., "Fluvial Geomorphic Responses to Holocene Climate Change," in ibid., 61.

6. Miller et al., "Fluvial Geomorphic Responses," 38.

7. Tausch, Nowak, and Mensing, "Climate Change and Associated Vegetation Dynamics," 39. Here, the authors cite several previous studies.

8. Douglas Fox, "Omens from a Vanished Sea," *High Country News,* October 31, 2011, 11–17.

9. Tausch, Nowak, and Mensing, "Climate Change and Associated Vegetation Dynamics," 40.

10. Jeanne C. Chambers and Jerry R. Miller, *Great Basin Riparian Ecosystems: Ecology, Management, and Restoration* (Washington, DC: Island Press, 2004), 1.

11. Tausch, Nowak, and Mensing, "Climate Change and Associated Vegetation Dynamics," 39.

12. Schwalm, Schaefer, and Williams, "Reduction in Carbon Uptake," study reported in "Chronic 2000–2004 Drought."

13. A reservoir becomes a dead pool when the water level falls below the dam's outlet pipes. See Tim P. Barnett and David W. Pierce, "When Will Lake Mead Begin to Dry?," *Water Resources Research* 44 (March 29, 2008). Subsequent studies by these authors and others moved the window a bit further out, but not by much. For a discussion of the controversy, see deBuys, *Great Aridness,* 138–39.

14. Schwalm, Schaefer, and Williams, "Reduction in Carbon Uptake," study reported in "Chronic 2000–2004 Drought"; Peter Folger, Betsy A. Cody, and Nicole T. Carter, "Drought in the United States: Causes and Issues for Congress," *Congressional Research Service* (August 15, 2012), 19, http://www.crs.gov, RL34580.

15. G. T. Pederson et al., "The Unusual Nature of Recent Snowpack Declines in North America," Northern Rocky Mountain Science Center, http://www.nrmsc.usgs.gov/northamericasnowpack, original article published in *Science,* June 9, 2011, doi: 10:1126/science.1201570.

16. Douglas Fox, "Omens from a Vanished Sea," 10–17.

17. Folger, Cody, and Carter, "Drought in the United States," 19.

18. Andrew Ross, *Bird on Fire: Lessons from the World's Least Sustainable City* (New York: Oxford University Press, 2011), 139ff.

19. Sarah Zielinski, "The Colorado River Runs Dry," *Smithsonian Magazine*, October 2010, http://www.smithsonianmag.com/science-nature/The-Colorado-River-Runs-Dry; Tim P. Barnett and David W. Pierce, "Sustainable Water Deliveries from the Colorado River in a Changing Climate," *Proceedings of the National Academy of Sciences* 106, no. 18 (2009).

20. Folger, Cody, and Carter, "Drought in the United States," 11.

21. Jack Healy, "Thin Snowpack in West Signals Summer of Drought," *New York Times*, February 22, 2013, http://www.nytimes.com/2013/02/23/us/in-drought-stricken-heartland.

22. Bureau of Reclamation, US Department of the Interior, *Colorado River Basin Water Supply and Demand Study Phase 4: Development and Evaluation of Opportunities for Balancing Water Supply and Demand*, November 2011, http://www.usbr.gov/lc/region/programs/crbstudy/OptionsSubmittalReprot.pdf.

23. Henry Brean, "Pipelines Seen as Threat to Great Basin National Park," *Las Vegas Review-Journal*, November 9, 2011; news release, *Great Basin Water Network*, October 31, 2011; Great Basin Water Issues, "Water Grabs Threaten the Future of Rural Communities and Wildlife Throughout the Great Basin," *Great Basin Water Network*, http://www.greatbasinwater.net/issues/index.php.

24. Nationalatlas.gov, "Water Use in the United States."

25. Timothy Egan, *Lasso the Wind: Away to the New West* (New York: Alfred A. Knopf, 1998), 160, 100.

26. Ibid., 103 (emphasis in the original); quoted in Zielinski, "Colorado River Runs Dry."

27. Zielinski, "Colorado River Runs Dry"; Environmental News Service, "Severe Drought Predicted to Grip the Global by 2040," http://ens-newswire.com/2010/10/22severe-drought-predicted-to-grip-the-world.

Contributors

ALICIA BARBER, PhD, writes extensively about the history of Nevada and the American West, place identity, and cultural tourism. Her book *Reno's Big Gamble: Image and Reputation in the Biggest Little City* (2008) analyzes the relationship between the city's reputation and its economic and physical development.

CHRIS BLANCHARD earned his PhD in urban studies at Portland State University. His applied planning work has appeared in *Planning and Urban Land* and his environmental research in *Journal: American Water Works Association*.

JESSICA L. DESHAZO is an assistant professor at California State University –Los Angeles in the Department of Political Science. Natural resource management and environmental policy are two of her research areas.

DENNIS R. JUDD spent his first eighteen years on a dairy and sugar beet farm near Vale, Oregon, and after a winding path ended up in his present position, professor and interim head of the Department of Political Science at the University of Illinois at Chicago. For many years he has been a leading contributor to the literature on urban development, national urban policy, and urban regeneration in Europe and the United States.

BRIAN LAURENT is the data management supervisor for the Alaska Department of Education and Early Development. He received his master's in public administration from Boise State University in May 2012.

ERIN DAINA MCCLELLAN is an assistant professor in the Department of Communication at Boise State University. Her research on the intersections among rhetoric and urban life appears in *Understanding Occupy from Wall*

Street to Portland: Applied Studies in Communication Theory (edited by R. G. Heath, C. V. Fletcher, and R. Munoz); a special issue of **lo Squaderno**; *Storytelling, Self, & Society*; *Liminalities: A Journal of Performance Studies*; and *Active Voices: Composing a Rhetoric of Social Movements* (edited by S. Stevens and P. Malesh).

ELIZABETH RAYMOND is a professor of history at the University of Nevada, Reno. Her publications reflect a long-standing fascination with the Great Basin, including *Changing Mines in America* (2004, with Peter Goin) and *George Wingfield, Owner and Operator of Nevada* (reissued 2013).

TODD SHALLAT directs the Center for Idaho History and Politics at Boise State University. His books on technology and the environment include *Structures in the Streams: Water, Science, and the Rise of the U.S. Army Corps of Engineers* (1994), *Secrets of the Magic Valley* (2002), and *Surviving Minidoka* (2013).

CHRISTOPHER A. SIMON (PhD, 1997, Washington State University) is a professor of political science at the University of Utah and co–book review editor for the journal *Public Integrity*. He is coauthor (with Brent S. Steel and Nicholas Lovrich) of *State and Local Government: Sustainability in the 21st Century* (2011).

ZACHARY A. SMITH is a Regents Professor of Environmental and Natural Resources Policy and Administration in the Department of Politics and International Affairs at Northern Arizona University. A consultant, both nationally and internationally, on natural resource and environmental matters, he is the author or editor of more than twenty books and many articles on environmental and natural resource policy topics.

BRENT S. STEEL is a professor and director of the Public Policy Graduate Program at Oregon State University. He is coauthor of *State and Local Government: Sustainability in the 21st Century* (2011) and editor of *Science and Politics: An A to Z Guide of Issues and Controversies* (2014).

ANAHIT TADEVOSYAN is a PhD candidate in the Department of Political Science at the University of Illinois at Chicago. Her work examines refugee policy and integration at state and city levels.

STEPHANIE L. WITT is a professor of public policy and administration at Boise State University. Her books include *The Urban West Revisited* (2012) and *People Skills for Public Managers* (2014).

ERIKA ALLEN WOLTERS is an instructor in the Political Science Department at Oregon State University. Her research interests include water policy, environmental policy, renewable energy, consumption, and climate change. Recent publications include "Attitude–Behavior Consistency in Household Water Consumption" (2014) and "Oregon Water: Assessing the Differences Between the Old and New Wests" (2014).

Index